Mary's Mother

Mary's Mother

Saint Anne in Late Medieval Europe

Virginia Nixon

THE PENNSYLVANIA STATE UNIVERSITY PRESS

UNIVERSITY PARK, PENNSYLVANIA

Library of Congress Cataloging-in-Publication Data

Nixon, Virginia, 1939–
   Mary's mother : Saint Anne in late medieval Europe /
   Virginia Nixon.
      p.   cm.
Includes bibliographical references and index.
ISBN 978-0-271-05812-2 (pbk. : alk. paper)
ISBN 978-0-271-02466-0 (cloth : alk. paper)
1. Anne (Mother of the Virgin Mary), Saint—Cult—
Germany—History.
2. Germany—Religious life and customs.
I. Title.

BT685.N59 2004
232.9'33—dc22
2004000482

The Pennsylvania State University Press is a member of the Association
of American University Presses.

It is the policy of The Pennsylvania State University Press to use acid-free
paper. Publications on uncoated stock satisfy the minimum require-
ments of American National Standard for Information Sciences—
Permanence of Paper for Printed Library Materials, ANSI
Z39.48–1992.

Contents

List of Illustrations

Title, dates, and other information are those supplied by the institutions owning the works of art. Sculptures, unless otherwise noted, are of wood.

1. Tilman Riemenschneider, *Anna Selbdritt*, 1490–95. Sandstone. Photograph Rolf Nachbar. Reproduced by permission of the Mainfränkisches Museum, Würzburg.
2. Hans Leinberger, *Anna Selbdritt*, 1513. Kloster St. Johann im Gnadenthal, Ingolstadt. Photograph and permission to reproduce Kloster St. Johann im Gnadenthal and the Kulturamt, Ingolstadt.
3. Leonardo da Vinci, *The Virgin and Child with St. Anne*, ca. 1510. Louvre, Paris. Photograph and permission to reproduce Reunion des musées nationaux / Art Resource, New York.
4. Mosan, *Anna Selbdritt*, ca. 1270/80. Photograph and permission to reproduce Liebighaus Museum Alter Plastik, Frankfurt am Main.
5. Hans Greiff, *Sainte-Anne Trinitaire Reliquary Statue*, 1472. Silver gilt and enamel. Musée national du Moyen Age—thermes et hôtel de Cluny, Paris. Photograph and permission to reproduce Reunion des musées nationaux / Art Resource, New York.
6. *Saint Anne Reliquary*, fourteenth century, with later additions. Silver gilt. Annakirche, Düren. By permission of Katholische Pfarrgemeinde St. Anna, Düren
7. Thomas Anselmus, *Holy Kinship*, 1501. Woodcut. Pforzheim. Photograph and permission to reproduce Staatsbibliothek Bamberg.
8. Master of the Legend of Saint Barbara, *Virgin Enthroned with Angels*, 1470–1500. Photograph Brian Merrett, Montreal Museum of Fine Arts. Reproduced by permission of the Montreal Museum of Fine Arts.
9. Hans Holbein the Elder, *Anna Selbdritt Katharinenaltar*, 1512. Augsburg Staatsgalerie. Photograph and Permission to reproduce Bayerische Staatsgemäldesammlungen.

Preface and Acknowledgments

GROWING UP IN a Catholic milieu in Ontario and Quebec, I assumed that I was
familiar with the imagery of Mary's mother, Saint Anne. The images I knew were
depictions of the Education of the Virgin and statues of Saint Anne holding the
child Mary, the first having roots in English medieval art, the second drawing on a
tradition of French sculptures going back to the Saint Anne statue at Chartres. It
was years before I discovered there was an entire body of Anne imagery that I knew
nothing about. Exploring churches and museums in Germany, I saw statues and
paintings in which an adult Anne carried both Mary, depicted as a child, and the
Infant Jesus, in her arms. I was curious to know why the artists who created these
works had rejected the normal generational chronology of grandmother, mother,
and grandchild and depicted Mary as a little girl not much older than her son.

The sense of surprise I experienced was partly the result of the strangeness of
these images, but it also came from the realization that there was a whole aspect of
Saint Anne that was unfamiliar to me. Consultation of the available art historical
literature did not answer my questions; in fact, most of the sources I looked at did
not mention the issues that interested me. Before long, however, an opportunity
arose for me to do extensive research on those German Saint Annes to find the
answers to my questions. Indeed, when I began to research these German depictions of Saint Anne with Mary and Jesus, I found that unraveling her story involved
considerably more than I expected. Far from being a purely art historical project, it
turned out to be as much about the history of religion, and indeed about history in
a general sense, and, as well, to have links with issues addressed in women's studies.
And though the subject of Saint Anne in Northern Europe—the area this book
deals with—remains far from exhausted, this book expands and clarifies our
understanding about the responses of late medieval Christians to the images and
texts that expressed the late medieval cult of Saint Anne, and about the people who
promoted the devotion in the period 1480–1530.

Turning to practical matters connected with the organization of the book, I want first to comment on what will seem like an inconsistent approach to the translations of primary texts, which, except where otherwise noted, are mine. Some primary texts are given in translation only, while in other cases the translation is accompanied by the original text. The decisions to include or not include the original text were not as arbitrary as they might seem. They are based on the following principles, though it must be admitted that decisions in actual cases sometimes had to be arbitrary. First, in cases where an argument rests on the specific nature of particular texts, notably in Chapter 6, I believed it was essential to include the originals. Second, I did not want to lose the distinctiveness of style that marks certain writers, among them Luther, but also the less well-known and sometimes anonymous authors of the fifteenth-century lives of Saint Anne. In addition, I believed it was important for readers familiar with German to see exactly what people were writing and reading in the late fifteenth and early sixteenth centuries. I thought it was good, too, to show some of the regional differences in the language, differences that would have been obliterated in translation.

Another matter that requires comment is the absence of page citations in the endnote references to some of the texts from the fifteenth and early sixteenth centuries. I omitted these for several reasons. In some cases the books do not have numbered pages. Sometimes the same texts were printed in different versions and sometimes they were combined with other texts. Thus the page numbers for different copies of the same work can differ. All this is complicated because the same text might not always have the same title. What I have done, for those who want to check, is provided the libraries or archives where the books I looked at are located. I have generally followed the principle of reproducing texts as they are, though certain printed symbols from some have been replaced with umlauts or in-text letters. With respect to terminology, in this book the early Middle Ages designates the period ca. A.D. 500–1000 the High Middle Ages ca. 1000 to the later 1300s, the late Middle Ages the late 1300s to the early 1500s. Romanesque, Gothic, and so on, refer to these styles as commonly understood. The term "Germanic-speaking" is used to refer to speakers of German in all its late medieval varieties, Dutch, and Flemish. "Flemish" is used in most cases to refer to the entire South Netherlands.

I want now to express my thanks to the many people who helped me in the production of this book. My thanks go first to Pietro (Pierre) Boglioni, Ellen James, and Lionel Rothkrug for their expert and generous help and constant encouragement. Very special thanks go to colleagues and fellow Anne researchers in Holland,

Willemien Deeleman–van Tyen and Ton Brandenbarg, for their extraordinary generosity with their time and their own research findings. Sharing Willemien's knowledge of European Anne imagery and enjoying her hospitality continue to be one of the most enjoyable aspects of my research. Thanks go also to the late Lène Dresen-Coenders in Holland and to Anne researchers in Germany Klaus Arnold, Angelika Dörfler-Dierken, Werner Esser, Bernadette Mangold, and the late Matthias Zender. My gratitude goes also to Rolf Kiessling and Hans-Jörg Kunast in Augsburg.

In Montreal I valued enormously my conversations about saints and art with fellow medievalists Joan Friedman and Rosemary Hale. I thank Anne Winston-Allen for her careful reading of my manuscript and her many extremely helpful comments, and Jim Bugslag for similar much appreciated help. Among others who shared information and research are Marianne Kalinke, Steven Sargent, Pamela Sheingorn, and Joanne Ziegler in the United States, and Frank Chandler in Australia. Help also came from feedback at the medieval conferences at Kalamazoo and Leeds and from the much smaller, convivial conferences of the Canadian Medieval Art Historians Association and the Hagiography Society conference at Groningen in 2000.

Library personnel helped me throughout. I thank in particular Herr Novak at the Augsburg Staats- und Stadtbibliothek, who went out of his way to notice things he knew would be useful in my research; the staff at the Sächsische Landesbibliothek in Dresden for extraordinarily kind and expeditious service; and the Inter-Library Loan Department at Concordia University. Thanks are also due to Gabriel Baugniet for checking my Latin translations and to the Concordia University Part-Time Faculty Association for a grant to cover the cost of illustrations. I owe immense gratitude to Peter J. Potter and Peggy Hoover of Penn State University Press, who saw this project through with what seemed like effortless ease and organization, e-mails sometimes answering e-mails within the hour. My most special thanks go to my husband, Laurence Nixon, for continuing critical discussion of my work, and to my children, Martin, Sarah, Judy, Anna, and David, for assistance with research and with computers and for their enthusiastic involvement with Saint Anne, seeking out *Anna Selbdritts* in their travels and creating family portraits in the guise of the *Selbdritt* and the Holy Kinship. I should also mention that none of the research for this project could have taken place had it not been for my introduction to the German language and literature in the undergraduate classes of Ernst Oppenheimer at Carleton University in Ottawa. Dr. Oppenheimer gave me a foundation in the language and an enduring fondness for German culture that were there, much later, when I needed them.

Introduction

In the late 1400s and early 1500s, artists in Northern Europe produced an extraordinary body of paintings, sculptures, and prints depicting Mary's mother, Saint Anne. Responding to the demand created by the unprecedented popularity Anne enjoyed in the decades between 1470 and 1530, artists outdid one another in ingenuity of composition and richness of iconographic detail. The subject certainly provided scope for detail and ingenuity, for medieval writers gave Anne not one but three husbands, and not one but three daughters, all named Mary. Anne's daughters produced a formidable progeny that included, along with the Saviour, five apostles, and a disciple, plus John the Baptist and the early Rhineland bishops Servatius and Maternus. Sculptors, painters, and printmakers in Germany, Flanders, and Holland depicted these family groupings, whether the larger Holy Kinship group or Saint Anne holding Mary and Jesus, with the realism and luxuriance that marked the genius of the Late Gothic art of the fifteenth and early sixteenth centuries—the toys, clothing, and other accoutrements of the comfortably-off urban middle classes rubbing shoulders with subtle nuances of theological meaning. Images of a similar type were produced in other parts of Europe too, in particular Poland, Bohemia, and Scandinavia, and to a lesser degree France, Spain, and Italy. However, the much greater production of images in the Germanic-speaking areas, and the fact that the cult in these regions formed a cohesive phenomenon, renders them a logical choice for investigation.

The different compositional formats of the images made different statements about the role of Saint Anne in the redemptive drama that forms the heart of Christian belief. In a Tilman Riemenschneider sculpture completed between 1490 and 1495, now in the Mainfränkisches Museum in Würzburg, a pensive Saint Anne extends one arm to loosely encircle her daughter, shown as a child of about ten, seated on her left knee, while her other hand supports the muscular Christ Child standing on her right knee (fig. 1). Mary's motherhood is alluded to in the visible presence of breasts in her childish figure, but her age and miniaturization subordinate her to the

FIGURE 1. Tilman Riemenschneider, *Anna Selbdritt*, 1490–95. Sandstone. Mainfränkisches Museum, Würzburg

enveloping presence of Anne, who seems to be presented as the physical source of both Mary and Jesus. The composition of an *Anna Selbdritt* carved for the convent of Sankt Johannes Gnadenthal in Ingolstadt by Hans Leinberger in 1513 makes a different statement (fig. 2). Seated on a bench, Mary and Anne share the child between them. Anne is shown not as dominating Mary but as equal with her in her relationship with the Christ Child, for the child's body is in contact with both women.

FIGURE 2. Hans Leinberger, *Anna Selbdritt*, 1513. Kloster St. Johann im Gnadenthal, Ingolstadt

Although there are fine examples in North American museums, it is surprising that the *Anna Selbdritt*, as the depiction of Anne with Mary and Jesus is called in German, and the Holy Kinship are not well known outside Germany. They rarely appear in survey or general art history works. Indeed, German art itself is neglected in English-language art-historical publishing. Ironically, the most widely reproduced version of the *Anna Selbdritt* is an atypical Italian reworking of this Northern compositional schema: Leonardo's *The Virgin and Child with Saint Anne* (fig. 3).

FIGURE 3. Leonardo da Vinci, *The Virgin and Child with St. Anne*, ca. 1510. Louvre, Paris

Along with their considerable visual appeal, the *Anna Selbdritts* present some curious compositional features. Why do they so frequently disregard normal chronology and depict Mary as a child? Why are both Mary and Jesus so often miniaturized compared with the oversize proportions of Saint Anne? Why do Mary and Anne not look directly at Jesus? Why are the husbands and fathers in so many Holy Kinships placed behind the women, often separated from them by the physical barrier of a low wall? And why did artists in Northern Europe produce such enormous quantities of these works during the relatively short period between 1480 and 1530?

When I began to ask these questions, I found that the existing literature on Saint Anne did not adequately answer them. The most frequently encountered explanations—that the *Anna Selbdritt* depicted the doctrine of the Immaculate Conception and that the late medieval expansion of Anne's cult was the result of popular devotional enthusiasm—explained very little, and in any case were supported neither by evidence nor by methodological rigor. The foundational studies of the cult and imagery of Saint Anne by E. Schaumkell, Paul-Victor Charland, and Beda Kleinschmidt all date from before the Second World War, and though they correctly connect the late fifteenth-century flowering of the cult with the contemporaneous publication of the new lives of Saint Anne written by Northern humanists, their findings must be treated with caution, for methodology is inconsistent and conclusions are sometimes drawn from extremely modest quantities of data.[1] Subsequent articles on individual *Anna Selbdritt*s shed little light on the circumstances of the cult's expansion, as they tended by and large to accept Kleinschmidt's association with the Immaculate Conception.

In the 1980s a new generation of scholars working simultaneously but independently in Germany, Holland, and the United States turned their attention to Saint Anne. The North American researchers were interested in new questions and approaches generated by women's studies and cultural and interdisciplinary studies. The variety of these approaches, and the wide range of themes discernible in the cult of Saint Anne, are illustrated in the conference papers published in 1990 in *Interpreting Cultural Symbols*, edited by Kathleen Ashley and Pamela Sheingorn. Around the same time that these papers were being written in the United States, a handful of European scholars were embarking on more comprehensive examinations of Saint Anne's cult that were oriented in some cases toward systematic study of groups of images and in other cases toward the late medieval texts connected with the cult. In 1986 Werner Esser completed a dissertation on the Holy Kinship that proposed a genealogy of the image type and began the work of establishing a geographical typology. In 1990 Ton Brandenburg published *Heilig Familieleven*, which analyzes seventeen late fifteenth-century Netherlandish and Rhineland German lives of Saint Anne and explains their role in the carefully orchestrated promotion of Anne's cult carried out by networks of humanists and reforming clerics in these regions.[2] In Amsterdam, Willemien Deeleman–van Tyen cataloged Dutch sculptures of the *Anna Selbdritt*, while, in Passau, Bernadette Mangold did the same for Lower Bavarian examples, as did Peter Paul Maniurka for those produced in Silesia. The German scholar Angelika Dörfler-Dierken's two 1992 books, on the lay confraternities (also referred to as brotherhoods) dedicated to Saint Anne and on the numerous texts connected with her cult, with their systematic compilations of source information, form a contribution of enormous value.[3] Many of these projects, as well as the present work, made use of data on Saint Anne collected by the Bonn *Volkskunde* scholar, the late Matthias Zender.

This book draws on the work of all these scholars, though it differs from their work in that it asks and answers different questions. It began as a study of the works of art, but as these can be understood only by examining the texts and records that speak to us about how Saint Anne was used and understood in the late Middle Ages, this is as well a book on the history of religion, and given the role of religion in the Middle Ages, it is as well a book about history. It is also a book about people. A good deal of space is devoted to "listening" to what people of the fifteenth and early sixteenth centuries had to say about the saints and images that played such a large role in their lives. I am interested in what they did with images, what they felt them to be, and how they perceived them. The listening is done attentively, with an awareness of the slipperiness of language but with an appreciation too of the fact that the deferral of signification does not decrease the potential of texts for releasing or generating meaning; it increases it—problematic though the task of extricating that meaning may be.[4]

The arguments in this study group themselves into four clusters. One group addresses the extraordinary success of the cult of Saint Anne, arguing that her clerical and humanist promoters saw her cult as a means for controlling lay, especially female, piety, and that they built on—and encouraged—anxiety about salvation to do so. I show that they created for Saint Anne a new image as a saint who had power not merely to intercede like other saints but also to actually assist her devotees in getting into heaven. In the liturgical offices and lives they wrote, Saint Anne is used to simultaneously arouse and assuage salvation anxiety. This power is evident in contemporary texts, and I argue as well that her role in the economy of salvation is alluded to in the compositional formats and iconography of the works of art depicting her.

Another set of arguments looks at economic factors in the spread of the cult. Church institutions were suffering financial stresses in some late medieval cities, and I show that the spread of late medieval saints' cults sometimes had less to do with popular piety than with the economics of staying alive—for clerics—in an increasingly competitive ecclesiastical landscape. Beautiful works of art, powerful relics, attractive confraternities, and generous indulgences all brought people into churches, stimulated donations, and encouraged endowments, and the cult of Saint Anne was bound up with all four.

A third group of arguments has to do with the numerous points at which the Saint Anne cult intersects with ideas about female sexual and social behavior. Brandenbarg has shown how new models of middle-class marriage were incorporated into the new Anne lives, and Dörfler-Dierken has demonstrated that the new writing embodies new ideas about sanctified marriage. I propose that, in addition, the Anne texts continued to express long-standing ideas about the incompatibility of sexual activity and holiness. It is an index of the richness of the cult that all three interpretations are compatible.

Finally, an important section of the book proposes a model of how late medieval Christians used and perceived images. I argue that medieval Germany was a culture in which power was more readily ascribed to objects, and images more easily conflated with their referents, than was the case, for example, in England and Holland, where images were more likely to be perceived as *representing* rather than *embodying* their referents. Not only do contemporary speakers reveal, sometimes at length, their feelings about images, but texts and images often contain inadvertent betrayals of responses to images. The predilection to conflate the image with what it represented had important ramifications for the creation, use, and, as it came to be seen, abuse of images in Germany in the late medieval period.

One of the achievements of Brandenbarg's work was the dispelling of the idea that devotion to Saint Anne arose out of popular enthusiasm. My own study of late medieval German images and texts leads me to agree with him, and to conclude, as Peter Brown did for the Early Christian cult of the saints, that the distinctive and to modern eyes magical characteristics that mark some expressions of medieval religious practice are not expressions of the unlettered, or survivals of pagan practices, but are evident at *all* levels, and indeed were propagated in writings and practices produced and encouraged at elite, educated levels of society.[5]

A fundamental assumption in the shaping of this book is the view that works of art are not transcendental objects with mysterious powers. Works of art, both works of genius and works of more modest achievement, are not only art objects but also social artifacts whose operations and means of signifying can be analyzed and to a certain extent understood. At the same time, I am all too aware of the ease with which present conceptions can be imposed on the past. In particular, I have been cautious not to apply nineteenth- and twentieth-century ideas of what constitutes piety, or the lack of it, in assessing fifteenth-century religious practice. As Lynn Hunt has pointed out, subjectivity and the self are not timeless and unchanging; they have histories.[6] I have tried to remember too that the people who lived in the midst of the discourses of the Reformation and of the Immaculate Conception did not "see" these laid out in the orderly formulations that modern historians are able to construct; living within events creates different, often multiple, sometimes conflicting perspectives for the individuals involved. I would also emphasize that the relationship of a work of art to its culture is not a simple case of the one being influenced by the other. A work of art is best understood not by setting it *against* its cultural or historical backgrounds but by looking at it as part of the dialectics of its culture.[7]

In the same way that the written word can yield information, so too can the repeating and changing patterns and correspondences in images. In pictures and in sculptures, in texts and in human actions, the presence or absence of themes and motifs, emphases, overdeterminations, and omissions are clues that provide points of entry for investigations into how people thought and felt. At the same time, it is crucial to remember that structural analysis reveals patterns not answers. Never self-evident, the meaning of the patterns uncovered must be sought with the aid of additional tools and data and supported with concrete evidence.

A final question for the researcher seeking to understand the language of medieval works of art concerns the relationships among images and texts. It is doubtful that it is possible to draw up a clear set of guidelines that will apply to all cases, for images are neither visual descriptions of reality nor simple reflections of texts. Textual sources can be found for many of the motifs in the imagery of Saint Anne, but not infrequently a search produces multiple texts with varying, even contradictory, meanings. In any case, works of art have their own history, with their own patterns, rhythms, and lines of descent. Habit, convention, even misunderstandings on the part of artists and patrons, help shape iconography, and artists draw on traditions of past images as well as on present discourses. On the one hand, compositional features seem related to underlying traits of the culture that produced them; for example, the fact that the realism in Dutch *Anna-te-Drieens* is consistent with the realism in the Dutch Anne texts suggests something important about Dutch culture. On the other hand, an iconographic or stylistic feature may simply reflect the availability of a model, the inspiration of a gifted individual, or the preference of a patron. The fact that Swabian compositions dominate Saxon images may have to do with the fact that the Saxon artists, who had less in the way of a tradition of their own to draw on, simply had access to a plentiful supply of Swabian prints.

Different forms of expression were created, paid for, and used by different groups, and while images and texts are closely related they do not speak in parallel voices. Sometimes they seem to contest one another; for example, at the same time that the painted and sculpted *Anna Selbdritts* and Holy Kinships embody images of female power, lives of Anne urge docility and restraint in women's behavior. Why are they not telling the same story? This book hopes to show that an examination of images and texts of different kinds, intertwined as separate parts of an overall discourse, can be, if not definitive in its conclusions, richly and often unexpectedly revealing.

Beginning with an account of the origins and early history of the devotion to Saint Anne, this book introduces the late medieval flowering of Anne's cult through the activities of particular individuals: a patron commissions an image; a priest promotes devotion at a local level; a prominent humanist writes a book that helps spread the cult at an international level; a pilgrim visits a site where a famed healing relic is displayed; a theologian reminisces. Chapters 3 and 4 address salvational issues in the text and images. Chapter 5 examines the motives and methods of the cult's promoters, in particular their desire to channel lay piety, their interest in presenting Anne as a model of restrained sexual and social behavior for women, and their strategy for presenting her as a salvational helper. Chapter 6 shows how Saint Anne's cult, and by extension other saints' cults, played important economic roles in some late medieval cities, looking in particular at Augsburg and Annaberg, the new silver-mining town named after Anne in the Saxon Erzgebirge. Chapter 7 looks at what people did with and thought about images of Anne and other saints. Chapter 8 returns to Saint Anne herself, showing how early modern ideas about gender, family relations, and the nature of humankind's relationship with God coincided with major changes in the imagery of Saint Anne as she began to lose her special powers and become a mere, if saintly, grandmother. The final chapter describes the images of Saint Anne and proposes interpretations of some of the details of their iconography.

1

The Early History of the Cult of Saint Anne

The Texts

Although Saint Anne was to enjoy special prominence in the late Middle Ages, she was far from ignored in earlier periods of Christian history. And as the themes that mark the early phase of her cult remained embedded in its later phases, an account of her early history helps to clarify later events. Saint Anne is not a biblical figure. She first appears in the second-century apocryphal infancy gospel, the *Protevangelium of James*, as part of the story of Jesus' birth and maternal ancestry.[1] In the ancient Mediterranean world, the genealogy of a hero was an important part of his story, and the author of the *Protevangelium* borrowed from Greek tales of the childhood of heroes for the unedifying but picturesque accounts of the Christ Child murdering playmates who interfered with his games. For Jesus' grandmother the author drew on the more benign biblical story of Hannah—hence Anna—who conceived Samuel in her old age, thus reprising the miraculous birth of the Jesus with a merely remarkable one for his mother.

In creating the story of Anne, the author of the *Protevangelium* did more than rework a familiar tale. He crafted sympathetic characters and a narrative infused with poetic images and human interest. The humiliation that Joachim suffers when his sacrifice at the Temple is rejected because of his failure to produce offspring is movingly conveyed, and his subsequent flight to the solitude of his pastures serves as an effective plot stimulus for Anne to lament both her sterility and the loss of her husband. Anne's lamentation, which is prompted by the twittering of a nesting bird, acquires a deeper pathos in light of the sneers of her maidservant in an ironic domestic repetition of the public humiliation of Joachim:

> And Anna sighed towards heaven, and saw a nest of sparrows in the laurel tree and immediately she made lamentation within herself: Woe to me, who begot me, What womb brought me forth?
> For I was born as a curse before them all and before the children of Israel

And I was reproached, and they mocked me and thrust me out of the temple of the Lord.

Woe is me, to what am I likened?

I am not likened to the birds of the heaven; for even the birds of the heaven are fruitful before thee, O Lord.[2]

God hears their prayers. Joachim in his fields and Anne sorrowing at home are told by an angel that Anne will become pregnant. Mary is conceived and born and, like Samuel, in fulfillment of a parental vow, is brought to spend her childhood in the Temple.[3]

During the Middle Ages, Anne's story circulated in the numerous books that retold the life of Christ.[4] The first Northern European writer to treat it was the tenth-century Benedictine canoness Hroswitha of Gandersheim in the long poem *Historia nativitatis laudabilisque conversationis intactae Dei genitricis*.[5] Later, the work's inclusion in such works as Vincent of Beauvais's thirteenth-century *Speculum historiale* and in Jacobus de Voragine's fourteenth-century *Legenda Aurea* ensured its dissemination throughout western Europe.[6] All the accounts of Anne's life from the late antique and earlier medieval periods singled out as their main theme the older, sterile woman blessed by God with a child, while a second theme, especially prominent in Greek writing, drew attention to Anne as the generator of the flesh that provided the flesh of the Redeemer.[7]

The Early History: Cult, Images, and Pilgrimage

Anne was not only a textual creation. By the sixth century, she was the object of cultic attention in Jerusalem and Constantinople. No study of her cult in its Early Christian and Byzantine settings has yet been done, but it would appear that the idea of Anne's flesh as the source of the flesh of Mary and the Redeemer struck a resonant note among theologians, while the possibility of attracting pilgrims to the house of Mary's birth interested others.[8] None of the five churches and chapels that some sources say were dedicated to Anne in Constantinople before the year 1000 has survived. Paintings have fared somewhat better, with cycles of Anne's life, as part of the life of the Virgin, recorded from the sixth century on. The earliest extant separate image of Anne holding the infant Mary was painted on the walls of the presbytery of Santa Maria Antiqua in Rome around 650, and she was depicted again there ca. 760 as one of the three holy mothers along with Mary and Elizabeth.[9]

Economic factors as well as theological issues affected the development of Saint Anne's cult in its early phases. The survival of two twelfth-century crusader churches dedicated to her, one erected in Jerusalem ca. 1130, the other built later in the century in Sepphoris, a town on the main route between Nazareth and the port of Acre, indicates that her cult was being promoted with a view to the pilgrim trade.[10] Travelers' references to the Sepphoris church as the birthplace of Mary suggest that it may have been in competition for pilgrims and their alms with a church in Jerusalem that was making similar claims. The fact that part of a floor in the Sepphoris church is formed of living rock—a feature customarily found in places purporting to be sites of sacred events in this part of the world—heightens the likelihood that it was claiming to incorporate the house of Anne and Joachim; indeed, Folda cites several travelers who mention Sepphoris as Anne's or Mary's birthplace.[11] Such an undertaking on the part of the church would not have been surprising. The numerous references to relics brought back by twelfth- and thirteenth-century crusaders and pilgrims tell us that Anne's cult was being successfully promoted in the Holy Land among visiting European Christians. Some of the relics those visitors brought back were later to form the nucleus of cult centers in the developing pilgrimage networks in western Europe.[12]

The Cult in the North in the Central and High Middle Ages: Saint Anne and the Immaculate Conception

By the twelfth century, Saint Anne's cult was established in Northern Europe. Though the sequence of events that marked its progress cannot be followed in detail, it is not difficult to discern the familiar strands of theological interest in Anne's significance as the source of Mary's flesh and of the development of cult centers dedicated to Anne.

The question of Anne's role in the conception of her daughter is a recurring theme in the late medieval discourse surrounding Anne. The theologians of the Central and High Middle Ages viewed the question of Mary's conception and birth with an increasingly heightened awareness of the implications of the various conclusions that might be drawn about it. What exactly was the nature of the conception that generated the Mother of God? Had it been attended by the original sin that accompanies every act of human generation? Or had Mary somehow escaped the stain of original sin? These questions about Mary inevitably directed attention toward Anne. By the eleventh century, a new feast of Mary's conception in the womb of her mother, probably introduced into southern Italy in the ninth century by Byzantine monks, was being celebrated in some English monasteries and very likely in Normandy as well. Around the same time, a feast devoted to Anne herself was established in western Europe.[13]

As the feast of Mary's conception began to extend out from the English and northern French centers, concerns continued to be raised over its theological implications. It seemed not unreasonable to conclude that Mary's great holiness and purity necessitated a special kind of conception for her. But what precisely was being honored when people celebrated that conception? The question of what composed Mary's incomparable purity had not greatly concerned Byzantine theologians, but Western European theologians wanted definitions. Some thinkers, probably first in England, proposed that Mary had been immaculately conceived in the womb of Anne, that is, conceived without the transmission of original sin. This idea was opposed by most of the eminent theologians of the day, among them Bernard of Clairvaux, Peter Lombard, Alexander of Hales, Albertus Magnus, Bonaventure, and Thomas Aquinas, who argued instead that Mary had been freed from original sin after her conception but before her birth—a doctrine referred to as the maculate conception. Aquinas expressed a fundamental objection when he asked how Mary's freedom from original sin could be reconciled with the fact that all human beings stood in need of redemption: "It is simply not fitting," he said, "that Christ should not be savior of the whole human race. Hence it follows that the sanctification of the Blessed Virgin was after her animation."[14]

In addition, the proposal that Mary had been immaculately conceived had to confront the entrenched Augustinian notion of an ineluctable original sin transmitted through bodily sexual generation. According to medieval theology, even legitimate marital sexual intercourse carried with it some degree, however small, of sinfulness. Bernard made this point succinctly in a letter criticizing the canons of Lyons for their unseemly haste in adopting the new feast: "If therefore it was quite impossible for her to have been sanctified before her conception, because she did not then exist; or in the act of her conception, because of the presence of sin; it remains that she was sanctified after her conception, when she was already in the womb, and that this sanctification excluded sin and rendered her birth, but not her conception, holy."[15] Aquinas invoked Augustine on the same point: "Even if the parents of the blessed Virgin were cleansed from original sin, the blessed Virgin contracted it since she was conceived in sexual desire and the joining of husband and wife. Augustine says, all flesh born of intercourse is of sin."[16]

Immaculatist thinkers countered these objections in different ways. A few argued that Mary had been conceived without sexual desire on the part of her parents, in which case, according to their reasoning, original sin would not have been passed on; others argued simply that God had made an exception for Mary; still others, particularly in England, were paving the way for eventual resolution of the problem with proposals that centered on concepts of time. Anselm the Great, while he emphasized that all human beings were born in sin, raised the possibility that Christ's salvific action might have cleansed Mary in advance.[17] This idea culminated in the early fourteenth century in the concept of preventive atonement first put forth by Robert of Ware and subsequently developed by the English Franciscan John Duns Scotus. This solution reconciled the Immaculate Conception with the doctrine of original sin and the universality of Christ's redemptive sacrifice: Mary did indeed require salvation like other humans, but Christ fittingly saved her in advance.

Scotus's formulation, at the same time that it ensured Mary's preservation from original sin, increased the magnitude of God's redemptive power: "Mary would have had the greatest need of Christ as Redeemer; for by reason of her procreation, which followed the common mode, she would have contracted original sin had she not been kept from it by the grace of the Mediator, and just as others are in need of Christ for the remission, by His merit, of sin which they have already contracted, so Mary would have been in still greater need of a Mediator preventing her from contracting sin."[18]

Scotus's formulation was propagated at Oxford and at the University of Paris, especially by the Franciscans, usually through the medium of commentaries on the *Sentences* of Peter Lombard, which argued against the doctrine of the Immaculate Conception.[19] However, despite the ultimately decisive intervention of Scotus, the Immaculate Conception continued to be the subject of strife throughout the fourteenth and especially the fifteenth centuries. At the same time, in many quarters the idea of what exactly the Immaculate Conception was remained vague; it is not uncommon to find a writer who announces himself an immaculatist expressing himself in words that express a maculist position.[20]

It is clear that, as Mary's mother, Anne was implicated in the discourse of the conception of her daughter. Indeed, both the composition of the *Anna Selbdritt*, which emphasizes the link between Anne and the two generations of offspring, and the chronology of the image, coinciding as it does with the spread of the feast, suggest that the image was intended to allude to Anne's conception of Mary. However, the frequently encountered statement that the *Anna Selbdritt* was intended to represent the Immaculate Conception is not tenable. The textual evidence does not support the idea that the image represents or refers to the doctrine that Mary was conceived without being stained by original sin. To begin with, while texts arguing *against* the Immaculate Conception often bring in Mary's parents, mentioning their sexual intercourse as an argument against the doctrine, texts arguing *for* it written before the late fifteenth century, at which point the discourse takes some new turns that will be discussed in later chapters, only infrequently mention Anne. Further there is no evidence to suggest that the doctrine was a concern at the level of the parish churches and even private homes, where some of the earliest extant images were located. And many of the early works were produced in areas far distant from the centers where the doctrine was being discussed. Conversely, in England, where the doctrine was firmly rooted and perhaps more clearly conceptualized than anywhere else, Anne was normally depicted not in the *Selbdritt* composition but alone with Mary. Anne's role in the high medieval discourse of Mary's conception was clearly important, but she was not at this point associated definitively with either the pro- or anti-immaculatists.

The Trinubium: *Anne's Three Marriages*

A second issue related to Saint Anne's family relationships, the number of her husbands and daughters, was also reformulated in Northern Europe in this period. Less complicated than Mary's conception, and less forcefully contested by eminent theologians (though Aquinas and Fulbert of Chartres were among those who raised unsuccessful protests), this was the idea that Anne remarried twice after the death of Joachim, producing two additional daughters, each named Mary.[21] In the ninth century, Haimo of Auxerre, the first writer to make this claim (as part of what was hoped to be a clarification of Jesus' family tree), connected Jerome's statement that the brothers of the Lord were the sons of his mother's sisters with the notion that the three Marys were sisters.[22] According to Haimo, Anne's second marriage, to Cleophas, produced Mary Cleophas, who married Alphaeus and gave birth to James the Lesser, Jude Thaddeus, Simon, and the disciple Joseph the Just, the disciple who lost out to Matthias when lots were drawn to replace Judas. Anne's marriage to Salome produced Mary Salome, who married Zebedee and became the mother of James the Greater and John the Evangelist. The family tree included other relatives too: Elizabeth, Mary's cousin and the mother of John the Baptist, was the daughter of Anne's sister Esmeria, whose son Eliud was an ancestor of Saint Servatius, a fourth-century bishop of Tongres in the Rhineland. Despite its rejection by Aquinas, the Holy Kinship became firmly established, its appearance in the works of such writers as Peter Lombard, Petrus Comestor, and Jacobus da Voragine helping to spread the details of Saint Anne's three marriages and their saintly offspring.[23]

The High Middle Ages: Anne as Shrine Saint

These variations on older themes were not the only forces shaping the devotion to Saint Anne in Northern Europe. By the High Middle Ages, Anne had begun to take on new roles as local shrine saint and as maritime patroness that do not seem to be related to her earlier history, but rather represent her insertion into existing Northern religious practice. Thus, though Anne had entered the Christian pantheon through her physical relationship with Mary, and though in theological and devotional texts and in images, the story of her life remained joined to that of her daughter, devotion to Anne now became in many instances a separate cult. She was increasingly singled out and honored in her own right. The primary cult role that emerges from the sources of the High Middle Ages is that of local shrine saint, the saint whose relics, located and promoted in a particular shrine, are sought out by pilgrims seeking miracles of healing, rescue, victory, and the like.[24] This is the dominant paradigm of saint worship in the Central and High Middle Ages, and this is the pattern found in a description of a visit to the shrine of Saint Anne d'Armour in Brittany in the medieval Breton poem *Les Brez*. In that poem Anne helps and protects the hero in battle. No emphasis is put on her role as mother of Mary. The hero's relationship to her follows the characteristic devotee-saint pattern, with its promises of gifts and devotional rituals in return for her help:

> If I come home again, mother Saint Anne, I will make you a present:
> I will make you a present of a cord of wax that will go three times around your walls,
> Three times around your church, three times around your cemetery,
> And three times around your lands, should I arrive at home.
> And I will give you a banner of velvet and white satin with a pole of polished ivory.
> And I will give you seven bells of silver to sing gaily night and day above your head.[25]

Five typical shrine-saint motifs are mentioned here. The hero seeks Anne's protection in battle; in return he promises her not only devotion but gifts; the saint's protection is contingent, not automatic, for the hero "woos her" with promises of devotion; there is mention of the "measuring" motif—both pilgrimage souvenirs and offerings at shrines sometimes involved candles or threads made to specific measurements, whether of holy places or objects, or of the supplicant; and finally, the references to "your walls . . . your cemetery . . . your lands" point to the local saint associated with a particular piece of territory that is "owned" by her.

The High Middle Ages: Anne as Maritime Patroness

By the High Middle Ages, if not before, along with more general patronages, Saint Anne had taken on a particular role as a maritime protectress, a saint to be prayed to before voyages or during storms. Her cult is marked in coastal areas. Of seven confirmed references to Anne brotherhoods in existence before the 1470s in Angelika Dörfler-Dierken's 1992 study of Anne confraternities, four were in cities on or near the North Sea coast, while another was on an important shipping river. Of fifteen unconfirmed earlier references to brotherhoods, at least eleven were on or near the North Sea coast or on important rivers, while one, that of the *vischkoopers* (fish merchants) in s'Hertogenbosch, was associated with a maritime occupation.[26] Further, Anne was often paired with Saint Nicholas, another saint associated with marine rescue. Her maritime role and her not infrequent association with Nicholas continued into the late Middle Ages, and indeed after. In fifteenth-century Lübeck, sailors belonged to the Annabruderschaft, and sea captains to the Nikolaibruderschaft.[27]

Throughout the High Middle Ages, Saint Anne seems to have enjoyed fairly widespread popularity in Northern Europe. In France, although her best-known images, at Chartres and at Notre Dame, depict her with Mary alone, a number of *Ste.-Anne Trinitaires*, as the *Selbdritt* is called in French, were produced in the fourteenth, fifteenth, and early sixteenth centuries, and a certain number of confraternities, most of them occupation-related, were founded.[28] The English cult shows similar structural features, but here the images most often depicted Anne with the child Mary; Jesus was usually not included. In neither country did the cult undergo the elaboration that it did in Germany, Flanders, and Holland. In France the period of greatest growth occurred in the seventeenth century. Ex-votos depicting Anne's help at sea were abundant in the coastal regions of France in the post-Tridentine era, and the tradition continued in Quebec, where the French form of the cult was imported in the seventeenth century.[29]

The Medieval Images of Saint Anne with Mary and Jesus

The dual concerns of theology and devotional practice that shaped the development of Anne's cult also informed the development of the imagery depicting her. Most notably, the invention of the *Anna Selbdritt*, the portrayal of Anne with Mary and Jesus, in contrast to the earlier works of art, which show Anne with Mary, suggests a new interest in the theme of Anne as the ultimate source of the flesh of Christ, the theme that will come to dominate the Anne discourse in the later Middle Ages. The earliest examples of the *Anna Selbdritt*, a handful of sculptures dated to the late thirteenth and early fourteenth centuries, show the different solutions artists adopted in

FIGURE 4. Mosan, *Anna Selbdritt*, ca. 1270/80. Liebighaus Museum Alter Plastik, Frankfurt am Main

responding to this new perception of Anne. The typical solution was to base the new trio on existing formats for depicting the Madonna and Child. A late thirteenth-century miniature sardonyx cameo relief in the Museo Nazionale in Modena, for example, incorporates an additional child into a classic frontal Romanesque Throne of Wisdom. In a late thirteenth-century Mosan example in the Liebighaus Museum in Frankfurt, the artist resorted to two separate figures, a tall Anne standing beside what is in effect a miniaturized standing Gothic Madonna and Child (fig. 4). In the early fourteenth-century *Anna Selbdritt* in Erfurt Cathedral, and in some other fourteenth-century sculptures, it is Anne (holding Mary, who in turn holds the Christ Child) who is modeled on the standing Madonna. In some early *Anna Selbdritts*, Anne is modeled so closely on Mary that the two women are almost identical, Anne's "Marian" appearance in some cases being so pronounced that it led some art historians to surmise that the sculptures were originally Madonnas later reworked as *Anna Selbdritts*.[30] Most likely, the similarity simply points to the familiar process of adapting an existing compositional type to new uses; another familiar device—ascribing to the imitating figure (Anne) the qualities or prestige of the figure imitated (Mary)—may also be at work.

The Fifteenth Century: New Forms of the Anna Selbdritt

As the fourteenth century gave way to the fifteenth, artists worked out a separate iconography for Anne, and a number of new compositional formats were added to the existing repertoire. No longer merely a variant of the Mary figure, Anne acquired the body type, face, and costume of a mature married woman of the upper levels of the middle class. Mary wears the same kind of clothing she wears in other late medieval Northern art works, garments that are beautiful and often of luxurious material, but often somewhat more austere and more generalized in terms of class and period than those of other saints. She usually does not wear jewelry apart from the crown or circlet, though jewels are sometimes incorporated into her crown or her clothing.

The fine clothing of the women of the Holy Kinship is displayed to splendid effect in many of the late fifteenth- and early sixteenth-century paintings, especially those showing Anne and Mary seated on a bench with the child between them, a compositional arrangement that achieved popularity all over Germany and Flanders. More often, the new formats coming into use tended to show regional differences, although some are found in more than one area. By the later fifteenth century, a variety of types and subtypes were in production, as interest in Saint Anne and the desire for representations of her slowly, and at first unevenly, began to grow. The stage was set for the final and most splendid phase of her cult.

2

Changes in the Late Fifteenth Century

Until late in the fifteenth century, Saint Anne had functioned as a saint among other saints. By the 1470s, however, there are signs that Northern European Christians were beginning to pay somewhat more attention to her, and attention of a different kind. Traces of this change make their appearance in written sources of many kinds—documents, books, notes, and journals—and in the works of art themselves, sometimes stating a program in plain words, sometimes leaving a suggestive hint in an offhand remark.

Anna Hofmann: An Urban Bourgeois Client
One of those who left traces of their interest in Saint Anne was Anna Hofmann, the wife of Hans Hofmann, an official of the court of Upper Bavaria. In 1472 Frau Hofmann commissioned a silver gilt reliquary 48 centimeters high in the form of a figure of Saint Anne holding Mary and Jesus (fig. 5). For this important and expensive commission she went to Hans Greiff, a leading goldsmith in the Bavarian town of Ingolstadt, where she lived. In Greiff's creation Saint Anne is seated on a throne-like chair surmounted by a baldaquin; Mary is seated on her left knee; the Infant Jesus stands on her right knee. Mary is miniaturized so that she more or less matches Jesus in size, and together the two children hold up a small box meant to contain a relic. Anne wears the head covering and neckband that Frau Hofmann would herself have worn at this mature stage of her life.

Though the image, which is now in the Musée de Cluny in Paris, shows Anne with Mary and Jesus, in the inscription he engraved on the back of Anne's chair Greiff describes it simply as "Saint Anne." For him it was Anne who was the important one, and this seems to have been the way most late medieval Germans viewed the triple representation, for there are many such references. Some late medieval texts refer to the images simply as "Anne with the two children." Indeed, the very name of the image puts the emphasis on Anne, for *Anna Selbdritt* means literally "Anne herself the third" or "Anne with two others."

FIGURE 5. Hans Greiff, *Sainte-Anne Trinitaire Reliquary Statue*, 1472. Silver gilt and enamel. Musée national du Moyen Age—thermes et hôtel de Cluny, Paris

Anna Hofmann could afford an expensive work. From 1447 to his death in 1480, her husband had been *Rentmeister* (revenue collector) for Heinrich the Rich of Landshut and subsequently for Ludwig the Rich, dukes of Upper Bavaria.[1] Hence her choice of gold and silver as material, and her choice of one of the top craftsmen in a region famous for its work in precious metals. Greiff may have viewed the work as special also, for he included an unusually large amount of information in the inscription he engraved on it. Goldsmiths often marked their works, but few inscriptions are as long as this one, which, besides the date of 1472 and the name of the maker, gives the weight and value of the commission (which included two patens as well), its subject matter, and the name of the commissioner:

> Hans Greiff goldsmith made for Anna Hofmann, wife of the *Rentmeister*, the image of Saint Anne and two patens, and it weighs as nine marks for gold [and] silver and payment set at 100 Rhenish guilders. Done on Saint Michael's Day in the year 1472.
>
> [hanns greiff golczsmid hat gemacht anna hofmanin rentmaisterin / Das pild sant anna und zbay paczein und biget als IX marck fir gold silber und lon gestet c gulden reinis geschechen an sant micheltag m cccc und lxxii iar.][2]

Why did Anna Hofmann commission her reliquary, and what did she do with it? The two patens, which are liturgical vessels, suggest that a donation to a church was intended, though it would not necessarily have included the reliquary. However, the choice of gold and silver as material, and the relatively large size of the work, point in the direction of a donation. While statues of precious metal were sometimes made for domestic settings, they were especially welcome acquisitions for church treasuries, not only because of their splendour and the status they demonstrated but also because they could be used as security, sold, or pawned should the need arise. Silver images and reliquaries abound in woodcuts depicting relic collections belonging to churches, monasteries, and princes, and church account books routinely list them with their weight and monetary value, which is always more than that of paintings or wood sculptures.

The author of the catalog for a 1988 exhibition of Ingolstadt gold work proposed that Frau Hofmann might have commissioned the reliquary to give to her parish church of Saint Moritz or to the Heilig-Geist-Spital in Ingolstadt.[3] It was a reasonable proposal, for people often made such gifts of works of art, which were deemed to earn the same spiritual merit as alms. In fact, Frau Hofmann did give her reliquary to a church, but it was not her parish church. The gift went instead to Sankt Johannes Gnadenthal, the Ingolstadt Franciscan women's convent dedicated to the two Saint Johns; documents compiled in the convent in the mid-sixteenth century, which drew on earlier sources, inform us that a Frau Anna Hofmann had given the nuns a "beautiful silver image of Saint Anne valued at about 80 florins."[4]

It is not really surprising that the reliquary did not go to Frau Hofmann's parish church. Covering as many bases as they could in their attempts to secure their salvation, late medieval German testators characteristically divided up their religious bequests among a number of different churches and convents. There are other reasons too why she might have chosen Saint Johannes; she undoubtedly knew the convent well, for the Hofmann house was almost next door to it.[5] Indeed, because the convent was a favored place for young women of her class, Frau Hofmann likely knew some of the nuns and their families personally.

Familiarity, however, may not have been the main reason Frau Hofmann gave her valuable reliquary to the Franciscan sisters. The convent had a reputation as a place of special holiness and austerity, and as such its prayers would have been viewed as having heightened efficacy. Over the centuries, the nuns of Sankt Johannes Gnadenthal had cultivated this reputation. Founded unendowed, possibly as a beguine house, they subsisted initially on alms and their own handwork. Sometime in the early 1300s they came into an association with the Franciscans. In the 1460s the convent was reformed—the first in the district to be reformed—so that it now came under a regularized Franciscan rule as a tertiary house. Reformed convents and monasteries were considered more holy than unreformed ones and were preferred by the wealthy laity as places of burial. From this time on, according to the convent chronicle of 1540 written by Sister Elisabeth Peringer, the sisters enjoyed a growing reputation for strict observance, copious flagellation, severe fasts, a meager diet, and other mortifications of the flesh. Their perceived holiness increasingly made them a focus for the alms of Ingolstadt's patrician families and for new recruits. In 1489 seven of the nuns were enclosed, in a memorable public ceremony attended by the entire town; the reason more did not take the veil, according to convent sources, was that some had to be free to go out to collect alms. The sisters were viewed as very holy, and support and donations, including gifts from prominent and noble families, increased enormously. Their most generous benefactors were the *Rentmeister* Johannes Kleshamer and his wife, Barbara, whose numerous gifts included a new toilet costing seventy-eight florins; in 1509, gifts enabled the sisters to build a bathhouse.

But despite the gifts, many of them salvational bequests, the discourse presented in the sources continues to report that the sisters suffered great physical need— sometimes having no supper on their table apart from "blue milk soup" with cabbage. Convent lore described a gift of ten florins brought by an angel, and on another occasion a visit from the Virgin personally delivering food to the hungry nuns. The combination of the two themes of holiness and poverty, doubtless exaggerated, continued to mark their self-presentation for some time. Only in the late 1480s does the theme of need seem to diminish.[6]

The gifts were not simply a reward for their sanctity, for holy nuns were powerful nuns. The long tradition of recourse to vicarious spiritual works in Germany was bound up with an assumption that the holier those who did the praying, the more powerful the prayers. At the lowest end of the intercessory spectrum, the elderly women who were given shelter in the *Seelhäuser* were required to pray for their bene-factors and to live a nun-like life, and they were expected to turn up to pray at other people's funerals too, in return for a few extra pennies.[7] The nuns of Sankt Johannes Gnadenthal—holy, wellborn, and virgin—were at the other end of the interces-sional spectrum; one might describe them as a kind of giant spiritual battery that generated efficacious holiness.

The proposal that the sisters depended heavily on their reputation for their income is supported by the fact that they do not seem to have gone after the kinds of things some other late medieval convents and churches did. There are no records of wonder-working images here. No caches of marvelous relics were unearthed in the convent cellars. There are no records of the church offering significant indul-gences. What they had to offer was holiness. And that evidently served them in good stead.

We can do more than merely assume that Anna Hofmann gave the sisters her reliquary in hopes of benefiting from their prayers. Convent sources state that this was the case; the gift was to be reciprocated by prayers for Frau Hofmann from the sisters. Nor was it the only gift. Over the years she had been a generous benefactor, concerned to make sure the sisters had enough to eat and drink, contributing toward building funds, and providing the necessities for the celebration of mass:

> And . . . old Frau Hofmann, the wife of Duke George's *Rentmeister*, along with many other benefactions of food and drink, gave 22 florins for the building of the new house, 10 florins toward the building of the church, along with a beautiful silver image of Saint Anne of a value of 80 florins, and in addition a chalice, three mass vestments, four altar cloths, a mass book, two angel staffs, and two lights, as well as other church ornaments. This woman did much good for the building of the convent and church, honoring them with altogether 300 florins with the request that the sisters should include her in their prayers.[8]

There is no mention of relics. Whether this is because the reliquary was given without its relic, whether it (or they) had been disposed of by the time the account was written, or for some other reason, is not known. As for the gold-and-silver statue, it would seem that the sisters eventually did take advantage of its considerable monetary value. When it left their hands is not known, but the Musée de Cluny acquired it from a private collector in 1861.[9]

Ironically, a far more beautiful representation of the *Anna Selbdritt*, a wood sculpture carved around 1513 by the celebrated Hans Leinberger—the gift of two Bavarian patrician families, the Peringer and the Riedler, whose daughters entered the convent in the early 1500s—is still in place in the convent church (fig. 2). Though it is more celebrated today for its aesthetic qualities than the Greiff work, being of wood, the Leinberger *Anna Selbdritt* did not have the same value as an object of exchange. Veit Peringer, who had been mayor of Ingolstadt several times, and his wife Anna, were the parents of two of the nuns. Margaretha died in 1561 with a reputation for holiness; Elisabeth, who came to the convent at the age of eight in 1497, became a novice in 1505, made her profession at thirteen, and in 1540 authored the chronicle that listed the gifts of Frau Hofmann. The co-patrons, the Riedlers, were a Munich patrician family whose daughter Barbara had come to live in the convent at the age of nine, making her profession at thirteen.[10] The arms of the two families are incorporated in the work.

With a date of 1472, the reliquary Frau Hofmann donated is a relatively early example of a Southwest German *Anna Selbdritt*. Its composition, with a child on either side of Anne, echoes one of the few very early examples of the *Anna Selbdritt* in Bavarian art, a stone sculpture dated 1290–1300 in the Diözesanmuseum Saint Ulrich in Regensburg, and it anticipates a formula that would be widespread in Southwest Germany in the fifteenth century. The crown that Mary wears is common in Bavarian depictions of Anne, less so the dark-blue, flaring enameled cloak worn by the Child Jesus. This cloak, which barely covers the Christ Child's bottom, appears in several later Bavarian and Franconian *Anna Selbdritt*s, and it is also found on the child who carries the basket of roses in some German depictions of Saint Dorothy. Not at all typical is the flower-shaped jewel set with pearls and gems on a star-shaped wreath on Anne's abdomen. It is possible that the jewel refers to Anne's conception of Mary, but this feature is extremely rare in the iconography of Saint Anne. The Leinberger work in which Mary and Anne, both shown as adults, sit on a bench or wide throne with the Christ Child between them represents a later compositional type. Leinberger's work incorporates another new feature of the fifteenth-century *Anna Selbdritt*: the vertical spiritual trinity—of God the Father, the Dove of the Holy Spirit, and the Christ Child—intersects with the horizontal fleshly trinity of Mary, Jesus, and Anne.

Frau Hofmann's statue was commissioned before the cult of Saint Anne came into the period of full bloom initiated by the efforts of the Rhineland German and

Netherlandish humanists and reforming clergy. The new lives of Saint Anne had not yet been published, nor had the new confraternities been founded. As such it occupies a special place in the cult's history, for it opens a window onto the substratum of popular devotion on which the humanists constructed their promotion. Ton Brandenbarg has argued that they were building on an expanding popular cult, and Anna Hofmann is an example of that popular devotion. In terms of patronage, of the role of women in the cult, of the functions of the Anne images, and of its composition and iconography, Frau Hofmann's *Anna Selbdritt* introduces themes that will shape the discourse through the expansion and decline of Anne's cult in the last two decades of the fifteenth century and the first two decades of the sixteenth.

Johannes Knüssli: Honoring Anne in a Pastoral Context

Quite the opposite was the case with Johannes Knüssli, a Swiss priest who expended a good deal of energy, and money, in his attempts to encourage devotion to the Holy Kinship at the Saint Gallen Münster. Drawing on the annotations Knüssli made on his copies of one of the earliest of the new texts about Saint Anne and her family, an office of the Holy Kinship known as the *Basler Offizium*, published in Basel in 1476, and on endowment and other documents, J. Müller, in an article published in 1909, showed the steps an individual priest took to promote devotion to a group of favorite saints.[11]

On his arrival in Saint Gallen in 1478 to take up a position as one of the five chaplains of the *Frühamt* (the mass said early enough that day laborers could attend) at the Liebfrauenaltar of the Saint Gallen Münster, Knüssli embarked posthaste on a program to correct what he saw as the neglect into which the liturgy at that altar had fallen, in particular the omission of the collects that were supposed to be said in honor of Joseph, Anne, and Joachim.[12]

As part of a considerable personal financial investment in his project, Knüssli himself endowed the daily singing of the office of Mary and her kinship.[13] His devotion to the Holy Kinship also informed the choices he made in drawing up plans for offices and masses to be said for his own soul and those of members of his family. As well as endowing these and other liturgies dedicated to members of Anne's family, he left funds for the preaching of sermons on the feasts of Joachim and Joseph with the express purpose of informing people about the Holy Kinship: "For their salvation's sake, and so that the praiseworthy and noble kinship, stem and root of the heavenly queen and mother of all mercy, the virgin Mary, will be worshipfully proclaimed each year, and so that the common folk would understand." Provision was made for the sermons to be announced beforehand, and for the brotherhood—probably a confraternity of the Holy Kinship or of Saint Anne—to be informed and its members reminded that they were to be present and ready to follow instructions concerning their participation. A third sermon was to be preached on the feast of Saint James, Saint Anne's grandson, to proclaim "the good roots, noble stem, and blessed and holy tree, Saint Anne and her three daughters and their seven sons."[14] Knüssli died in 1491. The preaching continued through the 1500s.

Knüssli had been given permission to set up an altar in the charnel house chapel and to dedicate it "in the honour and praise of holy saint Joseph, also to saint Mary Cleophas, James, and [Mary] Salome."[15] This may have been a family altar, but more likely it was the altarpiece of the brotherhood mentioned above, which was located in the charnel house. The reformer Johannes Kessler, writing in 1529, recalled a Saint Anne altar at which each morning around 5:00 a mass had been sung (with the schoolboy Kessler among the choirboys). According to Kessler, the primary altar was dedicated to Mary and her kinship, "but the people called it the Saint Anne altar, for the painting of the *Anna Selbdritt* was there . . . holding the two most holy children who have ever been born, Jesus and Mary, in her arms."[16]

Kessler's situating of Mary at the center of the kinship, in contrast to what he seems to describe as a popular focus on Anne, echoes the language used by Knüssli. In contrast to the terminology used by the Ingolstadt goldsmith Hans Greiff, which privileged Anne, not even mentioning Mary and Jesus by name, Knüssli's reference to the Holy Kinship as the kinship of Mary—"the Queen of Heaven and Maid Mary and all her kinship"—situates Mary rather than Anne as the link among these saints.[17] This emphasis on Mary in the midst of her kinship is consistent with other evidence that a more equitable distribution of attention to the members of the kinship may have characterized Switzerland in the 1470s and possibly earlier. But at the same time that one can point to the Marian emphasis as a survival, the emphasis on the genealogy of the Holy Kinship, its size and nobility, is a new theme. One that is prominent in the offices, it will be used to emphasize the power and honor not so much of Mary but of Anne, in the new lives shortly to be written. Knüssli's case illuminates the links and tensions that marked the period around 1470 when the cult was, by medieval standards, changing rapidly. Though we see a move to highlight Anne, underlying that emphasis is a focus on Mary. Knüssli remarks that when he urges parents to name their children after members of the kinship, he is doing it because naming children for members of Mary's family is a way of honoring her.[18]

Living in Switzerland, Johannes Knüssli was well placed to come in contact with the Basel office. The liturgical texts of the 1470s, which contain liturgical and other material, were one of the sources for the new Anne lives that would be published in the 1480s and later, for they contain not only themes and emphases but also incidents and even phrases that would be found in the latter.[19] The offices likely drew on still earlier liturgical texts.[20]

Angelika Dörfler-Dierken has argued that the fifteenth-century devotion to Saint Anne may have originated in Carmelite circles.[21] The offices do point toward the Carmelites inasmuch as one of the kinship offices, the *Historia nova pulchra devota et autentica de sancta anna matris dei genitricis marie*, published by Anton Sorg in Augsburg in 1479, contains sections in its Joseph office "Sequitur hystoria sancte ioseph ..." that are the same as those in *Das alte Regensburger Office*, a Saint Joseph office of 1434 that Joseph Seitz describes as a Carmelite work.[22] If Dörfler-Dierken is correct, the original intent of the new type of life would not have been to call attention to Anne but to bolster the Carmelite order's claim to ancient and illustrious origins.[23] Lacking a charismatic founding saint such as the Franciscans and Dominicans boasted, they made up for this by devising the story that the order had been founded by Elijah on Mount Carmel and that it was Carmelite monks who advised Anne's mother, Emerentia, to marry rather than follow her own inclination to virginity—a decision without which there could have been no Redemption. However, working against the argument for Carmelite provenance are the facts that the early offices do not, as a rule, give pride of place to Anne, tending rather to spread the attention around to the kinship as a whole, and that they do not put special emphasis on Emerentia's visit to Mount Carmel. On the other hand, Carmelites do play a prominent role in the promotion of the cult in the 1480s and 1490, some of the earliest brotherhoods being located at Carmelite convents, among them Trier, Frankfurt, and Augsburg.

Johannes Trithemius: The New Cult and the Humanists
Whether the late fifteenth-century offices were intended to direct attention to the Carmelites' involvement in the affairs of the holy family's ancestors, or whether the offices derived from an interest in Mary's kinship that may have enjoyed particular vigour in Switzerland, is yet to be determined. In any case, both these focal points were subsequently obscured as attention came to be centered on Anne. The offices were followed in the 1480s by a second group of new works, lives of Anne in Latin and in the vernacular—substantial books in which the account of Anne's life is followed by prayers and, most interesting for the reader, numerous little stories relating how she helped those who honored her and punished those who did not.[24]

While the names of the authors of the first group of liturgical texts are not known, those of the men who took over and fastened the focus securely on Anne are. A central figure in this group was the abbot of the Benedictine monastery at Sponheim, Johannes Trithemius. A noted writer and bibliophile—Trithemius increased the monastery library's holdings from 48 to nearly 2,000 volumes between 1483 and 1505 (and the monastery dog, Eris, did tricks to commands in Greek)—Trithemius was a man wearing many hats.[25] Prolific in his religious output (equally persuasive in championing shrines to Anne or Mary) and active in the Bursfelder movement for monastic reform, he was also the man who fabricated the myth of Trojan origins for the Emperor Maximilian, citing as sources his own invented chroniclers Meginfrid, Hunibald, and Wastald. An expert cryptographer, according to some contemporaries, he was also a magician who summoned up the shade of Maximilian's deceased wife, Mary of Burgundy.[26]

Saint Anne, Trithemius had urged in his influential 1494 treatise *De laudibus sanctissimae matris Annae*, ought to be honored above all other saints.[27] With some help from his friends, he ensured that she was. He and his circle, which included the Ghent Carmelite Arnold Bostius, the Flemish Carthusian Petrus Dorlandus, and the Cologne Dominican Jakob Sprenger, not only collaborated in writing, translating, and publishing lives of Saint Anne, as well as liturgical offices and poems dedicated to her, but also created structures through which the devotion could be made to spread and endure.[28] Primarily this involved the founding of the lay organizations called confraternities or brotherhoods, but as well they wrote texts that served to advertise the confraternities, commissioned images and acquired relics for churches and convents linked with their circles, and secured indulgences to enhance the attractions of the above. The account of their activities as related by Klaus Arnold and Ton Brandenbarg presents a dizzying round of favors given and returned: Trithemius wrote the *De laudibus sanctissimae matris Annae* for the new Anne brotherhood at the Carmelite convent in Frankfurt at the request of Rumold von Laupach, the brotherhood's founder; when the Frankfurt Dominican Wigand Wirt took offense at the treatise's emphatic promotion of the Immaculate Conception and at its insulting remarks clearly aimed at the Dominicans (Trithemius suggested that those who were not able to understand the doctrine would best keep quiet on the subject), his fellow humanists rallied to his support with a volley of letters praising Anne and her conception of Mary. In Cologne an Anne confraternity was amalgamated with the Rosary confraternity that Sprenger had founded in 1475; in 1478 Sprenger acquired an Anne relic for the Dominican Church of Saint Peter, where the confraternity was located; another Dominican, Dominicus van Gelre, wrote an account of the miracles attributed to this relic from Anne's finger, and his account was subsequently published in the Anne lives written by Petrus Dorlandus.[29]

What these men did in the process was reinvent Saint Anne. No longer a mere shrine saint with a local dwelling, so to speak, she was made into a transregional saint who was not attached to any particular shrine. She did new things, she was given new honors, and she acquired new powers. Through the topoi disseminated by the texts, and through the network of shrines and confraternities set in place initially in convent churches, particularly Carmelite ones, in the Rhineland, and later in other parts of Germany and the Netherlands, Saint Anne's cult spread. The reasons for the humanists' intense interest in Anne, and the nature of the changes they inflicted on her, will be subjects of later chapters. The innumerable paintings, sculptures, and prints depicting her still extant in churches and museums in Germany and the Netherlands are the testimony to their success.

Philippe de Vigneulles: Saint Anne and the Pilgrims

By the time the Metz burger Philippe de Vigneulles and his wife and friends visited the Saint Anne shrine in Düren in the Rhineland, shortly before 1510, Anne's cult was in full swing, and the works of Trithemius, Dorlandus, and the others were in wide circulation. French versions of the new Anne lives had been published, and de Vigneulles's party may have read them, though it is equally possible they had not, for their pilgrimage had less to do with the new aspects of the cult than with the deep-rooted tradition of relic pilgrimage that had been a characteristic feature of Rhineland piety for many decades. Aachen, Trier, and Cologne were the main centers, and pilgrims attending the immensely popular relic *Schauen*—the splendid ceremonial presentations of relics held periodically, every seven years according to some reports, in these cities—would usually have attended the *Schau* at the nearby Anne shrine in Düren, and they might well have stopped to pray at the widely publicized relic of Saint Anne at Saint Peter's Church in Cologne.

De Vigneulles makes mention of going to the Düren shrine to see "the head of the glorious Saint Anne, mother of Our Lady" (le chief de la glorieuse saincte Anne, mère à nostre dame).[30] And it is clear from his description of the crowds that they were far from alone in coming to see the relic of Mary's mother in its silver reliquary in the form of a bust of Anne. The relic was to be shown at seven o'clock in the morning, following a mass: "There were so many people and such a great multitude of folk along the road that it was a great marvel, and one could not—one could hardly, go forward" (Il y avoit très tant de gens et sy grant multitude de puple au loing du chemin que c'estoit grant merveille et ne so powoit—on à paine avancer), writes de Vigneulles, estimating that there were between eighteen and twenty thousand pilgrims at Düren.[31] Some had to sleep in the woods, though his party was fortunate enough to get lodgings with a priest in a nearby village. In the morning the excitement was intense:

> And then someone came to preach a short sermon as at Aachen and other places, and once that was done they brought out the jewels in the same order and manner as at the other [pilgrimage] places, then all the clergy came in order and showed the people—who were below—the said holy head and then they returned it to the prelate who holds it upside down in order to show the bone of the head uncovered, for it is decorated all over with silver, but on the head there was a little plate that lifts up, and then it seemed that everybody could have burst from the force of blowing their horns and piping, so much so that they wept as if from joy.

> [Et puis après l'on vint preschier ung petit sermon comme à Ayx et éz aultres lieux, et ce fait, toute en la forme et manière que l'on apourte les juaulx és aultres lieux, tout ainsy vint la clergie par ordre et moustre au puple qui est en bais, yceluy st chief et le retourne le prélat qui le tient, sens que dessus dessoubz, pour moustrer le tais de la teste tout nus, car il est tout guarni d'airgent; mais sus la teste il y ait une petite plaitine que se lièwe, et adont sembloit, que tout deust fendre de fource de courner et businer, tellement que l'on plouroit quasy de joye.][32]

The horns de Vigneulles refers to are the small ceramic horns that were sold at Rhineland shrines and blown by the pilgrims when the relics were shown. The pilgrims took the horns—which they perceived as retaining some of the power of the shrine—home, where they used them as "weather horns," to drive off storms.[33] De Vigneulles's description of the head reliquary is of great interest because he describes accurately and in some detail its rather peculiar construction (fig. 6). The head, made of gold covered with silver, was hollow. The rounded portion of cranium bone that was believed to be Anne's (Düren did not claim to own the whole head) was set in a separate silver frame that is attached to the top of the bust. The piece of bone is thus visible when the lid of the frame is lifted. De Vigneulles's description has been verified, for the reliquary is still in existence. Removed for safekeeping during the Second World War, it is now in place in the new church that replaced the Gothic Annakirche destroyed by bombs. The reliquary was probably made in Mainz in the fourteenth century, with additions from the sixteenth century, and the crown and plinth were added in the nineteenth.[34]

FIGURE 6. *Saint Anne Reliquary,* fourteenth century, with later additions. Silver
gilt. Annakirche, Düren

Originally in Mainz, the Düren relic had been stolen in 1501, according to its new
owners, by a devout laborer working in Mainz who was distressed by the lack of
respect Anne was receiving there. Though the story, which uses typical relic theft
motifs, may have been partly a fabrication, the theft was real enough.[35] In November
1500 a stonemason from Kornelimünster named Leonhard, who was working in the
Stephanskirche in Mainz, took the relic, in some versions of the story because he
was distressed at the lack of respect accorded it in Mainz, in other versions because
he was distressed at not being paid.[36] Leonhard brought the relic to the Franciscans
in Düren, who initially decided to return it to representatives of the Stephanskirche.

However, the moves to return the relic came to nothing as the town authorities realized the economic potential of the pilgrimages the relic seemed likely to attract. The pilgrimages constituted a financial windfall for Düren and the duchy of Jülich, and the town was determined not to return the relic. The dispute expanded and the matter went to the pope, who decided in favor of Düren. Julius II's bull of March 18, 1506, *Altitudo divini consilii*, explains that relics cannot be the property of human beings and that the pope can decide to change their place of residence if such be beneficial for the devotion of the faithful and the furtherance of the Christian religion. As well the Emperor Maximilian, who was financially beholden to the Duke of Jülich, put pressure on the pope to decide for Düren.[37] De Vigneulles's account of several versions of the story as it was told to him in Düren presents a slightly different picture from the official version:

> The head was miraculously brought to this good city of Düren as you will hear; for it is true that a little before, about the year 1500, I don't know exactly the correct day, there was a young mason at Cowelance, and this young mason was working in the church of the said Cowelance [the church was the Stiftskirche of Saint Stephen in Mainz] and every day said his prayers in front of some head images [probably head reliquaries]; these heads on the altar were not very reverently decorated or honored; among them was the head of this glorious saint Anne.
>
> Then one day when the clerk of this church did not want to pay this mason, as it has been told to me, and it was said and divinely revealed to him that he would pay himself and that he would take the head of this glorious saint Anne to the good city of Düren, as he did. Others say differently and say that the clergy made him take it thinking to mock him; but however he did it, it is true that the said mason brought the said head to Düren.
>
> [Lequel chief fut apourté mirauculeusement à ycelle bonne ville de Dur come vous oyrez; car il est vray que ung peu devant, environ l'an mil v.c. je ne sçay pas bien le jour à vray, il y avoit ung jonne maçon à Cowelance et owroit ycellui jonne maçon en l'église de la dite Cowelance et faisoit tous les jours sa prière devant aulcuns chiefs d'imaige, lesquels chiefs estoient sur l'autel aissez peu révèramment acoustrés ne honourés, entre lesquels estoit le chief d'icelle glorieuse saincte Anne.

Or avint ung jour que les commis d'icelle église ne vouloient pas paier yceluy maçon, comme il me fut dit, et tellement qu'il lui fut dit et révélé divinement qu'il se paiait et qu'il empourtait le chief d'icelle glorieuse ste Anne à la bonne ville de Dur, comme il fit. D'aultres en disent aultrement et disent que les ministres lui firent prendre se cuidant moucquer de lui; mais comment qu'il en fût, il est vray que le dit maçon apourtait le dit chief à Dur.][38]

De Vigneulles's description of the showing of the Anne relic conveys a vivid picture of the intense response that relics could arouse at these famed shrines. At Aachen he had witnessed a similar reaction when the priests held out Mary's chemise to the crowds on a lavishly decorated flagpole:

> And then the prelates took the said chemise, which is folded as stated, and with great honor and reverence loosed it from its folds and held it out all along the length of the said alleys on a flagpole of gold, in view of each person, and you would say that everyone trembled with the great noise of the horns and the shouts of the men and women who cried mercy, and there was not a man whose hair did not stand on end and the tears flow from his eye.

> [Et adoncque les prélas prengnent la dite chemise qui est ploiée comme dit est et en grande honneur et révérence la laissent ailler de ses plois et l'etendent tout du loing au dehors des dites aillées sus ung altre drapz d'or, à la veue d'ung chacun et adoncque vous diriez que tout le monde tremble du grant bruit des cornets et du cri des hommes et femmes qui crient miséricorde et n'y ait homme que les cheveulx ne luy dressent en la teste et que les lairmes ne viengnent à l'euil.][39]

Though churches and individuals in other parts of Germany amassed large relic collections in the fifteenth century, the perception of the power of relics seems to have been especially intense in the Rhineland shrines. By the same token, although indulgences always helped attract pilgrims, they seem to have been proportionately less important here as compared, for example, with Anne shrines in eastern Germany. For de Vigneulles, indulgences were important—in one sense they underlay the whole trip, as he explains to his readers at the conclusion of his description: "Now you have heard how one can go to Notre Dame at Aachen and win indulgences" (Or avez oy comment on peult ailler et venir à nostre dame à Ayx et gaignier les pardons).[40] But he does not have a great deal to say on the subject. He reserves his eloquence and prolixity for the elaborately orchestrated displays of the relics, especially at Aachen, and for the tremendous crush of the enthusiastic, bell-ringing, horn-blowing crowds trembling with awe as they beheld Mary's tunic paraded among them by prelates dressed in gold and silver. He also mentions alms, very occasionally repeats stories of miracles, refers to fine paintings depicting the events of saints' lives, and comments on the beauty of the towns he passes through. But the real excitement in de Vigneulles's writing is in his descriptions of the crowd's experience of viewing the relic displays.

From Düren, de Vigneulles's party went on to Cologne, where they saw the relic of Anne's finger at the Dominican church, of her head at the church of Saint Cecilia, and the remains of the Three Kings, and Mary's hair, in the cathedral, where they also might have noticed the stone *Anna Selbdritt* memorial tablet of the converted rabbi Victor von Carben.[41] Indeed, they would have found plenty of *Anna Selbdritts* and Holy Kinships to admire on their trip through the Rhineland, for the region had been an early cradle of the cult, and the overall production of images there was very large. Few if any churches would have been without at least one image of Saint Anne, whether in family, confraternity, or guild side chapels, as occasional images placed against walls or piers, or in the side panels or predellas of main altarpieces. Sculptures would have predominated for the *Anna Selbdritt*, while paintings were the usual though not invariable medium for the numerous Holy Kinship images produced in the region.

It would not be surprising if de Vigneulles's party had bought one of the numerous woodcuts, often with prayers printed on them and often indulgenced, that depicted Anne, such as the elaborate *Anna Selbdritt* printed in Pforzheim in 1501 with verses by Trithemius and his friends Konrad Celtis, Theodore Gresemund, and Jodocus Badius (fig. 7). In this bench-type composition Anne holds out an apple to the Christ Child, who stands on Mary's lap, while above him, framed in a round-arched window, are God the Father and the Dove flanked by angels. Joseph and Anne's three husbands stand behind the back and arms of the wide bench. The woodcut is unusual in that it includes not only the verses but also an iconographic detail drawn from the new lives: the triple-pronged candlestick placed in front of the perspectival space of the scene refers to the three candles that the new lives urge Anne's devotees to light in front of her image. The pilgrim kneeling at the side raises the possibility that the work might have been produced for one of the Anne shrines.

FIGURE 7. Thomas Anselmus, *Holy Kinship*, 1501. Woodcut. Pforzheim.
Staatsbibliothek Bamberg

Though de Vigneulles does not pay special attention to the miracles supposed to
be worked by the relics, miracles were an important aspect of the shrine activity that
was so abundant in the Rhineland. Indeed, all the substantial and detailed extant
contemporary reports of miracles produced by Anne relics come from Rhineland
shrines. It is also here in this cultically rich region that we find different strands
mingled in the developing late medieval devotion to Saint Anne. Old and new

motifs meet, flow together for a time, and then move apart to form new configurations. The changes wrought on the older devotion can be seen clearly when one compares older and newer types of reports of miracles performed by relics of Anne. Those described in the miracle book compiled at the Saint Anne shrine at the Wilhelmite Convent in Limburg retain the older approach, whereas those reported for the relic of Anne's finger at Saint Peter's Church in Cologne present features of the new form of the cult. Although the founding of the Limburg shrine was late, probably in the early sixteenth century, the writers of its miracle book followed a long-established tradition in the type of miracles they describe—largely miracles of healing.[42] By contrast, while the compilation of miracles performed by the relic of Anne's finger at Saint Peter's Church in Cologne, which was written by the humanist Dominicus van Gelre, includes healing miracles, it also contains miracles of a new and different type, among them deliverance from temptation to sexual sin. Van Gelre's choice of miracle here echoes themes from the new lives of Saint Anne, in particular the emphasis on the development of personal holiness, which is an aspect of the middle-class piety the cult sought to address.

Martin Luther: A Change of Heart About Saint Anne

The writings of Martin Luther shed further light on the transitional phase in the devotion to Saint Anne in Germany. In later life, Luther described Anne's advent in his town as a novelty:

> As I recall it the big event of Saint Anne's arrival happened when I was a boy of fifteen. Before that nobody knew anything about her; then a fellow came and brought Saint Anne. She caught on right away, and everybody was paying attention to her.

> [Bej meinem gedencken ist das gross wesen von S. Anna auffkomen, als ich ein knabe von funffzehen jharen wahr. Zuvor wuste man nichts von ihr, sondern ein bube kam und brachte S. Anna, klugs gehet sie ahn, den es gab jederman darzu.][43]

As Luther was born in 1483, this would put her arrival in Eisleben at around 1498, a date consistent with the pattern of the cult's expansion out of the Rhineland into eastern Germany. For a period at least, Luther must have been a reasonably enthusiastic devotee himself, for it was to Saint Anne that he made his vow in the thunderstorm in 1505: "Help, dear Saint Anne—I'll become a monk" (Hilft du sankt Anna, ich will Monch werden).[44] Twenty years later he had soured toward her. Critical of her inordinate popularity, he complained: "This Anne is exalted almost above the Blessed Virgin."[45]

But even earlier he had been no fool. In another reminiscence he contrasts his skepticism over a Saint Anne miracle reported at a relic shrine in the same part of the Rhineland as Limburg and Düren (he does not identify the shrine) with the iron faith of the inhabitants of the region:

> I was once in a place where they called on Saint Anne, and they put out a written public announcement of a miracle that Saint Anne had done at that place, that a child had been two days in the water and yet had not drowned, but had remained alive. I, as a young theologian, contradicted it, but the innkeeper said: "Make out of it what you want, the child was day and night in the water. The Duke of Jülich wanted to take Saint Anne's bones [the shrine's relic] and bring them to another place—and all his horses died!"

> [Ich bin einmahl an einem ortthe gewesen, da wurde S. Anna angeruffen, und gieng darvon ein auffschreiben offentlich aus von einem wunder-zaichen, so S. Anna an selbigen ortthe gethan hatte, das ein kind zwo nacht im wasser gelegen war und dennochs nicht ersoffen, sondern lebendig blieben. Ich als ein junger Theologus widerfocht es, aber der Wirdtth sprach: "Macht draus, was ir wollet, das kind ist tag und nacht im Wasser gewesen. Der Herzog von Julich wolt das gebeine S. Anna aufheben und an einen andern orth bringen, do sturben ihme alle seine pferde."][46]

Luther's description confirms the old-fashioned mode of the cult in this region. The nasty punishment the saint inflicts on someone who tries to interfere with her relics—a motif familiar from the stories of the Miracles of the Virgin—is a throw-back to the piety of the High Middle Ages. Luther's remarks also remind us that attitudes toward miracles were far from uniform.

The older type of healing shrine did not, of course, disappear at the end of the fifteenth century. Its role in the cult of Saint Anne, however, did diminish in comparison with the new emphases that were now dominating both the proliferating textual discourse and the practices of the confraternities dedicated to Anne, which by this time had expanded into virtually all parts of Germany. In the new texts,

Anne was increasingly promoted as a saint who could help with the problems of urban bourgeois life, including those having to do with money and status, and with a problem that was being increasingly promoted—and perceived—as pressing and urgent: that of salvation. The next chapter shows how the new texts conveyed the message that Jesus' grandmother had special powers to help the anxious soul into heaven.

3

Saint Anne and Concepts of Salvation in Late Medieval Germany

Within a few years, churches and convents throughout the Germanic-speaking regions were following the model set by the Rhineland cult of Saint Anne. Lives were rewritten, translated, and republished, confraternities were founded, and fine new altarpieces were commissioned.[1] By the late 1400s Saint Anne's popularity had spread throughout Germany, Switzerland, Flanders, and Holland, making substantial inroads as well into Poland, Bohemia, and Scandinavia.[2] Anne's name, we are told, was on everyone's lips. The Bern municipal scribe Valerius Anshelmus's 1508 description of the spread of Anne's cult and the extraordinary intensity of Anne's popularity echoes Luther's observation about its relative newness:

> Saint Anne, who was previously hardly thought about, for the common contemptible misfortunes of earthly poverty, the wretched pox and painful lameness, has now pushed her daughter, the worthy mother of our Lord, and all the saints behind her, so that in the German lands everybody is crying, Help Saint Anna Selbdritt, and in all the streets, cities and villages, images, altars, chapels, churches—on the Schreckberg in Meissen a city— and everywhere brotherhoods are founded in her honor.

> [Sant Ann, deren vor wenig gedacht, zu diser Zyt, für die g'meinen, unwerthen, unlydigen Bresten der zytlichen Armuth und der elenden Blatteren und pynlichen Lähme, gar nach ihre Tochter, die wirdige Mutter unsers Herren, und alle Heiligen hinter sich geruckt, also dass ihr in tütschen Landen Jedermann zuschrey: hilf Sant Anna selb dritt! und uf allen Strassen, in Städten und Dörfern, Bilder, Altar, Kappellen, Kirchen, uf dem Schreckberg in Myssen ein Stadt, und um und um Brüderschaften sind ihren ufgerichtet worden.[3]]

The reasons for the cult's success are not difficult to determine. As both Ton Brandenbarg and Angelika Dörfler-Dierken have shown, Anne's cult flourished because it was vigorously promoted. Untangling the reasons the promotion succeeded at various levels, however, introduces a number of other factors. Clerical and humanist promotion of Anne, merchant class response, imperial enthusiasm, and a popular response that cut across all levels of society seem to have drawn on and expressed a wide variety of intentions, interests, fears, and assumptions. Some of these were specific to particular groups or regions. Others were shared among several groups. But one factor was common throughout the broad territory implicated in the cult. That factor was salvation.

The desire to ensure personal salvation was a major element in the promotion of the cult of Saint Anne; Anne's promoters presented her as able to address this concern, able to help her devotees attain heaven. Salvational help was available through membership in Saint Anne confraternities, but in a more encompassing and perhaps ultimately more important way, it was available as well through salvational powers attributed to Saint Anne herself.[4] Absent in older accounts of Anne's life, such as the account in the *Golden Legend*, the idea that Anne could wield salvific power in her own right was a new theme in Christian hagiography, appearing for the first time in the late fifteenth-century offices and lives of Anne.[5] Earlier writers had linked her with salvation in terms of her role as the generator of the mother of the Redeemer.[6] Indeed, though they do not ascribe salvational power to Saint Anne herself, liturgical prayers and hymns to her in German manuscripts of the fourteenth and fifteenth centuries often close by linking her presence with the safe passage to heaven.[7] The new texts emanating from the humanist and clerical circles of the late fifteenth century built on this preexisting association, extending the motif to include a causal relationship and employing it with a pervasiveness that had not been seen earlier.

The decision to incorporate a salvational element in the cult is not surprising, given the intense concern with personal salvation that characterized late medieval religion in Germany. Where formerly evidence of active concern for the fate of the soul in the afterlife had been most strongly concentrated in monastic and aristocratic circles—the latter in effect paying the former to pray for them—by the later fourteenth and fifteenth centuries the evidence presented by indulgences, confraternity sources, wills, and other documents settling money on churches indicates that salvation was now a major concern for the middle and even the lower levels of society. As the early fifteenth-century Swabian chronicler Burkhard Zink so succinctly put it, "Everybody wants to go to heaven" (Dann iederman wolt gen himl).[8]

Indulgences had already been established as important coin in attaining this goal. In the fifteenth century lay brotherhoods became another means of helping smooth the road to heaven. Luther had criticized the salvational stance (real or perceived) of the brotherhoods in a text better known for its scathing description of the carousing that took place at the gatherings of these organizations:

> First we should look at the wicked works of the brotherhoods, among them this—that they organize a feast and a boozing; they have a mass or several held, and after that the whole day and night and the next day as well are given over to the devil for his own. . . . What do the names of our dear lady, Saint Anne, Saint Sebastian, or other saints' names have to do with your brotherhood, which is nothing more than a gobbling of food, boozing, useless squandering of money, crying, yelling, sweating, dancing, and wasting of time? If one were to set up a sow as patron of such a brotherhood, she wouldn't put up with it. Why do you seek out the dear saints like this, misusing their names to such shame and dishonor and slandering their brotherhood with such evil things?

> [Zum Ersten wollen wir die bossen ubung der Bruderschafften ansehen, Unter wilchen ist eyne, das man eyn fressen und sauffen anricht, lesst eyn mess odder ettlich halten, darnach ist der gantz tag und nacht und andere tag dazu dem teuffell zu eygen geben. . . . Was soll unser lieben frawen, Sanct Annen, sanct Bastian odder ander heyligen namen bey deyner bruderschafft thun, da nit mehr dan fressen, sauffen, unnutz gelt vorthun, plerren, schreyen, schwetzen, tantzen und zeyt vorlyren ist? Was man eyne saw zu solcher bruderschafft patronen setzt, sie wurd es nit leyden. Warumb vorsucht man dan die lieben heyligen so hoch, das man ihren namen zu solchen schanden und sunden mispraucht und yhre bruder-schaffte mit solchen boessen stucken voruneeret und lesteret?][9]

But Luther does not stop at accusing the brotherhoods of being no more than an excuse for collecting money for beer ("eyn geltt samlen zum bier"). He singles out as a more important problem their misguided boast that whoever is a member will not suffer damnation:

> That they publicly boast and say that whoever is in their brotherhood can-not be damned, exactly as if baptism and the sacrament, laws ordained by

God himself, were less significant and less uncertain than what they have thought up out of their blind heads.

[Das sie offentlich ruemen und sagen, welcher yn yhyrer bruderschafft sey, mueg nit vordampt werden, gerad als were die tauff und sacrament, von gott selb eyn gesetzt, geringer und ungewisser, dan das sie aus yhren blinden kopfen erdacht haben.][10]

No such extravagant claims are made in the written materials put out by the confraternities; whether members in the heat of satisfaction interpreted their situation thus or whether such ideas came from verbal suggestions is not known. But the repeated references to salvational benefits in the membership form printed for the Saint Anne confraternity at the Carmelite church in Augsburg certainly confirms the important role those benefits played in the confraternity's appeal. The good works of Carmelites throughout the whole southeastern part of the empire, the form reminds members, will be at their disposal to help them gain the kingdom of heaven: "with many good works, blessings, and merits, to gain the kingdom of heaven, . . . and for the salvation of your soul" (mit manigen guoten wercken säligklichen verdienen das reich der himel Zuo volpringen, . . . vnd zuo hail ewrer sele).[11] The confraternity will see to posthumous rituals that will further assist members' souls:

And as a special grace for all brothers and sisters who are departed out of the above-named praiseworthy brotherhood, quarterly on an appointed day a vigil will be held at night, and in the morning a requiem will be sung henceforth for all time in this worthy house of God. And after that they [the brothers] will sing a solemn office of the most worthy lady Saint Anne for the salvation of the living brothers and sisters of the aforenamed brotherhood.

[Auch auss besunder gnaden wirt man hinfür zuo ewigen zeiten in disem wirdigen gotzhauss all quattember alle brüder vnd schwester die auss der obgemelten lobsamen bruoderschaft: verschaiden sind besingen: auf ainen bestimpten tag: zuo nacht mit ainer vigilg: vnd enmorgens mit ainem gesungen seel ampt. Vnd darnach zuo hail der lebendigen brüder vnd schwester der vorgenanten bruoderschaft: singen ain loblich ampt von der hochwirdigen frawen sant anna.][12]

In addition, members and benefactors are eligible for indulgences if they give gifts to the brotherhood:

> Seven Augsburg bishops have confirmed the brotherhood, and six popes,
> namely Adrian II, Stephan V, Sergius III, John X, John XI, and Innocent
> IV, have given a large indulgence to all who join the brotherhood, to all
> who have repented of their sins and have confessed them, who assign land
> to the brotherhood and who give the above-named convent their help or
> support, or chalice, mass vestments, altar cloths . . . or in their time of death
> provide something for the convent.

> [Vii bishops zu augspurg habent bestat die bruederschafft und gross ablass
> geben allen die in die bruederschafft kument. namlich vi papst mit namen
> adrianus der II stephanus der v. sergius der iii. johannes der x. johannes der
> xi; und innocentius der iiii habent geben allen menschen die rew ueber ir
> sünd hand und gebeicht habent die sich land schreiben in die bruderschaft
> und de obgemelten closter ir hilf oder stair gebent. oder kelch. messgwand.
> alter tiecher hand zwechlen oder an irn lesten zeiten etwas dem closter
> schaffent.][13]

Aids to salvation were not, of course, restricted to the Saint Anne confraternities; all brotherhoods provided indulgences, posthumous masses, and other benefits. But what is distinctive about the rhetoric surrounding Saint Anne is that her ability to help the viator reach heaven now extended beyond these benefits. To reiterate the points made earlier in this section, according to the new texts, because of her flesh-and-blood relationship with the Redeemer and his mother, Saint Anne was able to exert an intrinsic power of her own that could help the soul achieve salvation. In implying this special ability on Anne's part, the promoters of the cult were introducing a new element into the Anne discourse: employing a battery of rhetorical strategies, they implied that she could help the worshiper broach the doors of heaven. The writers do not state the message explicitly, much less present it as a theological proposition, but the strength and the peculiar quality of Saint Anne's power is forcefully conveyed through repeated use of images and narratives that embody it, through implications and equivalences, through the appropriation of Marian tropes and motifs, and through assumptions made in the course of making other statements.

Images and Narratives Embodying Salvation Messages

Other saints, however powerful they might be, are normally spoken of as interceding for the soul before God. Anne, by contrast, is frequently presented through images that imply that she exercises salvational power, as she does in a Flemish devotional work that describes her as opening the door of heaven: "O holy mother Saint Anne / show us eternal consolation and refuge in all our needs. And open for us the door of heaven" (O heilige moeder sinte Anne / weest ons een eewige troost ende toeverlast in allen onsen nooden. Enn doet ons op die poorte des hemels).[14] The words slip in sidelong, the unorthodox bestowing of eternal grace sliding in on the heels of the conventional bestowal of material benefits.

ASCRIPTION OF POWER: ANNE AS THE ROOT OF SALVATION

The potent image of Anne as located at the root of the salvational process appears in a number of works, among them the *Legenda sanctae Annae*, a life by an anonymous Franciscan first printed in 1496 in Louvain and widely translated and reprinted subsequently: "Evidently it is almost as if this chosen utensil was foreseen and chosen by God and as such was ordained to be mother of the bearer of God from all eternity by the most Holy Trinity" (Augenscheinlich ist es wie fast dises ausserwöhlte geschirn von Gott seye vorgesehen vnd erwöhlt worden; Als welche zu einer Muetter der Gottes gebörerin von Ewigkeit hero von der allerheiligisten Treyfaltigkeit ist verordnet worden).[15] The same emphasis on Anne's role at the beginning of the redemptive process appears in a quatrain by the humanist Theodore Gresemund, one of the works in Anne's honor that Trithemius had requested from his friends. Widely republished, these poems were sometimes printed on woodcut images of Anne: "Hail fortunate Anne parent of the Virgin Mary / Worthily you laid the warp of the work of our salvation" (Virginis Anna parens salueto fausta marie / Ordiri nostre digna salutis opus)[16] (fig. 7).

The image of Anne preparing the fabric of Mary's body, which goes back to Greek Christian writing, does not in itself ascribe special powers to Anne. But it becomes the basis of the new image when the author of the Augsburg confraternity life joins it with the motif of helping the sinner to repent, concluding his passage with an image of the *Selbdritt* as actually loosing the soul from the power of the evil spirit and leading it into heaven:

> Truly you are our gracious help with your most dear child, that we may win a holy life at our last end and attain for us repentance for our sins, a sincere confession, a complete absolution, and a worthy reception of the

Holy Sacrament, and in the hour of our death so come to our help and release us from the power of the evil spirit and lead us, Selbdritt, into the joy of eternal life. Amen.

[Also warlich seyest du gnädigklich vnser helferin mit deinem allerliebsten kinde das wir ain seligs leben mügend gewynen an vnserem letsten ende. vnd erwirb vns rew vmb vnser sünd. vnd ain ware beicht. vnnd ain volkomne büss vnd ain wirdige empfangung der hayligen sacrament vnd in der stund vnsers tods so kum vns zehilff. vnd erlöss vns von dem gewalt der bössen gayst. vnd fur vns selbsdryt in die freüd des ewigen lebens Amen.][17]

ASCRIPTION OF POWER: ANNE PRESIDES AT THE DEATHBED AND HAS POWER OVER THE DEVIL

Anne not only leads the soul into heaven, she is sought at the deathbed to help obtain a "happy death and end and after this life everlasting glory" (mortem & exitum felicem & post hanc vitam gloriam sempiternam).[18] The motif of her presence at the soul's entry into heaven, found in so many works, is often joined with a suggestion of more direct powers—the ability to vanquish the power of the devil—as it is in the passage from the Augsburg life cited above. An office published by Anton Sorg in Augsburg in 1479 expressed a similar confidence in Anne's power over the devil: "O holy Anne, in the hour of our death free us from the enemy" (O sancta anna tu in hora mortis nostre. nos ab hoste libera).[19]

ASCRIPTION OF POWER THROUGH EQUIVALENCES: LINKING ANNE WITH MARY

Power is often ascribed to Anne through association, her status (and power) heightened by compositional devices associating her with Mary. Frequent in the new literature are Marian prayers and epithets in which Anne replaces or is added to Mary, as is the case in the Rosary of Saint Anne (*Rosarium de sancta Anna*) by the humanist Jodocus Beisselius, a member of Trithemius's circle.[20] A liturgical work by another humanist linked with the circle, Johannes von Lambsheym, *Oraciones et alia pulcra ad sanctam Annam*, includes a "Salve Anna" that appropriates formulations from the Marian prayer *Salve Regina*: "Hail Anne, mother of mercy, . . . to thee do we cry poor banished children of Eve . . . O clement, O loving, O sweet mother Anne" (Salue anna mater misericordie . . . Ad te clamamus exules filij eue in angustijs constituti . . . O clemens. O pia. O dulcis mater anna).[21] Trithemius joins Anne to the salvational process by ascribing to her the topos of predestination, brought to its full

Marian development earlier in the fifteenth century. As pure as her daughter, he says, Anne was chosen by God before the creation of the world.[22]

Sometimes writers linked Anne with Mary by having them act in unison. Anne intercedes—on equal footing with her daughter—in the papal bull granting indulgences to the Anne brotherhood in Annaberg, Saxony, in 1506, which states:

> Anne, to whom the Savior himself granted so much grace that she was worthy to bear in her blessed womb his mother, the most holy Mary, & who with her daughter never ceases to intercede for the salvation of Christians before the throne of divine mercy.

> [Anne cui Saluator ipse tantam gratiam concedere dignatus est, vt mariam sanctissimam eius genetricem in vtero suo benedicto meruit portare, & que cum filia pro salute Christifidelium ante Thronum diuine clementie intercedere non cessat.][23]

The same device is found in an exemplum in the Augsburg life in which a familiar Marian theme, the rescue of the undeserving rich, is altered so that it is "Anne with her dear daughter Mary" who comes to the aid of the knight who had led a sinful life but had daily honored Anne. In this revision of a story from the collections of the Miracles of the Virgin, both women intercede before Christ for the sinner.[24]

The difference between the treatment of Anne, with her ability to help the soul after death, and the treatment of other saints in contemporary lives is striking. Most saints' lives included descriptions of how the saint could help those who prayed to him or her, like that from a late medieval printed life of Saint Brendan: "Now let us pray to him that he will pray to God for us that our life be brought to a good end" (Nun sullen wir im bitten das er auch got Für vns pit daz vnser leben zu einem gütten end pracht werde).[25] We find the same approach in a life of Saint Katherine written by the South-Netherlandish Carthusian Petrus Dorlandus, who also wrote several Anne lives. But whereas Dorlandus's Anne lives are replete with the kind of salvational implications mentioned above, his life of Katherine ascribes no special salvational powers to its subject.[26]

The gulf between the older image of the helping saint and the new image of a saint whose scope and competence approach that of Mary is large. But the fact that Anne could be seen as enjoying such a degree of power is not surprising when one considers the model of religion that prevailed among many Christians in late medieval Germany, a model in which power is contained in objects and people, in which it is increased by such things as quantity and by proximity to other power sources, and in which it can be accessed and manipulated through appropriate actions and rituals. It was a conception of the universe in which, as Richard Kieckhefer puts it, "by fulfilling certain outward and objective standards ritual could have automatic power."[27] Though this perception of the relationships between the material and heavenly realms appears in sources from all parts of medieval Europe, there is evidence that it operated with particular vigour and persistence in Germany. Bernd Moeller, speaking of late medieval Germany, invokes this model of religion when he states: "By capturing the mediators [the saints] between them and God men attempted to force a guarantee of salvation."[28] By no means restricted to popular religion, to the religion of ordinary or uneducated people, these "magical" practices were equally part of the elite religion of the clergy and the educated. And though such approaches were contested in the decades leading up to the Reformation, there is abundant evidence that at the end of the fifteenth century they remained widely prevalent. Within this paradigm, Saint Anne, through her contiguity, her bodily generative relationship to the ultimate sources of power, acquired a share in that power. In other words, Anne's power derived not from her personal holiness but from her physical closeness to the holy figures of Mary and Jesus. And like their power, hers too was used not only to soothe and help in the multiple cares of everyday life, but also to address the most important problem, salvation.

The same mode of thinking that permitted Saint Anne to enjoy such an exalted degree of power was also part and parcel of the concern with ensuring one's salvation that was such a noticeable part of late medieval German religious life. Medieval Christians everywhere shared the belief that salvation was effected by the sacrifice of Christ on the cross and that repentance for sin and the reception of the sacrament of confession were necessary in order to benefit from this salvation. The actuality of practice, however, shows that other things might be thought necessary too. The words and actions of late medieval Germans show that they tried with particular assiduousness to ensure their salvation through a massive attention to the performance of ritual actions. Sometimes these were vicarious actions performed by other people, paid to do so, whether masses said by endowed priests, or prayers said by *Seelschwestern*.[29] Indulgences were increasingly sought as another means to help secure salvation. The Basel artist and writer Nicholas Manuel, in the anti-clerical play *Die Totenfresser* (Eaters of the Dead), which he wrote in 1523, refers to the sums of money that even poor people gave to the church in the hope that their souls would reach heaven:

Church offerings, weekly, monthly, and annual masses for the dead
Bring us more than enough.
. . . .
Indulgences lend a hand
By making men fearful of penance.
We also put a lot of stock in purgatory
. . . .
The reason is that we must use every chance
To scare the hell out of common folk.
. . . .
So let us . . .
. . . be thankful to the dead
Who make it possible for us to fleece the living.[30]

Nicholas Manuel's observation on the role of the clergy in encouraging salvation anxiety alerts us to an important feature of this concern: it did not arise solely of itself out of the individualism of proto-modern consciousness, as has sometimes been suggested. On the contrary, the ubiquitousness of the message that security about salvation could never be assumed, a message that was propagated in late medieval German sermons, devotional texts, and the counsel given in the confessional, calls attention to the role of the clergy in fostering salvation anxiety. Charles Garside Jr., in his study of Zwingli, remarks on the ever-present encouragement to doubt:

> The Church could not extend to the people the comfort of complete assurance. Penance, obedience, and at best a relative certainty could be its only answer. As a result, the sacrament of penance assumed even greater importance, together with indulgences and good works. But no one could be certain that he had done enough in terms of any one of the three, for each was in itself relative. . . . And the Church, far from trying to calm this frenzy of ceremonial piety, encouraged [it] . . . while attaching to the saints, their relics, and the shrines to which such pilgrimages were made more numerous and more extravagant indulgences.[31]

Heiko Oberman draws the same conclusion in his study of the fifteenth-century nominalist theologian and preacher Gabriel Biel, remarking that for Biel "the viator never knows whether he is actually in a state of grace, or perhaps has unconsciously committed a mortal sin."[32]

Given these incitements to worry, it is hardly surprising that confraternity documents, wills, and documents assigning money or capital to pay for salvational liturgies all suggest that German Christians took very special care in their posthumous salvational efforts. Many medieval Christians left salvational bequests but, compared with their English and Italian counterparts, German wills left larger numbers of separate bequests for masses and prayers, and stipulated more precisely calculated durations of time.[33] And while English wills also left bequests for the poor, who were expected to pray for the deceased's soul, they usually did not prescribe specific ritual activities, or express concern about the purity or holiness of the recipients of their charity, as the German ones so often do. Typically, German endowment documents are hedged about with more elaborate safeguards to ensure that the churches or convents endowed to say the masses did not neglect their duties.[34]

Saint Anne's role as blood-and-bone grandmother of the Redeemer, and grandmother or aunt to more than half a dozen apostles and saints, gave her the kind of special power that could help the German Christian negotiate the web of obligations and pitfalls that composed the salvational enterprise. Her clerical promoters strengthened her (and their) hand by including in the lives exempla that, on the one hand, encouraged anxiety about salvation and, on the other hand, presented Anne as a remedy for it. Hence in the lives, power is also ascribed negatively: neglect Anne and lose salvation. In a story that appears in a number of lives, a bishop who opposes Anne's feast refuses to change his ways, falls off his horse, dies, and is damned. Earlier versions of the tale in older miracle collections ended happily with the repentance of the erring bishop; the authors of the Anne lives evidently found this conclusion insufficiently stern to get the message across.[35] In another fiercely pointed exemplum, a virgin who refuses to pray to Anne because of her three marriages finds herself on the path to damnation. Although the young woman is described as having raised "a valid argument" (ein gültiges Argument), in the next breath the author informs us that her opinion is "a vexatious depravity, altogether not to be pardoned" (ein ärgerliches vnd solches Laster welches ganz vnd gar nit mag entschuldigt werden). It is only through the merits and intercession of Saint Anne that she escapes hell.[36]

The argument for Anne's singular power is completed by the texts' explanation of the source of that power: as the biological grandmother of Christ, she enjoyed a closeness to the divine personages unmatched by any other saint. This point is made in a document describing the Anne relic acquired for the Carmelite church in Frankfurt: "It is therefore quite clear that there are no relics of a human body on earth that are closer to the body of our Savior and his mother, Mary, than that of the holy mother Anne."[37] The interconnectedness of Anne with Mary and Jesus is of course the distinguishing feature of the *Anna Selbdritt*, and it is emphasized repeatedly in the texts.[38] The anonymous Franciscan author of the *Legenda sanctae Annae* tells us in a marvelously worded contradiction of the gospel that if God is to be praised in his saints how much more is he to be praised in his parentage.[39] Expressions such as "God the Lord together with Mary his mother and his most holy grandmother Anne" (Gott dem Herrn sambt Maria seiner Muetter vnd seiner allerheiligsten Grossmuetter Anna) momentarily make us envision Anne as even more important than her divine grandson.[40] More conventional expressions of the connection are embedded in the short prayers that address Anne literally as "Anne with two others": "Hilf St. Anna selbdritte," or the Low German "Help sunte anna sulfdrudde."[41]

> *Power and Quantity: The Holy Kinship*

Though Anne's bodily connection with Jesus and Mary was the main source of her power, two other factors also contributed to it: the large size of her family, and her family's nobility. The confidence in sheer quantity, the belief that more is better, is marked in German piety, appearing in the fondness for groups of saints like Ursula and her Eleven Thousand Companions, the Fourteen Holy Helpers, the Three Kings, and the Theban Legion, and for large collections of relics. The gigantic collections of Frederick the Wise and Cardinal Albrecht of Brandenburg with its reputed 39,245,120 years of indulgences, are notorious, but many a less well-known church and cloister had its own large collection, often publicized in woodcut illustrations with the relics neatly arranged in labeled compartments.[42]

The *Anna Selbdritt* is another grouping of holy figures, a group that becomes even larger and more imposing in the Holy Kinship, and the texts frequently put emphasis on Anne's position at the center of this collection of holy people. The Augsburg confraternity life's conjoining of the Kinship with the deathbed help Anne is able to offer is typical of many such formulations: "I have also read that certain people daily honored Saint Anne and all her blessed kinship with five Pater Nosters and five Ave Marias, and when these people came to die, then Saint Anne came at their departing with all her blessed kinship and got for them a holy end with God."[43]

Another salient feature of medieval German hagiography was its tendency to equate holiness with nobility. Ortrud Reber, in her study of medieval women's *vitae*, remarks on the virtual absence of nonnoble medieval saints in Germany: "One scarcely finds a text on the saints that doesn't mention that they are from the nobility. . . . One wonders whether in the Middle Ages there were such things as German saints who were not nobles."[44] The Anne literature frequently ascribes royal or high status to members of the Holy Kinship. The lives and offices often state that Anne was descended from the Royal House of David.[45] In the 1479 office *Historia nova pulchra devota et autentica*, Anne's apostle grandsons are referred to as "senators of the whole world, princes of the people, and judges of the world" (senatores orbis. principes populorum iudices seculi), and Anne's descent is described as "royal and priestly" (regalis et sacerdotalis).[46] Her daughter Mary Salome is described as "of the illustrious tribe of Judah, of the famed house of David and third-born daughter of the most noble Anne" (de illustri tribu juda / preclara de domo david et nobilissime anne tercio genita).[47] As well, as Werner Esser points out, the term *Geschlecht*, which is used along with *Sippe* to refer to the kinship, in itself implied high social status, *Geschlechter* being the term used for the patrician families in the German cities.[48]

These examples—and each instance could be multiplied many times over— show how the readers of the late medieval literature on Saint Anne were assailed on a multitude of fronts with the message that Saint Anne, as well as being able to help in the cares and problems of daily life, was also able to be present and efficacious in the troubling area of salvation. Can the success of her cult be wondered at?

4

Salvational Themes in the Imagery of Saint Anne

Though not everyone would have read the new Anne lives, the sheer volume of translations and editions coming off German presses, many of them with catchy titles like *A Really Useful Little Book About Anne's Whole Kinship*, suggests that the message was reaching large numbers of people. Miriam Usher Chrisman's study of the role of books in late medieval Strasburg concluded that vernacular saints' lives were popular reading matter among literate artisans. Hans-Jörg Kunast's recent estimate of basic vernacular literacy in Augsburg at about 30 percent by the year 1520 suggests that a good many families would have been reading about Saint Anne.[1]

But even more numerous than the texts were the works of art. By 1500, sculptures and paintings of the *Anna Selbdritt* and the Holy Kinship were to be found in churches throughout Germany, Switzerland, and the Netherlands, and in terms of geographical range they would have reached more people than either the texts or the confraternities, for they were widely distributed in regions like Holland and eastern Germany, where Anne confraternities were rare. The independence of the works of art from the textual and confraternal traditions is further evident in the fact that, with the exception of a handful of altarpieces produced in circles associated with the Rhineland promotion of the cult, the Saint Anne artworks rarely depict incidents from the narrative or exempla of the new lives.[2] What is of interest to the artists is Anne herself and her family, whether Jesus and Mary, or the extended family of husbands, daughters, sons-in-law, and infant grandsons.

Usually these paintings and sculptures formed the central panels of the family, confraternity, and guild altarpieces in the side chapels that lined the aisles of churches, though they also appeared as secondary panels in main altarpieces. Depictions of Saint Anne—especially sculptures—were also affixed to piers and walls, and sometimes they were used in funerary monuments. And although the majority were found in churches, a small but significant number of families commissioned or bought domestic works, miniature altars of the *Anna Selbdritt*, or protective plaques and statues to be affixed to the exterior walls of houses. As well, the survival of large numbers of woodcuts indicates that Saint Anne found her way into innumerable households of lower as well as middle and higher socioeconomic levels.

These works of art undoubtedly spoke to people in different ways, iconography, style, and composition each playing a part in the conveying of moods and messages about Anne's maternal goodness, her closeness to the Virgin and to Christ, and the help she could offer for the problems of daily life. Another message that may well have been received was a salvational one, for just as the new texts implied that Anne could exercise salvational power based on her links with Mary and Jesus, so too did the artworks. German and Flemish *Anna Selbdritts* and Holy Kinships are characteristically structured in such a way as to present Anne as the physical source of salvation. Further, by appropriating for Anne compositional structures that presented Mary as co-redemptrix, they embodied an association between Anne and salvation, suggesting that like her daughter she too played a role in the redemptive process.[3]

The idea of Anne as the ultimate physical source of the flesh of the Redeemer is suggested by a number of different compositional devices. Above all, the frequent miniaturization of Mary and Jesus and their depiction as children emphasize their physical dependence on and subordination to Anne. By showing Mary as a child, the artist disrupts the natural grandmother-mother-grandchild generational connection in favor of an emphasis on the maternal role of Anne vis-à-vis both Mary and Jesus; thus, in these works, even while Mary is Jesus' mother she remains Anne's child. This message evidently came across clearly to medieval Germans, for they repeatedly refer to the *Anna Selbdritt* as "Anne with the two children."

In some works the dependence of Mary and Jesus on Anne is heightened by the enfolding of the two smaller figures in Anne's arms and cloak, as it is in an altarpiece from the workshop of Gerard David in the National Gallery in Washington. The *Anna Selbdritts* in which the adult Mary and Anne sit side by side on a bench or throne with the child between them join the three figures in a way that carries different but equally telling implications. Here, rather than showing the joint dependence of Mary and Jesus on Anne, the composition makes Anne equal and parallel with Mary in her relationship with the child. It is significant too that artists frequently made a point of showing Jesus in physical contact with both women. Held by one, he places one foot on the lap of the other in the "first steps" motif, or he touches the fruit in her hands.

Still another kind of equation is suggested in some bench and Throne of Grace *Anna Selbritts* through the addition of a vertical spiritual trinity that intersects with the horizontal physical Anne-Mary-Jesus trinity. Hans Leinberger used this composition in the *Anna Selbdritt* he carved for Sankt Johannes Gnadenthal in Ingolstadt, with a bust of God the Father, the dove positioned below it, appearing directly over the head of the Christ Child (fig. 2). The linking of earthly with spiritual trinity cannot help but suggest that the two are either equal or parallel in importance as part of the scheme of heavenly relationships. Even the crudest of the Anne images, deficient in realism, expressiveness, and beauty, displays one form or other of this all-important link between Anne, Mary, and Jesus, its importance reflected also in the fact that long after realism came to dominate Late Gothic art in Germany, the older types of the *Anna Selbdritt* with the miniaturized Mary and Christ Child continued to be popular.

Anne, Mary, and Salvation

The works of art do more than merely emphasize Anne as the physical source of Mary and Jesus. By appropriating features of late medieval Marian imagery, they suggest for Anne the same heightened role in the salvational process that fifteenth-century thinking gave to Mary. Fifteenth-century depictions of the Madonna in both Italy and the North characteristically show Mary looking into the space in front of her, or looking downward toward her son—who does not return her gaze. Basing their conclusions on textual sources and on iconographic details within the works, art historians have interpreted this gaze structure—so different from the smiling interaction of the High Gothic Madonna—as intended to suggest that Mary is contemplating the coming death of her son.[4] Mary, suffering with Christ, is shown as taking part in the salvational process.

Thus the long-standing practice of linking the birth and death of Christ, as in the early medieval depiction of Christ's manger as an altar, was intensified in Late Gothic art in such images as Matthias Grünewald's paralleling of a ragged swaddling cloth with the ragged loincloth of the crucifixion in the *Isenheim Altar*. As well, Late Gothic nativity-crucifixion parallelisms increasingly involved Mary, notably in the similarity of facial expression in depictions of Mary with the infant Christ and depictions of her with the dead Christ. The heightened role that Mary plays in painted depictions of salvation is matched by the treatment she receives in the sermons of the fifteenth-century preacher Gabriel Biel. Heiko Oberman's study of Biel's theology reveals a two-pronged treatment of Mary. In his theological works, Biel develops the idea of the predestination of Mary as the mother of the Redeemer, thus giving her an important but passive role in the redemption of humankind. However, in Biel's sermons this passive role is replaced by a more active one in which Mary is presented as predestined (as the result of her foreknown humility) to play a role as the hope of humankind, God having granted her the right and power of intercession. Thus, in the sermons Mary's *compassion* with Christ at the foot of the cross takes on a quite literal meaning, implying that she *helps* redeem humankind.[5]

The ideas expressed by Biel find visual parallels in certain pervasive compositional and iconographic features of Late Gothic art: the downward gaze of a typical the fifteenth-century Madonna such as the work by the Master of Saint Barbara in the Montreal Museum of Fine Arts coincides with the emphasis on Mary's humility, while the absence of the smile is consistent with her role as co-sufferer with her son (fig. 8). The concept of Mary's role as co-redemptrix is expressed with particular drama in Rogier van der Weyden's Prado *Deposition*, where the curve of Mary's swooning body parallels that of Christ. Even the hand positions are parallel—though the nail holes in Christ's hands make clear the difference in their roles. Yet the stronger message, from a visual point of view, is that carried by the parallelism of the figures and by the pathos of Mary's swooning body, the extraordinarily realistic drops of sweat on her forehead testifying to the intensity of her suffering.

An identical approach to compositional features appears in the fifteenth-century German and Flemish depictions of Saint Anne. Like Mary, Anne does not smile, and with rare exceptions she does not engage gazes with Mary or Jesus, or with the viewer, but instead looks obliquely at them or gazes into space. Often, particularly in Flemish works, Anne looks with lowered, hooded eyes at Mary, who looks in a similar indirect way at the Christ Child. Other devices too are employed to prevent the meeting of gazes. In Leinberger's Sankt Johannes Gnadenthal *Anna Selbdritt*, the glances of Mary and Anne, directed outward into space, cross each other in mid-air (fig. 2). Riemenschneider's sandstone Saint Anne of 1520 exhibits still another common pattern—three different, unmeeting trajectories: Anne looks outward, the miniaturized Mary on her arm looks down toward her book, and Jesus looks out into space in still another direction (fig. 1).

The fact that the visual treatment of the gaze structures in the Anne imagery imitates those of Marian images suggests that an analogous content might have been involved. For the viewer, the unengaged facial expressions work to deemphasize the narrative of human relationships in favor of one about the interaction that is part of the plan of salvation. The gazing of Mary into space is thus doubled in these works in which Anne too lays claim to a role in the sacrifice on the cross. Both Mary and Anne share in the salvational process, not only by producing the Redeemer but also by sharing in the foreknowledge and pain of his crucifixion. One can see how such a feeling might have been engendered by such works as the bench-type *Anna*

FIGURE 8. Master of the Legend of Saint Barbara, *Virgin Enthroned with Angels*, 1470–1500. Montreal Museum of Fine Arts

Selbdritt painted by Hans Holbein the Elder as part of an altarpiece for the Dominican nuns of Saint Katherine in Augsburg ca. 1512, in which the child looks out toward the viewer, Mary looks with hooded gaze at him, while Anne displays the inward, detached gaze (fig. 9). The distanced gaze structure here is paralleled by a configuration of physical gestures that are designed to forestall intimacy: heads incline slightly but backs remain upright, and hands clasp limply. The interaction of

FIGURE 9. Hans Holbein the Elder, *Anna Selbdritt Katharinenaltar,* 1512. Augsburg Staatsgalerie

the gazes of Saint Ulrich and the messenger who approaches him in another panel of the same work reminds us that the absence of interaction between Anne and Mary is a matter of choice on the part of the artist.

Parallels and Contrasts: The High Gothic

The significance of the parallels between the Late Gothic Madonna and the Late Gothic Saint Anne is underlined by the contrasting parallels that mark the High

Gothic Madonnas and the Anne images of the thirteenth and fourteenth centuries. The tilted heads, beckoning smiles (with chins tucked into necks, swelling under eyes, and the other clever new devices developed by artists in response to new demands), and the engaged glances, sometimes between mother and son lost in mutual love and fascination, sometimes between Mary or Jesus and the viewer, which we see in the Madonna from the Lorenzkirche in Nuremberg (fig. 10), all express Mary's High Gothic role as the courtly lady who accepts homage from her devotee and either answers his supplications herself or brings them to her son, the king. These works are the sculptor's version of the Mary of the Miracles of the Virgin, who intercedes to perform personal favors for her devotees—whether they deserve them or not—so long as they have served her as their lady. The same inter-action is found in High Gothic depictions of Saint Anne. In place of the distanced focus and straight mouth of the Riemenschneider *Anna Selbdritt* of the late 1400s, we find the inclining bodies and sweetly curved smiles of the Mary and Anne who look out at the viewer in the thirteenth-century Stralsund *Anna Selbdritt*, the near-identity of the two faces creating an intensely reassuring atmosphere of sweetness and security (fig. 11). The absence of the "salvational" gaze structure in the High Gothic versions of the theme is of course consistent with the fact that, in the thir-teenth and fourteenth centuries, Anne was not ascribed salvational powers.

Analysis of stylistic or iconographic change cannot by itself reveal the meaning of the changes in question. In the absence of texts to support such an argument, it would be foolish, and given what we know of how stylistic and iconographic trends spread and change, probably incorrect, to maintain that all fifteenth-century artists necessarily intended to make allusions to salvation in their depictions of Saint Anne. However, it does not seem unreasonable to propose that the broad range of ideas about her connection with salvation was given expression in visual form in the works they created. The hypothesis receives further support from the fact that in the sixteenth century, when Anne began to lose her salvific power, the lowered and unmeeting gazes and the affectless body positionings began to decline in frequency, eventually to disappear and be replaced by a new configuration consistent with the new role in the economy of salvation that Anne took on as her cult moved into the last phase of its late medieval flowering. Gazes now connect, and other strategies to convey maternal warmth become more numerous.

Parallels and Contrasts: England and Italy
The description in Chapter 8 of how and why this change came about will resolve the various themes, explicit and implicit, in Saint Anne's late medieval cult. This must

FIGURE 10. *Madonna and Child*, ca. 1310. Stone. Lorenzkirche, Nuremberg

wait, however, for other threads to be picked up first, for in the years under discussion, the late fifteenth century, Anne's cult was still in the full flowering of its expansion.

There is more to be said too about the question of salvational content in late fifteenth-century German and Flemish images of Saint Anne. To underline the structural argument still further, it should be pointed out that temporal consistency between text and image in Anne's Northern cult is matched by parallel consistencies—and contrasts—in her cult in England and Italy. To summarize, in neither England nor Italy was Anne ascribed salvational power, and in neither place was she customarily portrayed in ways that emphasized the triple link.

FIGURE 11. Northeast Germany, *Anna Selbdritt*, late thirteenth century. Molded plaster. Nikolaikirche, Stralsund

The majority of Italian depictions of Anne, the Virgin, and the Child use what could be termed a two-plus-one composition. The Italian *metterza*, though it depicts the three generations, uses eye and body language not to join but to separate the generations.[6] In Fra Bartolommeo's *Saint Anne Altarpiece* (1510–12), in the Museo San Marco in Florence, Anne raises her hands and eyes toward heaven, separating herself from the Virgin who forms a separate unit with the Child as the two of them look down toward the kneeling infant Baptist. Anne is thus distinguished from, not joined with, Mary and Jesus. In Leonardo's well-known treatment of the theme in the Louvre, it is the two women who are joined to form a group. Interacting with

one another, Mary and Anne share a mutual absorption in the youthful Christ
(fig. 3). The explanation of a cartoon that would seem to be that of the Louvre
painting given in a letter to Isabella d'Este by Fra Pietro da Novellara in 1501 is
emphatic in not linking the three figures and in not ascribing Anne an active role in
salvation:

> . . . a Christ child, about a year old, almost jumping down out of his
> mother's arms to seize hold of a lamb. The mother, almost getting up from
> the lap of Saint Anne, catches the child to take him away from the lamb
> (sacrificial animal) that signifies the Passion. Saint Anne, partly rising from
> her seat, looks as though she wants to restrain her daughter from holding
> the child back from the little lamb, which perhaps represents the Church
> which would not want to hinder the Passion of Christ.[7]

Here Anne has knowledge of salvation and plays a role in making it possible but has
no agency in effecting it. Peculiarly Italian is the theme of Mary's reluctance to accept
the death of her son, a theme that is perhaps best known through the thirteenth-
century Franciscan Jacopone da Todi's dramatization of the Passion, in which Mary,
on learning that her son has been taken, cries out in protest:

> MARY: O Pilate, do not cause my son to be tormented: for I can show you
>   how wrongly he is accused.
> THE CROWD: Crucify, crucify! A man who makes himself king, by our law,
>   defies the senate.
> THE VIRGIN: I beg you to hear me, think of my grief: perhaps even now
>   you begin to have misgivings.[8]

Generally speaking, in Italy Anne does not appear to have been seen in terms of a
joint link with daughter and grandson. In Florence, where levels of salvation anxiety
seem to have been relatively low and where, according to Richard Trexler, relationships with saints tended to follow the patron-client model that is based on chosen
rather than blood ties, Anne was not viewed primarily in terms of her ties with
Mary and Jesus, and she had no special connection with salvation.[9]

The cult of Saint Anne in England differed both from its Germanic form and
from its Italian form. Late fourteenth- and early fifteenth-century English stanzaic
lives of Anne, as well as poems and episodes in religious dramas concerning her, pay
little or no attention to the issues that distinguish the Northern texts, neither the

triple link, the absence of fleshly lust, nor salvational power receiving much attention.[10] The admonition in *Mirk's Festial* is typical in presenting Anne, like other
saints, as exercising purely intercessory power:"Wherfor ye schul now knele adowne,
and pray Saynt Anne to pray to her holy doghtyr, oure lady, that scho pray to her
sonne that he geue you hele yn body and yn sowle, and grace to kepe your ordyr of
wedlok, and gete such chyld that byn plesant and trew seruandys to God, and soo
com to the blys that Saynt Anne ys yn. Amen."[11] Typical too is the fact that the
description links Anne with Mary but not with Jesus. English prayers frequently
link Anne with her daughter, and English art does the same, especially in the image
of the Education of the Virgin, which was widely popular in England. But texts and
works of art that emphasize Anne, Mary, and Jesus together in the *Selbdritt* type of
composition are rare in England. The composition used in the Holy Kinship in the
thirteenth-century English Krivoklat Psalter, in which Anne is shown with her
three husbands in the upper register while the three Marys and their children are
placed in a separate register below, is not found in Germany. Yet it is entirely consistent with English texts, which place more emphasis than German texts on Anne's
happy home life with her husband.

A final example, that of Holland, rounds out the structural argument. In Holland, where the metonymic approach to salvation appears to have been less strong
than in Germany by the late 1400s, the *Anna Selbdritt* image began to take on the
appearance of a more intimate, genre-type scene many decades before it did so in
Germany (fig. 12). In place of the distanced gaze structures of the German and
Flemish images, Dutch sculptures of the *Anna Selbdritt* include an unusually high
proportion in which both gazes and body positions establish a sense of intimate
contact: Anne and Mary sometimes look out jointly toward the viewer; bodies
incline slightly toward one another; smiles are frequent. Rather than portraying her
as a figure of power, Dutch images are more apt to show Anne as an affectionate,
down-to-earth grandmother interacting with her adult daughter. The realism of the
Dutch sculptures is consistent with the attention paid to the details of human interaction in the *vita* portion of Jan van Denemarken's 1486 Dutch life of Anne, *Die historie, die ghetiden ende die exempelen vander heyligher vrouwen sint Annen.*

That Holland should differ so from Flanders and Germany may seem surprising
considering that the three territories shared in the creation of the late medieval
Northern phase of the cult, using and helping to develop the same common body
of iconographic and textual material. Indeed, Van Denemarken's was one of the first
of the new lives. However, there are indications that perceptions of Anne and the
development of her cult differed in some important ways in Holland. There is less

FIGURE 12. Jan van Steffeswert, *Anna-te-Drieen*, 1511.
Bonnefantenmuseum, Maastricht

emphasis on Anne's salvational power in Van Denemarken's life than in the German
and Flemish lives.[12] There is also less emphasis on the absence of "fleshly lust" in her
marital relations, and less concern with depicting her as a model for restrained
female behavior, the emphasis in terms of family life in the Dutch work focusing
instead on the obedience of children to their parents and on their instruction. And
though the large number of images of Saint Anne made in Holland testify to Anne's
great popularity there, the fact that there were proportionately fewer confraternities,
no major pilgrimage sites, and few recorded relics supports the suggestion that she
was not utilized to shape lay piety to the same extent that she was in Germany.[13]
Dutch clerics do not seem to have been implicated in the kind of coordinated organization of Anne's cult that marked Germany and Flanders.

5

Anne's Promoters

WHY DID THEY DO IT?

If the means Saint Anne's promoters used to spread her cult can be documented with a good deal of precision, the question of why they did it raises new issues. They themselves state that they did it for pastoral reasons, and though we may view these reasons from a different perspective, the evidence suggests that this was indeed what they were doing. For it appears that the Anne texts and confraternities were part of a broader move to shape and control lay piety at work in the late fifteenth and early sixteenth centuries. At the same time that the laity were seeking a personal piety suited to their circumstances, the clergy were enlarging both pastoral care and influence in the area of salvational practices, and also in such things as the expanded role of confession and the provision of new arenas for lay devotional practice. In so doing they were at the same time extending the range of their influence.

Pastoral Concerns and New Devotions

The cult of Saint Anne was part of this movement, but it was not the first of its kind. It had been preceded by two other new transregional devotions aimed at the laity: the Rosary and the Seven Sorrows. Recent studies by Anne Winston-Allen and Carol Schuler have revealed important similarities in the organization and aims of the three cults. All originated in the Netherlands and Rhineland area. All three differed from earlier devotions in being independent of particular shrines and churches and thus able to address themselves to people over a wide geographical area, for though individual brotherhoods probably drew membership primarily from their own areas, the cults' literature addressed devotees at large. Each built on a devotion already in the process of expansion. The founders of all three were prominent men who had contacts with ruling circles and, in the case at least of the Rosary and Anne cults, were involved in movements for clerical reform.[1] Like the Anne confraternities, those of the Rosary and the Seven Sorrows offered attractive and easy-to-join large-scale structures in which laypeople could seek the spiritual goods of most concern to them, help in daily life, and salvation. Winston-Allen notes: "As a self-help association providing supplementary insurance (in perpetuity) against the pains of purgatory, the brotherhood met a pressing need."[2] Schuler too comments on the shift away from an initial meditational orientation as the Seven Sorrows cult increasingly focused on apotropaic and salvational ends.[3]

The Saint Anne confraternities appear to have borrowed certain features from those of the Rosary and the Seven Sorrows. The Augsburg Anne brotherhood made the same offer as the Rosary confraternity, not only in publicizing the mutual benefits to be gained from the prayers and devotional activities of fellow members but also in announcing that members would benefit from the prayers of the monks of the religious order that sponsored the confraternity. In some cases, organizers of the Anne and the Rosary cults joined efforts, as they did in Cologne under Jacob Sprenger's aegis, and Anne texts sometimes included sections on the Rosary while Rosary texts might devote space to Anne.[4]

But along with their similarities the three cults also showed differences that reflected the specific intentions of the people behind them. Where the Anne confraternities reveal a middle-class orientation, the Rosary confraternity emphasized its accessibility to the poor. Its membership included working-class people, tradesmen, artisans, domestics, and peasants, along with people of higher social levels, and Sprenger issued a specific invitation to women to join the Rosary confraternity.[5] The following excerpt from a German Rosary confraternity handbook emphasizes the fact that all can join (including the dead), and a particular invitation is extended to the poor and to sinners: "This fraternity accepts all; it excludes no-one. It accepts religious and secular, young and old, poor and rich, just and sinners. And not only the living but indeed the dead" (Hec fraternitas omnes recipit, excludit neminem. Religiosos, Seculares, iuuenes et senes, pauperes et divites, iustos et peccatores hec fraternitas suscipit. Et non solum viuos immo et mortuos).[6] The fact that formal inscription was not necessary and that membership was free underlines the mass approach of the Rosary movement at the same time that it points up the contrast with the Anne brotherhoods, which did involve official inscription and fees.[7] In the case of the Seven Sorrows confraternity, the founder, Jan van Coudenberghe, imitated Sprenger's successful formula in eliminating dues and in offering simple devotional rituals that could be performed at home. The Anne confraternities, on the other hand, stipulated that devotional exercises should be performed at the confraternity altar in front of an image.

The difference in intended audience is evident in the written material produced by the three confraternities. Winston-Allen points out that the twenty-seven short testimonials in the Ulm Rosary confraternity book of 1483 include a number about the concerns of poor people: stories of crops being saved, of a poor woman becoming rich and sharing her wealth, of the conversion of prostitutes, moneylenders, and those who mistreated the poor.[8] By contrast, the poor and the marginal rarely appear in the exempla in the Anne lives, which are more inclined to tell stories about middle- and upper-level people who lose and regain fortunes, status, and reputations. A prayer in a life by Petrus Dorlandus reveals the same concern with status and reputation when it asks that worshipers be "freed from all disgrace and dishonor" (ab omni rubore & infamia liberati).[9] One of the few Anne tales that does involve a poor person, a widow with a sick pig, ends not with wealth but with restoration of the status quo—the pig recovers.[10]

Anne's promoters seem to have succeeded in reaching their intended audience, for though the distribution of images suggests a broad popularity at all levels, evidence indicates special success among the urban bourgeoisie, a population increasingly anxious for a fuller share in the benefits of both worlds.[11] As for the promoters, one cannot help but notice that their response to the laity's concerns seems to have been colored by worries about heresy and by fears that questioning of established beliefs and practices could threaten the basis of clerical authority, the clergy's custody of the means of salvation, and in the process, its income. The new cults thus can be seen as part of an attempt both to satisfy lay desire and to control it.

All this is not to suggest that heartfelt devotion to Mary's mother and confidence in her ability to help humankind did not play a part in the writing of texts and the founding and joining of brotherhoods. There is plentiful evidence that late medieval Christians of all social levels felt strong personal bonds with their saints. If the Lutheran reformer Johann Agricola, recalling how he used to run to the saints for comfort, could speak of the apostles in the diminutive as "apostlekins" (*Apostelchen*), surely Mary's own mother would have aroused a warm response. Indeed, the ubiquitous references to her as "Mother Anne" seem fair testimony to genuine affection.[12]

At the same time, one must be cautious in assuming that devotional intensity in a text reflects devotional intensity in the heart of the writer. The authors of hagiographical texts were professional writers who knew how to create the effects they wanted, and their writings abound with rhetorical devices designed to create response and belief in the reader; time and again hoary exempla from the Latin and Greek fathers are resurrected and attributed to trustworthy old monks whom the author has met personally—and modern scholarship is replete with examples of the success of such strategies.

Pastoral Concerns: Women

We have seen how the Anne cult took the middle classes as its primary target. Within that group, its promoters seem to have singled out a particular segment for special attention: middle-class women. A model for female behavior is usually included in the lives' descriptions of Anne as a modest and retiring wife, a stay-at-home who avoided occasions for gossip and foolish behavior. *Das Leben und Wunderzaichen der allerseeligsten Frawen Annae* describes the youthful Anne recoiling in horror from the frivolities of adolescence, which the author compares to poisonous snakes: "She fled the frivolities and wantonness of young girls as poisonous snakes, preferring rather to devote herself to godly reflection at home" (Sie der Jungen Maegdtlein leichtfertigkeiten vnd gailheiten nit anderst als vergiffte schlangen flohe so hat sie vil lieber anheimbs der Goettlichen betrachtungen obligen).[13] Trithemius, in the *De laudibus*, emphasizes the fact that she was rarely seen in public places, combining this observation with advice to mothers to keep their daughters at home:

> No one ever saw her running in the lanes and streets; no one ever heard of her uselessly chattering in the houses of neighbors; no one found her attending dances and shows. From her youth she learned to stay at home; she accustomed herself to work with her hands; she did not desire to be seen outdoors by people. She sought to observe concord in goodness and peace with her neighbors; she injured no one; she perturbed no one by words or deeds; rarely was she seen in public; she did not sit with foolish, chattering women in the streets; and in slanderous conversations she took no part.
>
> O mothers, teach your daughters to honor God: not to love the pomp of the world, to flee the shameful gaze of the people, to stay at home. . . . The archangel did not come to Mary in public but in secret: not in the street, chattering, but in her room, silently.

> [Nemo unusquisque per vicos et plateas discurrentem illam repperit: nemo in domibus vicinarum inutiliter fabulantem audiuit: nemo ad choreas et spectacula unusquisque illam astitisse inuenit. Domi manere a iuuentute sua didicit: laborare aliquid manibus consueuit. foris videri ab hominibus non quesiuit. Concordiam in bono et pacem cum vicinis obseruare studuit: nemini iniuriam fecit: verbo vel ope neminem perturbauit. Raro videbatur in publico: in plateis cum mulierculis fabulantibus non sedebat: et in colloquio detrahentuum non stetit:

Dicite o matres filias vostras ad honorem dei instituere: mundi pompas non amare: publicum turbe conspectum fugere: domi residere. . . . Ad mariam archangelus venit non in publico sed in secreto: non in platea loquentem: sed in camera tacentem.][14]

Brandenbarg notes that Anne as the good woman had her opposite number in the negative stereotypes that were increasing in popular and didactic literature in the late fifteenth century.[15] Figures like the foul-mouthed thrice-married working-class widow of the Flemish satire *Les Evangiles des Quenouilles* are the bad examples that are countered in the descriptions of Saint Anne.[16] Lyndal Roper has shown how stereotypes of sexually untrustworthy women began to affect the examination of witnesses in rape trials as the fifteenth century gave way to the sixteenth, the questioning of women who brought charges of rape being increasingly colored by an underlying assumption that they were not rape victims but prostitutes. Sometimes their mothers were questioned on suspicion of being procuresses.[17] Saint Anne—modest, virtuous, and sexually restrained—embodied an opposite image of female behavior.

Modeling virtuous behavior was not the only point at which the new Anne texts touched the issue of women's behavior. Angelika Dörfler-Dierken has shown how they presented a new paradigm of the relative claims of God and husband on the married woman saint. Whereas in earlier lives of married holy woman, such as that of the fourteenth-century Prussian mystic Dorothea of Montau, the marital relationship was depicted as a hindrance to sanctity, and the husband as a rival to Christ, in the Anne lives it is through the marriage relationship and in loving cooperation with her husbands that Anne lives out her holiness.[18] Yet I would add that, at the same time that they introduce this new theological ideal of marital sanctity, the lives also retain an older model of marriage, a model signaled by the repeated assertion that Saint Anne experienced "no fleshly lust" in her marital relations. This emphasis on Anne's sexual anesthesia coincides with the long-held idea that holiness is incompatible with sexual activity. Assuring us that although Anne produced her three daughters through normal sexual intercourse, at the same time the lives insist that she experienced no sexual sensations ("non libidine carnali") in doing so.[19] In *Das Leben vnnd Wunderzeichen der allerseeligisten Frawen Annae*, Anne explains that she married not out of "fleshly love but out of the demands of the law, solely . . . in the hope of having honorable heirs and descendants" (Ich nit auss fleischlicher lieb sonder auss zwang dess Gesatzs einem Mann genomen hab, allein der Hoffnung in deiner forcht erlicher Erben und Nachkömmling).[20] In the same book, in a formulation that would have delighted Freud, the reader is told that Anne held her husband Joachim in honor as her lord and loved him as her father, while he honored his wife as his mother and embraced her as his sister.[21]

Though its appearance in the Anne texts is new, the "no fleshly lust" trope is old. Historically it served to reconcile two things often perceived by medieval Christians as incompatible: sexual activity and sanctity. Rare enough in European hagiography, married saints were especially rare in Germany. When the first ones appeared, royal saints like Elizabeth of Hungary and Hedwig, wife of Henry I of Silesia, their *vitae*, according to Ortrud Reber's study of women saints, included statements that seem intended to disassociate them from their sexual activities. The *vitae* of thirteenth- and fourteenth-century married women saints like Elisabeth, Hedwig, and Birgitta of Sweden typically contain one or more of the following motifs: the saint preferred virginity but married in obedience to parents; she married for the purpose of producing children; she lived continently with her husband for a period of time; she and her husband lived continently after the birth of the desired children; like Sarah and Tobias they waited before consummating their marriage; the saint engaged in marital relations without experiencing "fleshly lust."[22]

All these reconciling motifs appear in the Anne lives. Several state that she married in obedience to the law or in order to give birth to lawful children. And the motif is applied to other members of the kinship as well. According to Jan van Denemarken, Anne's mother, Emerentia, married to bring forth fruit to the honor of God.[23] Cleophas, Anne's second husband, is described as marrying for similar sober reasons in one life: "He married Anne not out of fleshly love but rather in order to increase his lineage and his house / and because of the demands of the Law" (Er hatte sich auch nit auss fleischlicher Lieb sonder vilmehr sein Gschlecht vnd Stammen zumehren vnd aus zwang des Gesatzes mit Anna vermaehlet).[24] And Anne and Joachim are sometimes compared with Sarah and Tobias. The cumulative effect is to render credible the sanctity of a woman who married three times and bore three children.

Saint Anne and the Immaculate Conception

Another aspect of Anne's marital life that is part of the discourse of her cult is the question of the Immaculate Conception. The doctrine that Mary was conceived in Anne's womb without at any time being stained by original sin was discussed in Chapter 1 in connection with the birth of the Northern cult of Saint Anne. We meet it again in the late fifteenth century. In secondary sources, one frequently reads that Anne's popularity in the late Middle Ages was a result of renewed controversy over the doctrine in this period and that the *Anna Selbdritt* was intended as a representation of the doctrine.[25] The source given is usually Beda Kleinschmidt's influential 1930 book on the cult of Saint Anne, which describes the *Selbdritt* as "a popular and concrete expression" of the Immaculate Conception: "When one honored Mother Anne, represented her in images, and celebrated her feast, one celebrated at the same time the mystery of the Immaculate Conception."[26]

Kleinschmidt's belief that doctrine and cult were causally related sounds reasonable enough. The expansion of the cult did coincide with a period of dispute over the Immaculate Conception. And even more suggestive of a connection, the same German and Flemish humanists and clerics who were promoting the doctrine were also promoting the cult of Saint Anne; some at least of the early offices also promoted the doctrine.[27] But just as the argument that the Immaculate Conception was a causal factor in the inception of cult and imagery in the thirteenth century was false, so it is false in the fifteenth-century context: Anne's cult had an important incidental connection with the Immaculate Conception, but the connection was not integral and it did not *cause* the flowering of the devotion.

The evidence against an integral connection is varied and abundant. To begin with, Anne was promoted by immaculatists and maculatists alike, and her cult was sometimes fostered by the Dominicans, who opposed the doctrine. Conversely, some of the lives, including the earliest extant example, Jan van Denemarken's *Die historie, die ghetiden ende die exempelen vander heyligher vrouwen sint Annen*, take a maculatist not an immaculatist position, while the author of the Augsburg confraternity life shows no interest in the subject one way or another.[28]

The fact that some woodcuts depicting the *Anna Selbdritt* were published in two versions, one with an immaculatist prayer, the other with a maculatist one, is further evidence that the image was not automatically read by contemporaries as representing the doctrine. Meaning depended on context. Opponents of the Immaculate Conception used the *Anna Selbdritt* to illustrate their pamphlets; supporters of the doctrine did the same.

The assumption of a connection in part arose from the fact that many of the promoters of Anne's cult were also supporters of the doctrine. The most striking and influential example was of course the *De laudibus sanctissimae matris Annae*, in which Trithemius makes the immaculatist point repeatedly and insultingly, provoking the doctrine's opponents to a response in the form of the November 1494 riposte by the Frankfurt Dominican Wigand Wirt, which in turn led to the letter-writing campaign of support by the literary friends of Trithemius.[29] But despite the uproar and the debates, what is surprising is how little interest some of the humanists show in the theological arguments underpinning the doctrine. Trithemius would have made a poor showing in the debates of the thirteenth century with his contention that God as the author of nature is not bound by nature's laws.[30] His harping on the purity of Mary and her mother suggests that his real concern was with the more general question of sexual purity and its role in heightening the honor and glory of Mary and her mother than with the meaning or implications of the Immaculate Conception as a theological doctrine.

It must be kept in mind that the humanists were, after all, literary men, and their no doubt genuine desire to honor Anne and her family was accompanied by an equal delight in devising ingenious ways to do so. Arnold Bostius, writing to Konrad Celtis to encourage him to spread devotion to Anne's husband Joachim, is perhaps most ingenious of all when he argues that Joachim was closer to Jesus than Anne because he was the closest mortal relative, Anne's connection in the chain of blood relationships being interrupted by Mary:

> Why is it not fitting that she [Anne] and also he [Joachim] be venerated, honored, praised, loved, invoked? I don't know where our eyes were up to now that we didn't see this. Surely this is a great injury to the forebear of God, who among all men was the closest to our Savior and Redeemer, . . . he who shares this closer nearness only with the Virgin Mary. Just as she is the closest to Jesus Christ of all women, so Joachim is closer to him than all men, seeing that he was his sole male forebear, he who did not have an earthly father.
>
> This supereminent glory he shares with her [Mary]—however, his holy wife, Anna, is not closer to Jesus Christ than any other woman, even though she was his grandmother—because Mary comes between her and Jesus whereas no other man comes between Joachim and Jesus.
>
> [Quare non decet ut ipsa etiam ipse venerari, coli, laudari, amari, invocari? Nescio, ubi hucusque fuerant oculi nostri, quod haec non vidimus. Magna certe iniuria avum Dei unicum, qui prae viris omnibus Salvatori nostro et Redemptori proximus attinet (hucusque sic postergavimus), qui in hac proximiore attenentia Mariae Virginis, natae suae, solus communicat. Sicuti vero ipsa Jesu Christo propinquior est omnium feminarum, ita et ipse Joachim sibi propinquior est omnium virorum, cum eius unicus avus fuerit, qui terrenum patrem non habuit.

In hac igitur gloria cunctis supereminet solusque eam participat; non
autem sancta sua coniunx Anna Christo Jesu propinquior est omnium
feminarum, quamvis etiam ava sua fuerit. Maria enim inter eam et Jesum
mediavit, inter Joachim autem et Jesum nullus virorum.][31]

It is clear from the variety and complexity of the ways in which Anne is connected—or not connected—with the Immaculate Conception in late fifteenth-
century writing that caution is needed before designating a text as immaculatist or
maculatist. Whereas the Council of Basel's bull promulgated in 1430 stated the doctrine explicitly and concisely—namely, that Mary's soul was not "at any time or for
an instant of time subject to original sin"—the discussion in the later part of the
century often seems to be concerned with a more generalized notion of purity. To be
designated with certainty as referring to the Immaculate Conception, a text must
make its references clearly and unambiguously; references to purity or sanctity alone
do not suffice. Even the epithet "Tota pulcra es amica mea" (Thou art all fair, my
love), which is often used to refer to the Immaculate Conception, is not an infallible
indicator, for it appears in a reference to Mary's virginity in a Rosary handbook
stemming from Dominican sources.[32]

The humanists were not the only ones who wandered off the track in discussions
about the Immaculate Conception. There were also instances of contemporary misunderstanding of the meaning of the doctrine. Birgitta of Sweden, who more than a
century earlier had been the first to apply the "no fleshly lust" motif to Saint Anne,
declares herself a supporter of the Immaculate Conception, but she does not understand the doctrine as the theologians did. For as Anna Nilsen points out, in referring to God's sanctifying Mary's body after her conception at the time of the
insertion of her soul, Birgitta is actually describing a maculate, not an immaculate,
conception. Birgitta's application of the imagery of cleansing in her description of
the Virgin as a clean vase, yet because of her descent from Adam, an unclean one,
confirms her misapprehension of the Immaculate Conception:

> Mary was both a clean vessel and an unclean one; truly clean because she
> was all beautiful and not even enough stain was found in her in which to
> fix the point of a needle, but she was not clean because she stemmed from
> the root of Adam and she was born of sinners, although she was conceived
> without sin.

[Maria fuit vas mundum et non mundum: mundum vero fuit quia tota pulchra, et tanta immundicia non inueniebatur in ea, vbi cuspis acus infigeretur; sed non mundum fuit, quia de radice Ade processit et de peccatoribus nata est, licet sine peccato concepta.][33]

Birgitta's concern with the relationship between sexual purity and sanctity may well have been connected with her own project to reconcile marital sexuality with sanctity, though in this case the reconciling may have applied as much to Birgitta's own marriage as to Anne's. Mereth Lindgren shows how after Birgitta's death her followers portrayed her and her children in woodcut compositions that imitated Holy Kinship woodcuts, thus appropriating the sanctity of Anne's family and marital status and applying it to her.[34] Birgitta used Anne the same way during her lifetime. As a married woman and the mother of a number of children, striving to achieve sanctity in her own and others' eyes, Birgitta had an interest in arguing for the compatibility of sanctity and legitimate marital sexual activity. Hence the personal value for her of her vision in which Anne appears as a patron of "lawfully married" folk. And no doubt women readers, such as those who read the following Middle English version of Birgitta's vision, would have found relevance for their own situations: "I ame Anne, ladi of all weddid folke that were byfor the lawe. Doghtir, wirshepe God of this manere: Blissed by thou, Jesu Criste, the son of God that chesid the one modir of the weddinge of Joachim and Anne. And therefor, for the praiers of Anne, haue meraci of all thame that are in wedeloke or thinkes to be weddid, that thai mai bringe furth froite to the wirshipe of Gode. And kepe wele the relikes that thou hase of me."[35]

Was Anne a Women's Patron?

But was Anne a patroness of women's concerns in general? In modern writing one finds frequent references to her as a medieval patron of such things as marriage, fertility, and childbirth. However, though there are certainly examples of such concerns, the overall evidence of both the new Anne texts and the miracle reports suggests that Anne was not a particular patron of women's concerns in the Germanic-speaking realms in the medieval period.[36] Those who sought help from the relic of Anne's finger in Cologne came, according to the anonymous Franciscan, because of sickness, pain, pestilence, bleeding, aches, fever, and problems with teeth, head, and face.[37] Women's problems are not singled out, nor are they given special attention in a 1516 song about the miracles performed by Anne's relic at Düren, which lists recovery after the following: a fall from a horse, several cases of posses-

sion, two drowned children and a drowned youth, two cases of blindness, two children murdered by their father, a bewitched woman, and victims of pestilence.[38]
Later, however, Düren did become a shrine of special interest to women, for in 1667
it acquired a "girdle of Saint Anne," which it lent out to women desiring to get pregnant.[39] The forty-one miracles effected by the Limburg relic during a six-month
period in 1511 included healing from physical and mental illness, recovery from acci-
dents, and deliverance from possession.[40] Yet while many involved the healing of sick
and injured children (including the resuscitation of drowned children), only four
concerned birth or the resuscitation of stillborn babies, and none involved fertility
or help in childbirth or marriage. The incidence of miracles involving drowned children suggests a possible relationship with Anne's patronage of ships and shippers.

However, signs of a role as a women's patron are far from absent. An early
sixteenth-century prayerbook from a women's convent in the Rhineland recommends that a prayer to Saint Anne be held or worn by pregnant women and read to
women in childbirth. And there are mentions of such patronages in the lives, the
works of the Flemish Carthusian Petrus Dorlandus being especially rich in exempla
concerning women's problems.[41] My contention, however, is that numerically speaking women's concerns are relatively minor in comparison with Anne's other late
medieval patronages.

Judging from what contemporaries said about her, one of the things people
prayed to Saint Anne about seems to have been something that concerned both
women and men: wealth. Luther, ruing the fact that no one ever bothered to ask the
saints for patience, faith, love, or chastity, bluntly referred to Anne as the patron of
those who wanted to get rich:

> Where does one find a saint who is prayed to for patience, faith, love,
> chastity, and other spiritual goods, the way Saint Anne is for riches or
> Saint Laurence for the fever, this one for a bad leg, that one for this, the
> other for that?
>
> [Wo findet man jetzt einen Heiligen, der umb Geduld, Glauben, Liebe,
> Keuscheit, und ander geistlicher Güter wird angeruffen, als S. Anna umb
> Reichthumb, St. Lorenz für das Fewer, Der umb ein böse Bein, der umb
> dis, der ander umb das?][42]

His contemporary, the reformer Johann Agricola, rhyming off the specialties of the
saints, makes the same association between Anne (and Erasmus) and riches:

Saint Barbara, if I celebrate her feast and fast on the day before, is supposed to protect me so that I don't die without the Sacrament. Saint Roch is supposed to serve for the plague, Saint Sebastian for dandruff, while Saint Anna Selbdritt—if I set up a little lamp for her—and Saint Erasmus will make me rich.

[Da musste mich St. Barbara, wenn ich ihren Abend fastete und ihren Tag feierte schützen, dass ich nicht ohne Sakrament stürbe, St. Rochus musste dienen für die Pestilenz, St. Sebastian für Schüffe, St. Anna selbdritte, wenn ich ihr Lichtlein aufsteckte, und St. Erasmus musste reich machen.][43]

It is worth raising the question whether Anne's long-standing role as guardian of shipping, which continued to be important in the fifteenth century, may have been related to the late medieval association with riches: Anne not only protects wealth from sinking to the bottom of the sea, she now helps to increase it.

As well as presenting Anne as interested in the problems of the merchant class, the writers of the lives depict her and her husband as themselves wealthy members of that class. They are generous to the poor, God-fearing, and prompt to fulfill religious obligations and to pray for help in time of trouble, and they are assiduous in bringing up their daughters in the fear of the Lord and the knowledge of proper behavior. But though there are exceptions, meditation, raptures, weeping, asceticism, or other types of extraordinary religious practice rarely appear.[44] In fact, a popular story indignantly reported by Luther reveals just how far Mary's parents had been remade to fit the mold of the contemporary bourgeois family. The standard apocryphal version, in which Joachim and Anne gave one-third of their money to the temple, one-third to the poor, and kept one-third for themselves, is here revised to turn Mary into a wealthy heiress: "And it is not true, as some say, that Joachim and Anne Mary's parents were rich and bequeathed their goods in three parts, one to the church, one to the poor, and the third they left to Mary" (Und ist nicht, als etliche sagen, das Joachim und Anna ire [Mary's] oelttern sind reych gewesen und haben ire guetter in drey tayl gelassen, in die kirchen ain tail, das andere den armen and das dritte Marien gelassen).[45]

However, though women's issues do not seem to have been a specialty of Saint Anne in the late medieval North, there is some evidence that she may have enjoyed special popularity among women.[46] A survey of the contents of the German and Dutch manuscript books of hours in the Cologne Stadtarchiv, a large number of which are fifteenth- and early sixteenth-century vernacular books from women's

convents in the Rhineland, reveal that Anne was more likely than other saints to
be the object of extended devotions such as rosaries, the five joys, or the seven greet-
ings. Prayers to Anne outnumbered those to other saints by a wide margin: in one
sampling there were twenty-five to Anne, seventeen to the Three Kings, fifteen each
to Barbara and Rock, fourteen to Katherine, and thirteen each to John the Evangelist and Mary Magdalene. Overall there are far more references to Anne than to
other saints: Anne has fifty-four, Mary Magdalene twenty-one, the Three Kings
and Katherine twenty each, Sebastian nineteen, Barbara eighteen, and Ursula ten.[47]
However, the talk about Anne overshadowing Mary would have been decidedly
out of place in a Rhineland convent, for the number of prayers and devotions to
Anne in the sisters' prayerbooks does not begin to approach those addressed to
Mary and Jesus.

In closing this discussion of Saint Anne's complex relations with the female sex,
it should be noted that attention to women's issues—including the Immaculate
Conception—seems especially strong in the Rhineland, a circumstance that is
consistent with the long-standing tradition and concern with female piety in this
region. Manfred Beck, in a study of religious literature printed in Cologne in the
early 1500s, remarks on the high incidence of women martyrs' lives printed in
Cologne and on the prevalence of bloody martyrdoms ("slaughterhouse poetry")
here. Beck describes several female martyrs' lives in which the spilling of holy blood
is an important motif; in one legend, a gift of earth from the cemetery of the 11,000
virgins brought by Saint Irmgard to the pope is found to contain fresh blood.[48] And
Johannes Cochlaeus's 1512 description of the city makes reference to power residing
in the bodies of dead virgins whose blood has been shed.[49]

But admiration for the power of feminine holiness was accompanied by anxiety
related to perceptions of women as potentially dangerous and uncontrollable and by
consequent attempts to control both female sexuality and religious practice. The
Malleus Maleficarum is a well-known expression of this anxiety. Brandenbarg notes
that control over sexual impulses is a prominent motif in the miracles attributed to
the Cologne Anne relic.[50] It is therefore not surprising that the new Anne texts from
this region bear an extraordinarily rich burden of signification with respect to issues
pertaining to women and to female sexuality. By and large, it is in these works that
the issues of the Immaculate Conception and of Anne's sexual relations with
Joachim are most strongly emphasized, and the same is true with the modeling of
women's behavior.

6

Economic Factors and the Cult of Saint Anne

THE EXAMPLES OF AUGSBURG AND ANNABERG

While ideological factors helped shape the initial promotion of Saint Anne's cult in the Rhineland area, another set of factors entered the picture with the diffusion of the cult into the rest of Germany, factors that had less to do with concerns about lay piety than with the exigencies of raising money. This chapter examines the introduction of Anne's cult in two cities where it was newly introduced in the 1490s: the Swabian city of Augsburg, and the new mining town of Annaberg in the Saxon Erzgebirge, in each case paying particular attention to the way clerical and civic authorities orchestrated its potential for raising funds. The links between the financial and the spiritual were close and tightly wound—their manifestations diverse.

Saint Anne as Fund Raiser: Augsburg

Any Augsburg citizens who were out on the streets at three o'clock in the morning on the first of May 1516 might have been surprised to see the Dominican nuns of Saint Katharina, the most elite of the city's women's foundations, stepping out of their convent, crossing the present-day Maximilianstrasse, and going into the church of the Dominican monks some blocks away in the Dominikanergasse. The sisters were accompanied in their early morning excursion by the Dominican provincial, Johannes Faber; the mayor, Hieronymus Imhof; and several other prominent persons. The older among the fifty or sixty nuns were carried on wagons, reports the chronicler Wilhelm Rem.[1] This rare and no doubt welcome outing for the nuns, who had been somewhat unwillingly reformed several decades earlier, was undertaken to test the acoustics of the recently built Dominican men's church. In the process of building a new church of their own, the sisters were considering vaulting it like the monks' church, but they wanted to make sure the beauty of their singing would not be damaged by the innovation. They tested it by singing Matins; satisfied, at 5:00 A.M. they returned to their convent.

Why had the Dominican monks built their new church? Why were the nuns so
keen to follow in their footsteps? Why indeed were virtually all the churches in late
fifteenth-century Augsburg either rebuilding or renovating in these last decades
before the Reformation?[2] And what did all this have to do with Saint Anne? The
answer is: a great deal. Saints' cults were part and parcel of the syndrome that had
led to these decisions to rebuild, both developments arising out of the complex
dynamics of ecclesiastical life in late medieval Augsburg, for the city's churches and
convents, as well as embodying its population's changing class lines, were in competition with one another for status, clientele, and ultimately income. They addressed
this competition by attempting to outdo one another in beauty, in grandeur, and in
the various attractions they could offer the citizens of Augsburg.

Augsburg's city chronicles contain numerous references to new walls, new vaulting, the casting of new bells, processions, and other novelties introduced into the
city's churches in the later years of the fifteenth century. A few churches had suffered
fire damage, but most had not. Some argued structural problems, or a need for more
space in existing buildings. According to the Augsburg merchant Wilhelm Rem, the
Dominicans had justified their request for permission to offer an indulgence to raise
money for building with the arguments that, "first, the old church was so narrow
that they could no longer say mass in it; . . . the convent was falling down; . . . the
church was ready to collapse, and certain citizens here had given five thousand
ducats financial support for the building." But Rem considered the rebuilding
unnecessary and the reasons spurious. "The old church," he says, "was stronger and
better than the new one, it was not fallen down, this was all half nonsense. It's true it
wasn't very wide, but it was wide enough."[3]

Rem may have been right in his conviction that the rebuilding had not been
necessary from a structural point of view, for a wide body of evidence suggests that
Augsburg's building boom was less a response to problems in the material fabric of
the churches than a response to problems arising from structural strains in the city's
ecclesiastical fabric. In short, the new construction seems to have been part of an
attempt to attract the presence and alms of clientele in an increasingly competitive
ecclesiastical market place. Overall, the increase and diversification in the services
and attractions that churches were offering to the Christian public in the last few
decades of the fifteenth and the first decades of the sixteenth century, and the
inducements given people to avail themselves of these, suggest an attempt to meet
competition within a limited market.

The choice of expansion (rather than downsizing), the introduction of new and
varied attractions, the efforts to increase spending among both higher- and lower-

income population groups, the increasingly complex financing methods, and the measures taken by both civic and ecclesiastical bodies to control the market in what might be called nontangible religious goods, resembles the pattern that can be seen at work in a modern retail consumption market. As anachronistic as the comparison might sound, a consideration of the decisions made by ecclesiastical authorities in both Augsburg and Annaberg suggests that it is far from inappropriate.

As we saw at the beginning of the chapter, churches were being rebuilt—and they were being lavishly decorated, for beautiful works of art brought people into churches. But not everyone approved. The reformer Hieronymus Emser (1478–1527) complained that monks and priests "are more diligent (one is afraid) regarding their images (so that the churches will be decorated and have great congregations) than they are in caring about the living images, which are the souls of men who were created in God's image."[4] At the same time, indulgences, long used as a source of building funds, expanded their scope to offer increasingly enticing provisions. Claims for wonder-working relics and images multiplied, as did the sheer numbers of relics in relic collections. Lay confraternities were founded with their own chapels, spiritual privileges, liturgical services, and social activities. And, encouraged by devotional literature, sermons, and confessional counsel to worry about their salvation, increasing numbers of families were paying to have endowed chapels along the side aisles and elsewhere in churches. Confraternity membership offered the same kind of salvational benefits on a group basis, thus making them available over a wider economic spectrum. For the families or groups who endowed them, the chapels brought both prestige and the salvational benefits of masses said for the departed souls of members. The churches gained the more tangible benefits: first, the initial payment, plus the works of art that decorated the chapel and the necessary liturgical vessels and vestments, along with candles, maintenance, and cleaning, as well as the ongoing costs of the salary of the priest who said the masses, plus such things as payments to the singers who sang at the services. As well as serving the soul, churches were also serving the body, stepping up their activities in the selling of the life-insurance policies called *Leibdinge* whereby a sum paid to the church entitled the beneficiary to a stipulated amount of cash annually, or to food, firewood, and other necessities of life for the remainder of his or her days.[5]

References to activities of this kind are widespread in Augsburg sources. Clerics were digging up crypts and churchyards in the hope of finding bones, which were then identified sometimes with more optimism than evidence. The Augsburg chronicler Johannes Frank describes such an incident at the old Benedictine church of Saints Ulrich and Afra, where the body of Saint Digna had been discovered in

1454 and reburied with great solemnity, the head reserved in the sacristy in a silver bust reliquary.[6] Digna's body had been found in an ivory-covered box bearing her name, according to Frank, himself a monk at Saints Ulrich and Afra.[7] But there were also lead boxes with other relics, as well as an unidentified body about which he remarks cautiously:

> Item . . . in the year 1454 on that same day (Saint Bartholomew's Day), a grave in the church behind Saint Nicholas's altar, underneath, was opened up, and inside was found a whole body and on it a document, but there was nothing written on it. It was found in a hollowed-out stone sarcophagus, but no one knew for certain whose the holy body was. . . . In that same year they put the holy corpse back into the same coffin inside a lead box and wrote on a piece of paper, and also above on the coffin, "the body of Saint Nigarius Bishop," but they did not know for certain if this was true or not, especially since they had only heard it from several old people—therefore they wrote it doubtfully [*dubitative*].[8]

Such fortuitous discoveries were not unusual. In 1485 the nuns of the Bavarian convent of Hohenwart "recovered" a treasure trove that included, along with saints' bones, particles of the crucifixion sponge; earth from Calvary, from the site of the sepulchre, and from the launching site of the ascension; and fragments of Jesus' and Mary's shoes and clothing, parts of the burning bush, manna, Mary Magdalene's hair, and the bed where Mary had lain with the baby Jesus.[9]

Augsburg's cathedral, located at the other end of town from Ulrich and Afra, seems to have felt under pressure too, for its chapter had expressed concern over anticipated competition for mass attendance from a new brotherhood, founded in 1483, and a newly instituted procession notable for its figures representing the Passion of Christ, at Heilig Kreuz, another downtown church. Heilig Kreuz had its own problems; the new procession seems to have been organized in response to a pamphlet casting doubt on the authenticity of its famous wonder-working host, the *Wunderbares Gut*, doubts that, were they to spread, could affect the church's income.[10]

Heilig Kreuz and the cathedral solved their problem with the former timing its procession so that it did not interfere with the latter's main mass. But other confrontations may have been more heated. Johannes Trithemius, defending confraternities at convent churches against the charge that they took money away from parish churches, acknowledges that the confraternities were doing just that when he explains that if parish churches lose parishioners it is their own fault for not providing better service and example. At the same time, he invokes the laity's freedom of choice in deciding where they will go for their spiritual needs: "You lament that the parish churches are empty: the fault is no less to be imputed to you. You demand the milk and wool of the sheep of the lord: but you do not nourish these sheep as is proper, in the first place, nor do you care for them."[11]

Augsburg: The Carmelite Anne Brotherhood

The decision of Augsburg's Carmelites to introduce Saint Anne's cult into the city in the 1490s was part of this complex of events, and it is clear that the Carmelites' financial problems were a major factor in it. The succession of events offers a capsule version of the larger schema outlined above. Eberhart Schott's study of the convent's documents reveals that the relatively long-term financial stability that the brothers had enjoyed in the 1200s and 1300s had been followed by a period of instability in the early 1400s, succeeded later in the century by a period of prosperity, a prosperity that in turn drastically declined in the early 1500s.[12] An examination of these fluctuations seen in light of the changes in the convent's sources of income suggests that diversification of the goods and services it offered coincided with periods of financial stress. In the 1200s and 1300s the Carmelites had subsisted mainly on offerings given at mass, offerings for saying masses and hearing confessions and for preaching in the convent church, funds received for burial within the convent walls or inside the church, and money realized from fund-raising trips to outlying districts. However, as the fifteenth century progressed, regular mass oblations decreased significantly as a percentage of the annual total, while proportionately significant increases were noted in money (and income-producing property) given for masses and other postmortem salvational services, and for burial places or chapels. Proportionately significant increases were also noted in income from boxes placed in front of (possibly indulgenced) paintings and statues and at church doors, and from the membership fees for the new Saint Anne confraternity, while income from fund-raising forays continued to be important. Financial stresses were exacerbated when in the early 1500s Johannes Fortis (Johannes Stark), who succeeded Matthias Fabri as prior, put the convent in serious difficulties by selling too many *Leibdinge*.[13]

In any event, when the Carmelites founded their Saint Anne brotherhood in 1494 they made no bones about its purpose, which was, in Wilhelm Schiller's summary, "to call forth a greater devotion on the part of the people and to make them inclined to donate to the rebuilding of the church."[14] Nor did they fail to stress the salvational benefits available to confraternity members; the membership form, which gave automatic membership to wife and children along with the husband, who signed his name in the blank space provided, lists the liturgical and other aids that will be provided members in life and death by Carmelite brothers from Franconia to Hungary.[15] The life written for the confraternity describes the yearly services for members' souls: "to sing a vigil at night and in the morning and a requiem for all the souls that have departed the brotherhood, and after the requiem there will be a procession and Saint Anne's relic will be carried and after that a praiseworthy office of Saint Anne will be sung."[16]

Rebuilding and enlargement of the church began in 1487: the roof was raised; the church was lengthened by twenty-five feet; the choir, chancel, sacristy, and library were rebuilt; and a new coffered ceiling was installed.[17] Following the completion of the new church in 1497, further rebuilding began when the Fugger family chapel, completed in 1518 and remarkable both for its new Renaissance style and for its location at the western end of the nave, got under way.

But despite generous endowments from the upper strata of the city, the Augsburg Carmelites, who numbered around twelve to fourteen brothers plus a half-dozen novices, were, as we have noted, not a wealthy convent. And amelioration of this situation was clearly in the mind of the Carmelite author of the Augsburg confraternity life when he pressed his readers to gain the indulgence granted to those who joined the newly founded Saint Anne brotherhood, providing they confess their sins and, perhaps in addition, give or bequeath land, money, or goods to the convent.[18] The confraternity life reiterates the salvational benefits attendant on honoring Anne, noting that people who honor her along with her whole kinship can expect to be attended by the same on their deathbeds. The monks' further attempts to make use of Anne's potential included changing the name of the convent, which was rededicated November 15, 1485, "in honor of the virgin Mary and Anne the mother of Mary." Previously the church, which was usually referred to as "vnser lieben Frauen Brüder Kirche," had been dedicated only to Mary.[19]

Gifts to churches were well worth making, for in later medieval theology the giving of money for church building or decoration counted as alms in the same way that giving money to the poor or for the support of the clergy.[20] Works of art depicting Saint Anne graced the renamed church. In 1490 the brothers reported the acquisition of "a heavy silver image" of Anne, valued at 178 florins, and a second, smaller silver statue valued at six florins. In 1494 they replaced the Annunciation on the convent seal with an *Anna Selbdritt,* and in the same year they founded the confraternity.[21]

Not long after, an altarpiece was commissioned for the confraternity altar. The artist who painted it is not known, but painted it was, and not sculpted, for the instructions in the life to pray in front of it, say: "Thus you have in the painted image the whole kinship of Saint Anne and her sister Esmeria."[22] The reference to the family of Esmeria and to her descendants, the Rhineland bishops Maternus and Servatius, marks the altarpiece as a somewhat unusual composition for South Germany, where Holy Kinships do not usually include Esmeria's line of descent.

The exact location of the altar is not known either, but contemporary references indicate that it was in the choir.[23] The altarpiece's present whereabouts are another mystery. It was not destroyed, as some works of art were in the iconoclastic activity of the 1530s, for the Annenkirche had turned Protestant—the first in Augsburg to do so—some years earlier in 1525. Most of the artworks and other valuables were probably returned to the families who had given them, following complaints by the order's provincial that the convent was disposing of its treasures and other goods, though the silver images were taken into custody by the city.[24]

The quantity of late medieval offices of Saint Anne published is a reminder of the importance of liturgical celebrations in her cult. Notations on an organ codex dated 1511 belonging to the Augsburg church provide a glimpse into the services held by the Carmelite brothers' confraternity on Tuesdays, Anne's special day. On the days when the monks communicated, the Offertory and the last *Agnus Dei* were to be played more slowly, to take up the extra time.[25] On the Tuesday after Pentecost, the office was to be sung for the confraternity's procession with the Sacrament, while the instructions for the Feast of the Holy Innocents stipulate the mass *Gaudeamus*, which is presumably the mass from the office *Historia nova pulchra devota et autentica de sancta anna matris dei genitricis marie*, published in Augsburg by Anton Sorg in 1479, which begins: "Officium misse de sancta Anna. Gaudeamus omnes in domino die festum celebrantes in honore sancte Anne matris dei genitricis marie."[26]

The wealth of objects and activities associated with the cult at the Carmelite church should not lead one to imagine it had a monopoly on Anne. A woodcut of the *Anna Selbdritt* published in Augsburg in 1494 by a printer known as Casper suggests that others were making use of her popularity too (fig. 13). This work, which uses the popular southwest Germany format with the seated Anne holding Mary on her right knee and Jesus on her left, includes a plague prayer, but it devotes the bulk of its textual component to persuading the reader that the indulgenced prayer (10,000 years mortal sin and 20,000 years venial sin for those who say the prayer three times in front of the image) is authentic—Pope Alexander himself having personally nailed the indulgence to all the church doors in Rome. The fact that the Augsburg confraternity life promises the same indulgence to those who say a particular prayer in front of an image of the same type "that on the left arm has Mary and on the right arm Jesus Christ as is painted in the figure here" raises the possibility that the extreme

FIGURE 13. Casper, *Anna Selbdritt Plague Sheet*, 1494. Woodcut. Augsburg. Stockholm
National Museum

popularity of this particular way of depicting the *Anna Selbdritt* in this part of Germany may have been associated with a perception that images of this type carried an
indulgence. The use of the word "painted" (*gemalet*) also raises the possibility that the
life may be referring to the figure of Anne in the confraternity altarpiece.[27]

The form the cult of Saint Anne took in Augsburg—confraternity, life, and an
abundance of images—followed the Rhineland model. Its content and function,

however, were different. Whereas the clerico-political agendas of the Rhineland
humanists and reforming clerics had been important in fueling its expansion there,
its introduction into Augsburg seems to have been, as we have seen, largely the
result of financial factors. The differences are perhaps most evident in the Augsburg
confraternity life. Though this work is based on one of the Rhineland lives, its
author shows little interest in the tendentious subtexts and devotional intensity that
characterize the works by Trithemius, Dorlandus, and the anonymous Franciscan.
He recites the details of Anne's marriages and miracles in a hurried, perfunctory
manner that is in sharp contrast to the eloquence of Trithemius, the elaborate and
at times fanciful writing of Dorlandus, and the down-to-earth realism of Van Denemarken. He drastically abridges the exempla, sometimes so stringently that the
point is lost: the tale of the nun who declined to pray to Anne because of her three
marriages is hurried through without mentioning the reason for her disinclination.
The Augsburg life includes the unusual detail of explicitly insisting that Mary was
conceived through the semen of Joachim:"And Anne soon after conceived from male
semen from her husband Joachim." But overall, the author shows little interest in the
nature of Anne's marital relations—a prominent theme in the Rhineland discourse.
The "no fleshly lust" motif does not even make an appearance in the Augsburg book.
Mary's conception is presented as maculate rather than immaculate ("She was filled
with the Holy Ghost in her mother's womb"), and though the author does mention
that Anne shunned "all evil worldly joys," there does not seem to be any real attempt
to model female behavior.[28]

The role of relics also differed in the two regions. The Augsburg confraternity
owned a relic of Anne, but the brothers' extreme modesty about it suggests it was
not as powerful as its fellow body parts in the Rhineland. The miracles mentioned
in the life are not attributed to the relic, and the author gives no details about it
except to mention that it was carried in processions. In contrast to the precise lists
of miracles claimed for the Anne relics in Limburg and Düren, claims for the miracles performed by Saint Anne in Augsburg are vague in the extreme; the Augsburg
author in fact gives more details about the wonders at Düren than about those that
supposedly happened in his own church.[29] Keeping a discreet but tantalizing silence
about the author's identity, the life closes by saying: "A learned father confessor of
Augsburg, who knows the matter thoroughly, had this printed. Father confessors
know many secrets" (Die ding hat lassen trucken ain gelerter beicht vatter zuo
augspurg. der die ding gruntlichen waist. die Beicht vätter wissen vil haimlichait).[30]

In the short term, the confraternity at the Carmelite church seems to have been
successful in generating income for the monks. But there is no evidence that Anne's

cult put down strong roots at the level of church institutions in Augsburg.[31] Well into the first few decades of the 1500s, Augsburgers continued to call the Carmelite church by its old name, "Unser Lieben Frawen Bruder Kirche," when they left it money for masses or sued it over property squabbles.[32] And when Jakob Fugger (1459–1525) planned a burial chapel for himself and his brothers Ulrich and Georg, he had Christ represented on the altarpiece, not Anne, though Anne with the Christ Child is among the sculptures ornamenting the choir stalls.[33] And the Fuggers did commission a small altarpiece, now in the Saint Markus Chapel in the Fuggerei, with an *Anna Selbdritt* on one panel (fig. 14). At Saints Ulrich and Afra a new altar was dedicated to Augustine, Anne, and Agatha in 1497, but the Anne relic in this church's sizeable relic collection was not singled out for special attention.[34]

Augsburg: Changes in Late Medieval Piety

This does not mean Anne was not a popular saint in Augsburg. Indeed, the quantity of surviving images and their dispersion throughout the region, with many still in place in their original locations in parish churches, shows that she was a ubiquitous presence in the Swabian pantheon. But the evidence suggests that while she enjoyed a high degree of popularity, she was not singled out for major organized cult activity. It may not be without significance that some other attempts to generate active cults in Augsburg also met with no more than moderate success. Despite assiduous clerical promotion in the second half of the fifteenth century, the revived tomb cults of the city's founding saints, the martyr Afra, and the bishops Ulrich and Simprecht do not seem to have become major pilgrimage sites. And just as the Carmelites eschewed inflated claims for their Anne relic, so did the new life of Ulrich, Simprecht, and Afra printed by the church of Ulrich and Afra, which emphasizes instead the importance of asking the saints for help in bettering one's life; the saints are "intercessors . . . not only for bodily and earthly protection but also for the healing of the soul to attain eternal life."[35] The book is one of several signs that a strong attachment to saints as wonder-workers may have been less strong here at this time than it was in some other parts of Germany. The Ulrich, Simprecht, and Afra life also steps apart from prevailing medieval piety in describing Ulrich as someone who grew in holiness, not someone like Anne or Katherine who was set apart from other humans as a special holy being.[36]

Other instances of skepticism in the life of the city—and reactions to that skepticism—point to changes and stresses in perceptions of religious phenomena. In response to the controversy over the host relic at Heilig Kreuz, Heinrich Institoris, co-author of the *Malleus Malleficarum* and a man ever alert to questionings of clerical

FIGURE 14. Swabia, *Anna Selbdritt* (side panel, Fugger Altarpiece), mid-sixteenth century. St. Markus in der Fuggerei, Augsburg

authority and stirrings of lay independence, came to Augsburg to write and preach in support of Heilig Kreuz's *Wunderbares Gut*. In the thirty-six sermons he preached on the subject in 1491, he threatened anyone who encouraged people to doubt the miracle with excommunication, and he took advantage of the occasion to warn Augsburgers about witches in whose reality some "dangerous and untrained preachers" no longer believed even though hardly a village was free from witches. Augsburgers had already drawn Institoris's ire, ten years earlier in 1480, when he had brought to trial a group of women who were receiving communion daily, and sometimes even more often. The women were ordered to discontinue the practice, a judgment they and their spiritual director, Johannes Molitor of the elite Saint Moritz church, ignored once Institoris left the city.[37]

The objects of Institoris's worries—pious laywomen, heretics, witches, doubters of eucharistic miracles, and those who questioned church authority—are not unconnected to the situation described at the beginning of this chapter: the laity, increasingly inclined to deprive the church of its material and jurisdictional resources, also seemed increasingly apt to question miracles and authority, two foundations of the church's control over the means of salvation.

Saint Anne as Fund Raiser: Annaberg

As an old city undergoing major social and economic changes, Augsburg presents a complicated picture of interwoven and sometimes conflicting elements. The installation of the cult of Saint Anne in the new town of Annaberg in Saxony in the 1490s shows the pattern of a saint's cult used to generate income in more clear-cut lines. Founded by Duke George of Saxony in 1496 following the discovery four years earlier of a rich vein of silver in the Erzegebirge, the mountainous Saxon mining region, the town was named in honor of Anne, possibly because of her association with wealth, but in any case not because of her supposed patronage of miners, for she did not play this role to any significant extent in medieval Germany. In local lore, it was the prophet Daniel, not Saint Anne, whose help led to the discovery of Annaberg's silver ore.[38] In 1499 the building of a fine new hall church dedicated to Anne was begun. At the same time, Duke George embarked on an ambitious program of acquiring spiritual "franchises" that brought in the funds necessary to complete the church while simultaneously fostering Annaberg's renown, enhancing the spiritual well-being of residents and pilgrims alike, and substantially fostering the town's material prosperity. The church was completed in 1525 and lavishly decorated with an iconographic program in which Anne has a major part. Particularly valued in their time were the silver bust reliquary figures of Anne, Mary, Nicholas, and Christopher acquired in 1509 and 1510, but more visible to those who came into the church would have been the large and elaborate altar and the fine carved panels in the ceiling and elsewhere.[39]

As almost the only church in a new town, the Annakirche was in a very different situation from the Carmelite's "Annenkirche," for it did not have to compete with other local churches.[40] Instead, it competed for the spiritual clientele of the entire region, serving as the focal point for a complex of undertakings designed to draw pilgrims and money to the church, the town, and ultimately into Duke George's coffers. The means by which this was done echo the steps taken in Augsburg, with the difference that in Annaberg the civic and ducal authorities were able to implement more far-reaching measures to control the flow of the trade in nontangible religious goods and to integrate these measures with the town's overall economy.

Annaberg: The Saint Anne Confraternity

As in Augsburg, an Anne brotherhood was founded for the purpose of raising funds for building the new church. Hector Milisch, in a 1746 work on the city that draws on contemporary documents, states: "This brotherhood may presumably have had a rule that one paid to join, the money going to the building of the beautiful church of Saint Anne.... Man and wife could pay the same as a single individual."[41]

Annaberg also needed relics. Inspired by the collection of his cousin Frederick the Wise, which in 1509 numbered some 5,005 items, Duke George sought out relics for his new city. Some he begged from relatives, while some were acquired from the same Lyon Convent of Saint Anne that had supplied the Frankfurt confraternity with its relic. Further donations were made to the collection, apparently generously, for a list of relics displayed to worshipers in a procession in 1518 comprised 120 entries, some involving more than one item;[42] 11 were Anne relics. Whether the Annaberg relics were any more powerful than those in Augsburg is a moot point. The 1510 poem of Meistersinger Hans Schneider, on the building of the city of Annaberg, says that miracles took place:

> Saint Anna many wonders did
> For they a relic had of hers.
>
> . . . .
>
> Now further have I yet to speak
> Of wondrous signs that happened here.
> Written you have seen a lot,
> of children dead brought back to life.
> For Anna helps all in their need.
> Crippled feet and poverty,
> Saint Anne is merciful to these.
> Wax and silver images
> —They would be too much to describe—
> The waxen figures you can see
> Standing up as large as life.
> Of silver statues I should speak
> That in processions carried are.[43]

The mention of life-size wax ex-votos suggests that healings were experienced, but the very general terms in which Schneider describes the raising of children from the dead—as though it were almost an everyday occurrence—raises doubts about whether he is doing more than reciting a conventional list of miracles. The chronicles of Adam Daniel Richter and Petrus Albinus make no mention of specific miracles or of a miracle book, but sources agree that pilgrims came to Annaberg in great numbers.

In 1517 Duke George secured from Pope Leo X a Jubilee Year indulgence for the brotherhood issuable for twenty-five years. Schneider's poem, the "Carmen von der Stadt Annaberg Erbauung," mentions the indulgence as it embarks on a lengthy description of the church's size and beauty, and Richter's Chronicle speaks of it also in a description of the various ways the church raised building funds.[44]

Thus far the Annaberg situation sounds familiar: the introduction of a popular new cult for the purpose of raising funds; the founding of a brotherhood; the acquisition of relics, works of art, and an indulgence—and the absence of a miracle book. Where they differed was that the Annaberg cult was more successful than the Augsburg cult in raising money. Here it was the scope that was exceptional, for many towns shared in the funds raised by shrines located in them, at the same time taking steps to ensure that the shrines were run in a way that maximized these benefits.[45] But Duke George's orchestration of the financial aspects of the cult of Saint Anne achieved a level that surpassed the usual. In addition to the indulgence for brotherhood members, an indulgence for visitors to the twice-yearly Annenmarkt was obtained, as well as permission from the Curia for Annabergers to do business with the heretical Hussite Bohemians. Permission for residents of the city to work on holy days in cases of special need was also obtained. As well, Duke George tried to have the availability of other indulgences in ducal Saxony limited so that the donations of the faithful would go to the local brotherhoods.[46] The measures taken to keep money from leaving the region also included a law forbidding the collecting of money for nonlocal religious foundations within twenty-five kilometers of the town, the Antonite order being the only exception. All such undertakings cost money and required permission, because the times of masses, the right to call the faithful by means of a bell, the right to collect money outside the church, and the necessity of not infringing on the rights of other churches, among other like details were all subject to regulation by ecclesiastical authority.

Annaberg: the Indulgence

The financial outlay involved could be considerable. According to Aloys Schulte, 500 ducats were required for the privileging of the brotherhood, and a further 500 for the Jubilee indulgence, and that sum was increased following further demands by the duke. Half the Annaberg indulgence proceeds—or a set sum of 1,000 ducats—was to go to the building of Saint Peter's, though according to Schulte it may be that only one-third actually went for this purpose. Collection and administration were handled by Jacob Fugger.[47]

The attractions of Annaberg were further enhanced when in 1519 Duke George acquired some earth from the Campo Santo in Rome for the cemetery at the Church of the Trinity in Annaberg, with an accompanying indulgence. Once again it was the Fuggers who handled the arrangements and delivered the portion of the revenue destined for the papacy. It is possible that the Fuggers were also involved in the selection of Adolf Daucher, who had carved the altarpiece for their family chapel in the Carmelite church in Augsburg, as sculptor for the marble high altar in the Annaberg church. Duke George may have seen Daucher's work when he attended the Reichstags in Augsburg in 1518. Richter describes the installation of the altarpiece in 1522: "It was in Augsburg that this altar was made, by a citizen of that city, Master Adolph. It was brought here in wagons in sections and skillfully put together and set up free-standing in this church in the year 1522, Wednesday after Invocavit (First Sunday in Lent), and it took until Laetare Sunday, by its maker, Master Adolph."[48]

The pinnacle of Annaberg's attractions may well have been the indulgence acquired for the Annaberg Saint Anne confraternity. As an invisible product that required no labor or outlay to produce (though considerable to administer) the indulgence benefits, like the value of a work of art, can be increased with relative ease. The Annaberg jubilee indulgence can be seen as such a case of inflation. Very different from the indulgences available through the Augsburg confraternity, which provided varying quantities of remission of purgatorial punishment (calculated in equivalents of earthly time ranging from forty days to the plenary indulgence, which removed all the purgatorial punishment due), the Jubilee indulgence available in Annaberg also lifted some of the temporal punishments, but it also gave the recipient virtual permission to commit certain acts normally considered sins. Richter's summary of the provisions of the Latin bull for the Annaberg indulgence is worth quoting in full:

> In this bull the Pope, for the purpose of benefiting and aiding the construction of this parish church, grants in particular to the brothers of this brotherhood, along with other freedoms and indulgences, that the members of this brotherhood may themselves choose a confessor, even a member of an order or a secular priest, who shall have the power to exempt them

from all ecclesiastical punishments, even from the greater Bann; from these
and similar they may be exempted, even from the stain of simony. He shall
have the power once in their lives to absolve them from all sins, so great
and unabsolvable these may be, even from those for which one must go to
Rome to be dealt with, and from those which the pope alone has reserved
to himself; however, concerning other sins, he may absolve them, following
confession, as often as necessary giving them the appropriate absolution
and imposing a wholesome penance. However, all those sins are excepted
which are included in that bull that was customarily read out on Holy
Thursday. As well this confessor may, though only *in foro conscientiae* [in
cases of conscience], forgive those sins in which legitimate things are
acquired in an illegitimate manner and means, so that those who acquire
offices through illicit means may administer them freely without let or
 hindrance, and as well may keep and enjoy at their own pleasure ecclesiastical properties acquired through illicit means; they must contribute a sum
specified by their confessors, for the building of a specified parish church.
In addition, the confessor may also commute into good works all vows and
far distant pilgrimages, with the exception of this one, whether they be to
Rome or Compostella, along with the vow of celibacy, so long as this com-
mutation is designated to serve the purpose of the above-mentioned construction. Above all, he shall have the power once in a lifetime and the
other time in the last hour of death to pronounce free and absolved from
all sins those who heartily repent of their sins and who make their confession with the mouth. It shall also be permitted to such a confessor to dis-
charge from responsibility and to absolve from replacing things acquired in
an unjust manner, things that have been contested, or things that have
deteriorated through improper use. This also holds true if a usurer bor-
rows from another usurer and replacement is ordered on that account;
however, it would not be allowed again. Or in the case where someone has
certain goods in his possession, and either does not know, or is uncertain
about, to whom they belong, or indeed in the case of anything that he has
acquired through illicit or other means (not excluding that which belongs
to the poor or that designated for the use of ecclesiastical places) that he
may not have to replace these, as long as something is given for the building or for the other necessities of the often-mentioned parish church of
Saint Annaberg. Also, it is granted that this confessor may absolve from
excommunication those who knowingly or unknowingly marry within the

third or fourth degree of blood or legal relationship, including such alliances as are performed through fleshly mingling (insofar as it does not involve matters pending at law or does not result in a public nuisance arising from immorality) under the imposition of an appropriate fine, to be applied to the oft-mentioned building; and also *in foro conscientiae* to grant permission to the challenged parties, to marry one another anew and in such marriage to be able to live free and unhindered, and to legitimize the children born of such a marriage.

Finally he shall grant to the brothers of this brotherhood, and no less to the other inhabitants of the city, and to those who come here with their goods from other places, and also to those others who eat with them at table, that in times of fasting, and other times and days in which meat, eggs, butter, cheese, and other milk products, either by judiciary or through customary or other usage, are forbidden, permission to eat these same foods, even to eat meat.[49]

For the indulgence (*Ablass und Beichtbrief*) with the membership certificate, the confraternity member paid a ducat. An additional financial contribution, presumably provided for in the member's will, was required to activate the postmortem benefits of confraternity membership. Richter gives a paraphrase of the "Warning to the Members" to this effect, printed with the membership letter:

When, therefore, a member of the brotherhood dies, the letter by which he was accepted into the brotherhood must be delivered to Saint Annaberg, and in addition an alms must be sent according to his means, in order that the deceased be inscribed in the *mortirologium* of the fraternity.[50]

The letter raises the question of whether postmortem indulgences applicable to the *already dead* were available through the confraternity in Annaberg.[51] However, none of the contemporary or near-contemporary material from Annaberg mentions this type of indulgence, nor is there mention of applying indulgences to the deceased in the lives connected with Saint Anne confraternities elsewhere.[52]

With all these sources of income, it is not surprising that the confraternity quickly became wealthy, so wealthy that in 1534 it was able to lend the large sum of 1,600 Rhenish florins to the town administration, at 80 florins yearly interest.[53] The chronicler Petrus Albinus, writing in the late 1500s, relates an anecdote that suggests the citizens of Annaberg were well aware of their patron saint's exalted financial status. In 1511 the large Saint Anna bell had been put in place. On that occasion:

> Wolff Gerstenberger was pastor. Margaretha, Matz Hanffstengel's wife, made the baptismal garment for this bell. Valtin Hanffstengel brought it to the pastor, who asked what he ought to give his mother for it. Hanffstengel answered that his mother wanted to give it as a gift. "No," said Gerstenberg. "My dear son, Mother Saint Anne is much richer than your mother." And he gave Valten Hanffstengel a Schreckenberger [a coin] as a tip.[54]

As a fund raiser, Anne had indeed been efficacious. In Augsburg her confraternity had helped the Carmelites weather their financial storms, and in Annaberg her beautiful church, with its splendid panoply of images, not to mention its grand indulgence, had enriched both town and duke. Images helped in this process, and the next chapter examines how paintings, prints, and sculptures functioned for the men and women who made use of them.

7

Functions and Perceptions

HOW PEOPLE USED IMAGES

In an eventful exemplum that appears in several of the Anne lives, a young man is reduced to penury through the reckless spending of his inheritance. Praying for help, he is told by Saint James to take Anne, hitherto unknown to him, as his patron. Forced to abandon his homeland for a distant country, and reduced to near destitution, he maintains his devotion to Anne. She rewards him with the gift of miraculous if limited literacy: he asks her for the grace that, even though he has never studied, he will be able to learn to write the three names Jesus, Mary, and Anne. His prayer granted, he honors her with holy graffiti: writing and painting the three holy names on walls und other convenient places.[1] As a further token of devotion, the young man lights a daily candle in front of an *Anna Selbdritt* in a church. One day as he is leaving:

> the Child Jesus spoke to him, jumping up from the lap of his holy ances-
> tress Anne [the author is evidently thinking of an *Anna Selbritt*] saying: see
> here—every day you set up a burning light in front of my honorable ances-
> tress, but you bring nothing for me and my mother.

> [Alsbald redet ihn an das Kindlein Jesus / vnd springet gleichsam auss der
> schoss seiner H. Anfrawen Anna sprechendt: Sihe du thut alle Tag meiner
> Ehrwürdigen Anfrawen ein brinnendes Liecht auffstecken aber mir vnd
> meiner Muetter keines.][2]

Informed in no uncertain terms that poverty is no excuse for stinginess toward the family of God, the young man sells his few remaining possessions and returns with three candles. No longer able now to contribute money, yet ever desirous to find new ways to honor Anne, he turns artist himself, painting pictures of Anne with Mary and Jesus on towers sixty feet high.[3]

The devil causes him to fall off the tower, but Anne appears and rescues him in her cloak. After still further adventures, he is rewarded with the restoration of his fortune, and thenceforth he honors Anne on a grand scale:

> In his homeland [once again], after he had settled and arranged things in the house that had come to him as an inheritance, he had an exceedingly beautiful chapel built in which not only were the divine praises sung, but holy images and lights were endowed and paid for. He lived another seventy years, a man rightly renowned for his great understanding and his holy life. And it came about that he acquired such a reputation that he was chosen by the citizens as mayor, and even became the king's secretary and counselor. . . . He so moved and convinced the king that he had beautiful, elegant images installed in the churches of his realm along with lights, and he ordained that her feast be kept and celebrated every year.

> [In seinem Vaterlandt nachdem er alles richtig gemacht und expediert, hat er auss seinem Hauss so ihm in dem Erbtheil zugefallen der H. Anna ein uberauss schoene Capell aufferbawet in welcher er sowol das Goettliche lob als Heilige Bilder und Liechter auffgericht und gestifft hat. Nach disem hat er noch 70. Jahr lang gelebt; Ein Mann so wol dem Namen nach als an der that eines grossen Verstands und eines H. Lebens. Dahero er ein solches ansehen bekommen das er von Burgern zum Burgermaister erwoehlet wurde und noch neben dem des Koenigs Secretari und Rath war. . . . Den Koenig hatt er so weit bewegt und uberredt das er in allen Kirchen seines Reichs zu ehren der H. Anna schoen unnd zierliche Bilder sambt den brinnenden Liechtern verordnete / und ihr Fest Jaerlich begehn und halten liesse.][4]

Modeling a spectrum of appropriate image use as the hero goes through the cycle from riches to poverty to destitution, then to wealth, honor, and long life as a result of his devotion to Saint Anne, the exemplum calls attention to one of the striking aspects of Saint Anne's late medieval cult: the enormous emphasis it placed on images. Confraternity membership sheets prescribe devotional activities to be performed in front of images, and the lives urge their readers to commission them or contribute toward their purchase. The exempla convey the same message in vivid detail as Anne's devotees, rich and poor, contribute to the adornment of her sanctuaries according to their means, and are in turn rewarded—or, if they fail to honor her, punished.

The anecdotes describing image use emphasize different themes. Some stress Anne's primacy among the saints. In an exemplum in the Augsburg confraternity life, a sick woman who calls in vain on all the saints recovers only when she has an image of Saint Anne made, honors it, and advises others to do the same.[5] The motif of encouraging others to honor and commission images is pervasive. All convey the point that honoring Saint Anne involves works of art depicting her.

This emphasis is not surprising. Interaction with images served to sharpen mental focus and arouse devotional feelings—to engage the devotee with the object of his or her devotion. Images paid for by families and confraternities were also, as the previous chapter has shown, useful in attracting clients and income. Works of art could perform this function directly through the alms deposited in boxes placed in front of images, and indirectly by drawing people into the churches through their beauty and workmanship.

Contemporary writers remarked on the drawing power of images, not always with a favorable eye. The Catholic reformer Hieronymus Emser, though he supported their use, was critical of the fund-raising purposes to which they were put, and he was critical as well of the extraordinary beauty and skill that marked the artworks of the final flowering of the Late Gothic style:

> The more artfully images are made the more their viewers are lost in contemplation of the art and manner in which the figures have been worked. We should turn this contemplation from the images to the saints which they represent. Indeed, many are transfixed before the pictures and admire them so much that they never reflect on the saints. . . . The painters and sculptors make images of the beloved saints so shamelessly whorish and roguish that neither Venus nor Cupid were so scandalously painted or carved by the pagans.[6]

But worshipers, while they may have been aware of the clergy's use of images in the competition for their attention, came to them for their own purposes. The majority of *Anna Selbdritts* and Holy Kinships they encountered were located in parish and convent churches, either as altarpieces in the confraternity and family chapels along the side aisles, or as "occasional" images placed against the piers or elsewhere in the church.[7] The altarpieces served a liturgical function as the focal point of masses said for the souls of confraternity or family members, but as well, both altarpieces and other images were sought out by people making private prayers. Contemporary images show *Anna Selbdritts* and Holy Kinships in both settings.

Images of Saint Anne were also to be found on secondary panels of main altars, and in smaller numbers as reliquary images, and they were occasionally chosen to decorate funerary monuments. In all these cases, along with their particular liturgical or devotional functions, images created beauty, helped establish an atmosphere of appropriate religious decorum, and in a general way served to instruct, remind, and arouse the feelings as the theologians said they did. As well, they made statements of religious and sometimes political import, and they testified to the wealth, status, and possibly divine approbation of the people who paid for them.

Contemporary references to people speaking or praying to images tell us that people used works of art in a very direct way for personal prayer. Prayer instructions in the Anne texts suggest that these habitual modes of interaction with images were incorporated as prescribed acts for members of Anne confraternities. Prayer for medieval people involved the body, for they viewed bodily gestures as expressions of the worshiper's inner feelings, and the requirement to kneel in front of images at confraternity altars or elsewhere is often mentioned in the Anne literature. The requirement to burn candles before them is also part of the physical interrelationship with images. Not infrequently, three genuflections, three prayers, or three candles are mentioned in the lives, whereas for other saints it would be only one. Tuesday—*tercia feria* (the three-fold feast)—the day Anne was born, gave birth to Mary, and died, was especially recommended for the performance of devotional activities. The Augsburg confraternity book sums up its instructions in these matters as follows: "In honor of Saint Anne one should pray three *Pater Nosters* and three *Ave Marias* in front of her image every Tuesday. One should also burn thus three lights, one in honor of Jesus Christ, another in honor of our dear Lady, the third in honor of Saint Anne."[8] In an extension of the church's presence outside its walls, processions used images as focal points in these public events, which played important roles in proclaiming community and status. Important people might take part, as was the case in the Augsburg Carmelite's festive procession attended by the Emperor Maximilian on Anne's feast there.[9]

There were, however, some roles that images of Saint Anne appear not to have played. The visionary experience of the young man in the exemplum notwithstanding, the *Anna Selbdritt* does not seem to have been used as an *Andachtsbild* or meditation image, at least not in the strict sense of the term. Most conveniently defined in terms of their function as aids to prayer, meditation, and visualization, *Andachtsbilder* were often small images for personal use, though larger ones located in side altars or other places more accessible to the worshiper than a high altar also served this function. References to the use of such images for meditation are abundant in the writings of mystics. Elsbeth Stagel's description of her fellow nun Mezzi Sidwibrin's converse with an image of the Virgin makes clear the ease with which those who had inclination, encouragement, and conducive settings could use works of art to help them bridge the threshold between the earthly and the visionary world:

> She had a particular habit of bowing before the image of Our Lady in the Choir, and she remained there and looked around her, like someone who pays attention to nothing except God alone. And when the sisters would ask her why she was so often in front of our Lady's image, and if the image ever spoke with her, she answered with all simplicity: She often talks with me, and smiles at me; and I talk with her Son a lot too.

> [Sie hatte besonders die Gewohnheit, dass sie sich im Chorraum vor userer Frauen Bild neigte, und sie lag da und sah über sich, recht wie ein Mensch, der keiner Dinge acht hat als Gottes allein. Und wenn die Schwestern sie etwa fragten, warum sie so viel vor unserer Frauen Bild wäre und ob diese niemals mit ihr rede, so sprach sie aus einfältigem Sinn: Sie redet oft mit mir und lacht mich an; auch mit ihrem Sohn hab' ich viel zu schaffen.][10]

The *Anna Selbdritt* was probably not used as a devotional aid in this way because the attention of mystics was directed primarily to Christ and secondarily to Mary, with Mary herself often functioning to lead the worshiper to Christ, whether as the sorrowing mother in the *pietà* or as the mother who allows the devotee to hold, bathe, or play with her infant, as she does in the *Nonnenbücher*.[11] Descriptions of the few devotional visions or meditation visualizations involving Anne often place her in a similar supporting role. The English mystic Margery Kempe (born 1373), for example, asks Saint Anne if she can "adopt" her daughter:

> Another day, this creature gave herself up to meditation as she had been commanded before, and she lay still, not knowing what she might best think of. Then she said to our Lord Jesus Christ, "Jesus, what shall I think about?" Our Lord Jesus answered in her mind, "Daughter, think of my mother, for she is the cause of all the grace that you have." And then at once she saw St. Anne, great with child, and then she prayed St. Anne to let her be her maid and her servant. And presently our Lady was born, and then

she busied herself to take the child to herself and look after her until she
was twelve years of age, with good food and drink, with fair white clothing
and white kerchiefs.[12]

As well as appearing in a small number of first-person accounts of mystics, Anne
also appears in fictional visions related in devotional literature to make doctrinal or
political points. The vision described in the lives of the Franciscan reformer Colette
of Corbie, one written by her friend Sister Perrine, the other a now lost life written
by Pierre de Vaux in the 1440s but copied twice in the 1490s, seems intended to
convey a message about the validity of remarriage, but whether it had to do with
more than the fact that Colette is said to have criticized her own mother for remar-
rying is not known.[13] In any case, this meaning was clear enough when Margaret of
York commissioned the 1494 copy, which includes an illustration of Margaret praying
while Anne and the Holy Kinship appear to Colette; Margaret's marriage to Charles
the Bold of Burgundy was his third. In the vision, Colette, who has declined to
honor Anne because of her three marriages, is shown the error of her thinking by a
visit from a cross Saint Anne.

However, though the *Anna Selbdritt* did not serve as an *Andachtsbild* in the fullest
formal sense of the word, the writers of the lives encouraged their readers to look at
these images in a devotional manner. The author of *Das Leben und Wunderzaichen*,
for example, describes a worshiper who "very humbly performs his devout prayer in
front of his much-beloved image."[14] He remarks on the behavior of a crowd of worshipers in somewhat similar terms: "Day in and day out, in huge numbers the people
crowd to the image of Saint Anne and out of their great devotion they offer up their
oblations to it."[15] Clearly a feeling component is being ascribed to devotional activities. It is worth remembering too that, as Jeffrey Hamburger shows in his study of
the use of devotional images in the convent of Saint Walburga in Eichstätt, the line
separating the activities of the spiritual elite from those of at least some of the ordinary laity may not have been as sharp as is sometimes thought.[16] His description
of the interchanges through letters and gifts of religious images among nuns in
certain convents and their relatives, friends, and supporters outside the convent
suggests that encouragement to deepen one's piety was not absent in all laypeople's
lives. Whether the promoters of the cult felt their audience was not likely to
respond to exhortations to meditate, or whether they felt saints were not suitable
objects of really intense feeling, is not possible to say with certainty, although the
fact that there were vernacular texts that aspired to arouse devotional intensity over
the sufferings of Christ and Mary points toward the second suggestion. But what-

ever the reason, the exhortations in the Anne material are more likely to concern devotional behavior than meditation. What is asked for are physical acts of devotion, such as kneeling and lighting candles in front of images, saying prayers out loud, and maintaining an attitude that is appropriately "devotional" (*andächtig*). The works of art that depict Anne leave the same impression as the texts. While many Late Gothic paintings represent people who appear to be meditating in the presence of an image or vision of the Madonna or Christ, such compositions are rare in the imagery of Saint Anne, and the few works that may depict meditation usually involve clerics.

But one must not underestimate the experiences that were provoked by images of Saint Anne, for though the *Anna Selbdritt* was not used as a classic *Andachtsbild*, it may have been the focus of the kind of intense visual attention that seems to have been more characteristic of medieval society than of our own. Religious images were not the objects of passive attention; they were actively looked at. And though we may find no references to meditation connected with Anne, we can reasonably imagine that the advice the Strasburg preacher Johann Geiler von Kaisersberg (1445–1510) gave to an illiterate audience might be applied in some degree to images of Anne:

> Even if you cannot write or read, take a colored picture on which Mary and Elizabeth are painted as they met—you can buy one for a penny—look at it and think thereon, about how happy they were and about other good things and perceive this in/by faith.

> [Kanstu nit schreiben noch lesen, so nim ein gemalten brief für dich, daran Maria und elisabeth gemalt ston als zusammen kumen sein, du kauffst einen umb ein pfennig, sihe jn an und gedenk daran, wie sie frölich gewesen sein und guter ding und erken das im glauben.][17]

The text goes on to advise the reader to kiss the image on the paper and to bow and kneel in front of it.

The incorporation of looking as part of prayer is implied also by the combining of image and printed prayers on woodcuts of the *Anna Selbdritt:* the devotee looked at the image while reading the prayer. In fact, indulgence instructions sometimes mention that the prayer is to be said *while looking* at the picture.

We find a parallel with the *Andachtsbild* when we look at another category of medieval image function, that of *Gnadenbilder* or miracle-working images. Only a very small number of Anne images in the late medieval North, often Swiss ones, seem to have enjoyed public fame as wonder-working images in the late medieval period.[18] In the case of the more widely publicized Anne miracles, it was relics, not images, that were the agents, and the same is true of the fictional healings described in the exempla. Wax votive images representing body parts of supplicants, presented with prayers for healing or given as thank offerings for healings or for other favors, were left at Anne relic shrines just as they were at other shrines. Mentioned in connection with the Düren relic, they are also referred to in Jan van Denemarken's life of Saint Anne, and the Augsburg life describes a repentant sinner who made "a wax figure and gave it to his confessor, who had it hung up for Saint Anne." Van Denemarken also mentions an offering presented at an Anne altar following the rescue of a ship on the Flemish coast. Because this object is described as including a text and as being hung up in the church to publicize the rescue and to honor Anne, it was probably an ex-voto painting depicting the rescue. Even if these stories are invented, it is likely that they represent contemporary practice.[19] It is important to note that the practices described above do not involve the kinds of gifts customarily given to wonder-working images, notably clothing or jewels.[20] Anne was seen as able to help in healing and rescue, but it was she rather than particular images of her that answered prayers.

But if people did not go to images of Saint Anne expecting miracles, they did have, as with all holy images, a general confidence that such objects were of help in keeping the course of daily life running smoothly. A fifteenth-century description of the apotropaic activity of a ceramic image of John the Baptist, the "patron and protector" of the Dominican convent of Unterlinden near Colmar, illustrates how this kind of help might be experienced: "After the church was built they set up a heavy lead cross toward evening on the peak of the roof. On top of the cross was a handsome figure of Saint John, made, if I'm not wrong, of metal (*Erz*). When now and then a fire broke out that looked as though it threatened harm to the convent, it often appeared as if Saint John were breaking up the fire balls with his cloak and dispersing them far away from his house."[21] No actual miracles happen, but the image protects and prevents harm. The *Anna Selbdritt* with the date 1337 inscribed on it on a house front in Eichstätt probably aroused a similar confidence in its protective power, and the same is true of numerous other such reliefs and statues, many of them still in place, set in niches in the facades of houses and other buildings.

There is one case, however, where a more direct type of power is described: in an exemplum in a Low German life Anne appears to a man who is under the power of the devil and tells him that if he should be in need he should hold on to her image with all his might and not let go and her strength and power will help him.[22] Small

Anna Selbdritts, the right size for grasping with one's hands, were produced from the cheap mold-made ceramic statuettes manufactured in Siegberg in the Rhineland (some as small as four or five inches in height) and even cheaper papier maché figures, to expensive little figures of ivory, silver, or wood.

Contemporary descriptions tell us that people prayed in front of images, knelt before them, held them in their hands, at times spoke to them, presented them with gifts. What did they experience in these engagements with images? The writings of medieval mystics describe intense interior experiences, sometimes accompanied by interpretations of and commentaries on these experiences. This kind of writing does not appear in the chronicles and letters written by the lay population. To what extent was this because laypeople, at any rate those who were not members of the spiritual elite, did not have or cultivate such experiences? To what extent was it because they lacked a language in which to think about and express them, and, equally, lacked a tradition of describing them in written form? Participation in languages of spirituality, in hearing, recitation, and for some in writing, was part of the formation and regular activity of nuns and clerics. This was not the case for the laity.

In the writings of people who lived outside the walls of convents and monasteries, references to religious activity, when they occur, are more likely to take the following forms: references to devotional (*andächtig*) or pious (*fromm*) *behavior* rather than *feelings*; references to people shedding tears in response to religious stimuli; and short prayers requesting protection or giving thanks inserted into texts when death or misfortune—or good fortune—are mentioned. Philippe de Vigneulles described outbursts of intense emotion expressed in weeping and boisterous physical behavior at the shrines in the Rhineland. The Augsburg priest Johannes Frank describes the vast crowds who came to hear the Franciscan preacher John of Capistrano in 1454 as similarly affected, with "a great weeping and sorrowing from numerous devout people" (da was ain grosses wainen und trauren von fil andächtigen menschen).[23] Frank sets considerable store by physical expressions of devotion, repeatedly referring to the *andächtig* behavior of those who came to hear the famed preacher, and the late medieval Anne texts use this same language. What they do not do is suggest that people should attempt to cultivate inner development of the kind described in the classic texts of medieval spirituality. Praiseworthy people in the exempla are those who are "pious," a term that seems to be associated with the performance of devotional activities and perhaps the manner in which they are performed.

The above observations would lead us to conclude that lay piety for the average person was characterized by emotional lability and by physical, bodily, response to stimuli, rather than by the deliberate cultivation of interior feeling. Geiler von

Kaisersberg's assumption that his listeners will feel a response—distinct but not complicated—to an image of the Visitation corresponds to such a hypothesis. Yet one must be cautious about assuming a lack of complexity in lay religious feeling. The English mystic Margery Kempe, writing in the early fifteenth century, believes she is observing something more complex when she describes a group of women who are holding and dressing an image of the Christ Child. The woman who owns the image—she appears to be returning from a pilgrimage to the Holy Land—allows women in the Italian towns she travels through to pick it up and hold it. Observing the women enacting this popular ritual of *imitatio Mariae*, Kempe observes:

> And when the creature saw the worship and the reverence that they
> accorded the image, she was seized with sweet devotion and sweet medi-
> tations, so that she wept with great sobbing and loud crying. And she was
> so much the more moved because, while she was in England, she had high
> meditations on the birth and the childhood of Christ, and she thanked
> God because she saw each of these creatures have as great faith in what she
> saw with her bodily eye as she had before with her inward eye.[24]

Kempe is here making the distinction between meditation with images, which the women are doing, and her own imageless meditation on the infancy of Christ.

Along with affective responses to stimuli, another aspect of lay writing is the frequent enunciation of charm-like expressions of thanks or supplication. Such ejaculations are frequent in the diary the Augsburg merchant Lucas Rem kept from 1494 to 1531. Rem was the Antwerp representative (after 1509) of the Welsers, another Augsburg family firm and an important European dealer in spices, with offices as far away as Lisbon. Rem's references to the deity suggest a view of the universe as ultimately subject to God's benevolent power. Yet the repeated expressions of confidence, thanks, and praise that punctuate his description of a serious illness may also have functioned as protective, even propitiatory prayers, that the fragile good health might continue:"[I] had given myself up to God willingly in death.... But at the end of the month I was better. Praise God.... Honor, praise, and thanks to the almighty Lord in all his works. Amen!"[25] Otherwise Rem has little to say about his religious life. He bought and commissioned a number of religious paintings. When he had himself and his wife painted as members of the Holy Kinship by Quintin Massys, he may have expected the painting to help him in some way, and he probably felt a familiar affection for the personages depicted in them, especially since his wife's name was Anna. But he makes no mention of using this or any of the images he owned to generate personal religious experience. The *Tagebuch* tallies up the religious images and rosaries he received as wedding gifts with the same terseness and attention to monetary value that he accords his other gifts.

The author of another Augsburg chronicle, the scribe Burkard Zink, a man of lower social status than Rem who was writing in the early fifteenth century, is somewhat more voluble on religion than Rem, but ultimately his references to religious matters fall into the same categories: asking for God's help in the present; uttering requests for future help and protection; expressing confidence in God's goodness; and subsuming good religious behavior under the adjective "pious" (*frumm*).

Zink invokes mercy on the soul of his mother after speaking of her death in childbirth: "Item my dear mother died in childbirth in the year of Christ our dear Lord's birth 1401, God the Lord have mercy on her. Amen" (Item mein liebe mueter starb an ainem kind da man zalt nach Christi unsers lieben herrn gepurt 1401 jar, gott herr erbarm dich über sie. amen). On another occasion, lost in the woods on his little horse (*pferdlin*) while carrying a message, he calls out to Jesus and Mary for help: "I was alone in the vast immense forest and didn't know where or which way to go, and I called on God and his dear mother and crossed myself and begged God that he would help me, that I might find people" (Dann ich was allain in dem grossen ungeheuren wald und west nit wahin oder wa auss, und ward gott anrüefen und seine liebe mueter und gesegnet mich und pat gott, dass er mir hulf, dass ich zu leuten kommen möcht). Zink uses the word *frum* (pious) as his primary term of praise for the three good wives God gave him: "[And one] was called Dorothea, she was surely as pious and honorable a daughter as might be found in the whole city; God in Heaven be thanked for his godly gifts, that he gave me three such pious wives" (Die hiess Dorothea, die was sicher ain so frumme und erber tochter, als sie mocht sein in der gantzen stat; gott von himel sei gedankt sein göttlichen gnaden, das er mir drei so frum hausfrawen beschert hat).[26] Throughout he invokes the name of God when he mentions good fortune, attributes it to God, and thanks him for it. He acknowledges God's omnipotence and man's lack of knowledge. His frequent mention of the religious events in his personal life—baptism, confirmation, and extreme unction—and his (indeed, most people's) reckoning of time in terms of the feasts of the church remind us how integrally religion was a part of daily experience. Also noteworthy in Zink's language is the affectionate terminology ("lieb" = "dear") he applies to the Christian pantheon.

Perceptions of Images in Late Medieval Germany

As we have seen, an important aspect of the religious experience of late medieval German Christians was the interaction they enjoyed with images. This interaction was an intense one, for notwithstanding the fact that people *knew* perfectly well that the sculptures and paintings in their churches had been made in workshops by artists and had been paid for with substantial sums of money, they often *experienced* them as though they embodied the people they represented. Saint Anne, as well as being in heaven, was also perceived as being in some way present in her images. Medieval texts provide abundant evidence of the tendency among late medieval German Christians to conflate image and referent, to respond to works of art as though they were their referents. "The dear saints" (die liebe Heilige) were not the distant inhabitants of heaven; they were the dear, familiar figures who inhabited the churches.

Contemporary descriptions of what people did with images repeatedly refer to incidents in which people treat statues and sometimes paintings as though they were people. What people ought not to do with images was a central target of the reformers, and their lists of objectionable practices are informative in this regard, for they characteristically show people behaving toward images as they would toward people. The Swiss reformer Leo Jud names the following practices at the shrine of the wonder-working Saint Anne at Oberstammheim in Switzerland: "[They] accord such images great honour, and entreat them with ornaments, silver, gold, precious stones, with sacrifices and with reverence, that is, by taking off their hats, bowing, and kneeling before them, all of which, however, God has forbidden."[27] Zwingli provides a similar catalog of cultic acts involving behavior that points to conflation of image and referent: "Men kneel, bow, and remove their hats before them; candles and incense are burned before them; men name them after the saints whom they represent; men kiss them; men adorn them with gold and jewels; men seek consolation merely from touching them and even hope to acquire remission of sins thereby."[28] Ludwig Hätzer, in a work published in 1523, refers scornfully to the tendency to conflate image and referent when he says: "People call them saints—this is our lady, this is Saint Anne, etc. If they're holy, then every sculptor can make a saint."[29] Andreas Karlstadt also alludes to the tendency to behave toward images as toward people, in his treatise *On the Removal of Images*: "You bring them wax offerings in the form of your afflicted legs, arms, eyes, head, feet, hands, cows, calves, oxen, tools, house, court, fields, meadows, and the like, just as if the pictures had healed your legs, arms, eyes, heads etc. or had bestowed upon you fields, meadows, houses, honours, and possessions."[30] Karlstadt is even more explicit in his acknowledgment of the complex roots of his own conflationary mode of interacting with images. His poignant admission of the difficulty he has in putting away images reveals the depth of the predeliction, and his words make it clear that knowledge alone is not sufficient to change attitudes:

> And I want to confess my secret thoughts to the whole world with sighs and admit that I am faint-hearted and know that I ought not to stand in awe of any image. . . . But (I lament to God) from my youth onward my heart has been trained and grown up in the veneration and worship of pictures. And a harmful fear has been bred into me from which I would gladly deliver myself and cannot. As a consequence, I stand in fear that I might not be able to burn idols. I would fear that some devil's block of wood [i.e., an idol] would do me injury. Although, on the one hand, I have Scripture and know that images have no power and also have no life, no blood, no spirit, yet, on the other hand, fear holds me and makes me stand in awe of the image of a devil, a shadow, the noise of a small leaf falling, and makes me flee that which I should confront in a manly way. Thus I might say, if one pulls a man's hair, one finds out how firmly it is rooted. Had I not heard the spirit of God cry out against the idols and read his Word, I would have thought: I do not love any image; I do not stand in awe before any image. But now I know how I, in this case, stand toward God and images, and how strongly and deeply images are rooted in my heart.[31]

Texts also provide unintentional evidence of conflation. Karlstadt inadvertently proves the truth of his own words when he moves seamlessly from speaking of images "as if" they were saints to using language that identifies them as such:

> So they invoke idols in the house of God and seek health, support, and counsel from insensate dummies. And the people vilify God in his house, which is a good and important enough reason to drag idols out of the churches. Not to mention that many a man doffs his cap, which he would wear if his man-made god were not before him. I do not regard it lightly that they bend a knee before the saints.[32]

He goes on to address this very point:

> However, we are open in word and deed before the world to the charge that we take images for gods and give them names and venerate them. For we call the image of the Crucified One a lord god and now and again say

that it is the Lord Jesus. We also venerate it as though Christ himself were present. . . . We also say that this image is St. Sebastian and that one is St. Nicholas, and the like.[33]

Baltassar Fridberger addresses the depth of feeling involved in people's attachment to images in the public disputations in Zurich in October 1523, and like Karlstadt he himself conflates images with referents in the very words in which he rejects them: "They should be thrown away and laid down to sleep" (Das man die bilder hynweg thü und schlaffen lege).[34]

Evidence: Fluid Boundaries Depicted in Images

Evidence of conflation is not restricted to words and actions. Works of art them-selves embody fluid boundaries between image and referent when, for example, human beings are depicted in settings or with objects normally associated not with people but with images. One of the woodcuts printed with verses by Trithemius and his circle shows Anne, Mary, and Jesus as living figures, yet in front of them is the three-branch candlestick that would normally be placed in front of a painting or sculpture on an altar (fig. 7). Lucas Cranach the Elder's depiction of the Saint Anne reliquary from the collection of Frederick the Wise similarly conflates living saint and image by putting halos on the three figures even while the accompanying text describes them as "a silver gilded image of Saint Anne" (fig. 15). The humanist Rutger Sicamber, in a poem included in the *De laudibus*, can perhaps be seen as performing a similar operation when he addresses his words not to Anne but to an *Anna Selb-dritt*: "Rutger Canon Regular of Venray to the image of Saint Anne. Devoutly, with deeply bended knee I plead this prayer / Anna blessed parent seated with your pos-terity" (Hic profunde preces devote poplite flero / Anna parens vbi cum prole beata sedet).[35]

Evidence of Conflation: Iconoclasm

As misuse is an aspect of use, it is also appropriate to consider the behavior of German iconoclasts and to recall that when German Christians smashed images they often did so with displays of anger and disappointment, and they challenged, maimed, punished, and executed the images as though they were guilty living beings. Though the arguments of the Reformation theorists centered around the charge that images were worshiped as idols, at the level of ordinary Christians, the level that generated so much of the iconoclastic activity in Germany, the response seems less a rejection of idolatry than anger at discovering that images did not have

FIGURE 15. Lucas Cranach, *Relics of Saint Anne*, 1509. Woodcut (Wittenberger Heiligtumsbuch, book 581/82, p. 69)

the power they had believed them to have.[36] After the great crucifix of the cathedral in Basel had been carried to the marketplace, the crowd shouted, challenging its power: "If you are God, help yourself; if you are man, then bleed."[37] Even as the images were destroyed, they retained certain aspects of their character as living beings. The power of the rejected images to thus enrage their erstwhile worshipers was part of the continuum of response that accompanied the elision of images with their prototypes.[38]

Though it is most clearly evident in the conflation of image with referent, conflation is not restricted to this manifestation. An organizing principle that pervaded medieval culture in many parts of Europe, it manifested itself in many ways. It makes its appearance, for example, in the temporal realm, in the fluid approach to time, the absence of firm boundaries between past and present, that is a feature of the type of *Anna Selbdritt* in which Mary is shown as a child. The artist, by reducing the size of Mary or by showing her as a child, is able to refer simultaneously to the fact that she is both adult (Jesus' mother) and child (Anne's daughter). The visible presence of breasts beneath the dress of some of the child Marys serves as another marker of the Virgin's dual life stages (fig. 1). A similar use of varying body sizes to express different time periods is found in another characteristically German image, the *pietà*, especially in early examples where the body of Christ is often noticeably smaller than that of his mother in what would seem to be an attempt to refer simultaneously to the dead adult Christ and the infant Christ in his mother's lap. The *Schmerzenkind*, the late medieval representation of the suffering Christ child popular as a New Year's card, is another theme that conflates the childhood and adulthood of Christ in its representation of the infant Christ with crown of thorns and streaks of blood.

Temporal conflation is widespread in devotional literature, and the same is true of spatial conflation. In the exempla in the late medieval Northern Anne texts, fluidity of time and of space create a world in which present flows into past and the geography of heaven seems next door to that of earth. In the lives, Anne and her daughter and grandson repeatedly step in and out of the contemporary world of her worshipers, speaking to them, scolding, and rewarding. Fluidity of time is frequently encountered in German mystical writing. In the meditation/vision of the presentation of the Infant Jesus in the temple in Henry Suso's *Exemplar*, the fourteenth-century church dissolves into first-century Jerusalem:

> For Candlemas Day ... he prepared beforehand, with three days of prayer, a candle for the heavenly Mother in childbed. ... When the day of the blessing of the candles arrived, very early before anyone had gone into the church, he went up before the main altar and waited there in contemplation of the mother in childbed until she might come with her divine treasure. When she approached the outer town gate, in the longing of his heart he would outrun all the others and would run to meet her with the procession of all God-loving hearts. In the street he fell down before her.[39]

The propensity to conflate, although it was not confined to Germany, is especially noticeable there, and though it influenced the interactions of worshipers with
all types of religious images, it can be said to have played a special role in the cult of
Anne since her importance was so bound up with the metonymy inherent in the
power that derived from her bodily connection with Christ and Mary. This regional
specificity becomes very evident when one compares the cult of Saint Anne in
Germany with its counterpart in England, where Anne was a popular saint but not
one who enjoyed special prominence above other saints. What is significant is not
so much the differing forms the cult took in these two places, for these arose from
specific historical circumstances, but rather the details of images and texts and the
implications of these. The conflation of time so prominent in the German texts is
absent in the lives of Saint Anne written in England in the fifteenth and late fourteenth centuries; where the German lives present Anne's life in a miraculous present,
the English lives place it firmly in a historical past. An English stanzaic life written
in the early fifteenth century makes the point that Anne's story happened a long
time ago: "& forthermore as the story says / It befel in our elder days / In ierslum
was it swa."[40] Another English stanzaic life, the Trinity College manuscript life, puts
a similar emphasis on the clear separation of temporal periods when it announces
the aim of saints lives in terms that stress the edifying function of remembering
what happened in past times:

> Hyt ys a vertu to rede in storyes
> And holy seynts lyfes to translate.
> Hit causeth to be in the memoryes
> Of well disposyd pepyll in good state-
> To theym where grace ys nothyng desolate
> But by perseueraunce theym to apply,
> Sore repentaunce puttyng awey foly.[41]

The description of Saint Anne in this poem situates her clearly as someone who
formerly lived in the past and now resides in heaven:

> We halow and worshyp in euery land
> Of seynt Anne chefe the festfull memory,
> Whyche ys departyd and ys in glory
> And hath forsaken the carnall pryson

Of the body to the soule a dongeon.
Thys gloryous Anne, happy, full of grace,
Ys caryed vp most worshipfully
To the hyghest of seynts in that place.[42]

"Out of thys world she ys depertyd clene," says this English poet, in contrast to the German writers, for whom Anne is still very much here and for whom past and present are so easily mingled.[43] In German texts, Anne makes regular appearances and interventions in the lives of humans, helping those who honor her, scolding those who do not, and occasionally presiding over the death and damnation of those who persist in ignoring her and her feast. In the English texts, Anne's statue does not speak to people, and as a rule Anne does not make appearances to worshipers or meet them on their deathbeds. She is now in heaven, and though she responds to prayer and intercedes for worshipers, she does not step into their world.

Overall, the pattern of characteristics pointed out for Germany stands in contrast to the pattern found in England, for though in many respects medieval Europe formed an international Christian community, it was marked by important regional differences, differences that often turn out to be parts or symptoms of larger patterns of difference. And despite the many things they had in common, Christians in England and Germany appear to have experienced and thought about images somewhat differently, English Christians habitually distinguishing images from their referents more clearly than German Christians.

It would be wrong to suggest that no English Christians conflated images and referents—Lollard propaganda certainly complained that they did.[44] But generally speaking, English writing on images tends to address different issues. Fourteenth-century Lollard criticism often stresses the deflection of honor from God, the taking away of money that should be spent on the poor, and to a lesser extent the dishonor shown to the saints. An important concern in the English discourse was the possibility of the image to deceive, to present harmful illusions rather than truth. An early Lollard text states:

Though images made true that represent verily the poverty and the passion of Jesus Christ and other saints be lawful and the books of lewd men, in Gregory and other doctors, nevertheless false images that represent worldly glory and pride of the world as if Christ and other saints had lived thus and deserved bliss by glory and pomp of the world, be false books and worthy to be amended or to be burnt, as books of open error or of open heresy against Christian faith.[45]

In this kind of thinking the relationship between image and referent is not one of conflation but rather one of representation. When the English Dominican Robert Holcot ponders the potential problems with image use, these do not include conflation of the image with its referent. Holcot distinguishes between the image in front of which he prays, and Christ, the object of his prayer: "I worship not the image of Christ for that it is wood, neither for it is the image of Christ, but I worship Christ before the image of Christ for it is the image of Christ and moveth me to worship Christ."[46]

This facility in separating precise layers of experience is not restricted to the writings of churchmen. Margery Kempe verbally conflates image and referent when she states that she prays, for example, "at the Trinity," by which she means at an image of the Trinity. But when she describes her religious experiences it becomes clear that this is a figure of speech, for she consistently interprets images not as conflations but as representations. In the incident with the Christ Child image mentioned earlier in this chapter, she explicitly describes the image as a representation, which functions to provoke visualizations: "And they would dress it up in shirts and kiss it as though it had been God himself."[47] Kempe neither experiences the image as Christ, nor does she confuse the visualizations that took place during her meditations with visions. In fact, despite her lack of education she seems as well able to separate categories as Holcot is: she clearly distinguishes material image, what the image represents, and the mental images provoked by the use of material images.[48]

It is unlikely that such clear separation was present in all times and places in medieval England; England had some well-known wonder-working images with respect to which it is reasonable to assume perceptions involving conflation on the part of some people. But at the same time it is interesting to note that the correspondence dating from the 1520s and 1530s from the commissaries sent out by Thomas Cromwell to inspect the English monasteries (with a view to their eventual closing), to "deface" the church buildings, and to confiscate relics and images, frequently leaves the impression that devotion to images and relics was something associated with the past. The tone in the reports, rather than scandalized, is sometimes humorous ("all the rotten bones that be called relics") or when John ap Rice writes from Bury St. Edmunds of "the coals that Saint Lawrence was toasted withal, the parings of S. Edmund's nails, S. Thomas of Canterbury's penknife and his boots, and divers skills for the headache; pieces of the holy cross able to make a holy cross of."[49] And though there were certainly incidents of popular iconoclasm in England, much of the destruction there was carried out by appointed officials, sometimes aided by enthusiastic adolescent boys—in contrast to Germany and

Switzerland, where the destruction of images (as opposed to their removal) was usually carried out by angry adult citizens.[50]

Holland shares traits with both Germany and England. The repertoire of texts and images related to Saint Anne is part of the larger Germanic context, but Dutch perceptions of images seem more to resemble English ones. When Dutch writers worry about image problems, they worry less about idolatrous practices than about the possibility of naive believers confusing imaginary responses to images with visions. The fourteenth-century reformer Gert Grote makes a clear and explicit distinction between sign and referent, observing at the same time that many people do not make this distinction; for Grote, the problem lies not in idolatry but in human imagination. His description of confusions among material images, mental images, and visions distinguishes with great precision among different kinds of sense experiences:

> Thus a simple man will believe that he can sense the very corporeal presence of Christ, or seem to see him with his eyes or hear with his ears, or touch some saint he has imagined. Such deceptions are not without danger. Indeed here signs are employed as things, just as when someone believes an image of Christ to be Christ himself. Far be it from us to worship such a strange or newly invented God. Never! This is to offer honor to your own imagination.... Then too this form of imagination, with its apparent presence of Christ or a saint, can puff up the mind, which may begin to believe itself worthy of an appearance from Christ or one of the saints.[51]

Grote's lack of concern with the problem of power located in images as opposed to the problems inherent in human behavior is perhaps consistent with the Dutch tendency to create images marked by a down-to-earth realism. The creators of a great many sculpted Dutch *Anna Selbdritt*s used body positions and facial expressions to make Saint Anne and the Virgin look more like ordinary good people rather than the more beautiful, remote, and powerful figures of German and Flemish art.

Flemish religious culture seems to have more closely resembled German piety than Dutch, though there were important differences, among them the greater involvement in Flanders of civic lay groups. The distinctiveness of the fifteenth-century Flemish artistic achievement—where the concept of painting as forms on a two-dimensional surface developed rapidly (in contrast to Germany, where for

much of the period under discussion sculpture predominated and paintings sometimes have the quality of representations of sculpture)—suggests that there were
important differences in perceptions of images and their relationship to their referents.[52] Indeed, although image and relic cults were widespread in Flanders, there is
some evidence for a metaphoric rather than (or in addition to) a metonymic or
conflational mode of perception. In this connection one might mention the development of lay drama in Flanders, and the mimetic civic ceremonies such as the *tableau
vivant* of the *Ghent Altarpiece* performed by the citizens of Ghent on the occasion of
the entry of Philip the Good, Duke of Burgundy in 1458.[53] But whereas in Germany
the conflation-metonymy paradigm can be easily demonstrated (and in the case of
Holland, its widespread absence), the extent to which conflation and metonymy,
and the extent to which representation and metaphor, dominated in perceptions of
works of art in Flanders is not clear.

8
Anne's Decline

When, sometime before 1513, the Peringer and Ridler families thought to commission Hans Leinberger to carve an *Anna Selbdritt* to commemorate the entry of their daughters into the Franciscan convent of Sankt Johannes Gnadenthal in Ingolstadt (fig. 2), they could have been forgiven for thinking Saint Anne would go on forever. The sheer quantity of the newest sculptures and paintings depicting her, works that manifested the full glory of the realism and the mannered flamboyance of the last phase of the Late Gothic style, enshrined her presence in unprecedented splendour. The secure and established place Anne enjoyed in the affections and devotional life of Northern European Christians would have surely pleased, and perhaps surprised, Johannes Trithemius. And if the members of her confraternities did, as Luther claimed, spend a good deal of their energy collecting money for beer, they undoubtedly did so with fond nods to "Mutter Anna."

But even as the production of works of art and the founding of confraternities continued into the second decade of the century, the roots of Anne's power were coming under attack and her cult was beginning the process of a transformation that would reorient her relationship to the members of the holy household and to the Christian worshiper. The transformation began for Saint Anne with a triple loss: the loss of the *Trinubium*, the loss of her central role in the family of the Redeemer, and the loss of the immense and special power she had so recently acquired.

Anne Loses Her Husbands
The most tangible loss was the loss of Cleophas and Salome, the two husbands Anne married after the death of Joachim, and of Mary Cleophas and Mary Salome, the daughters she bore them. For while the *Trinubium* continued to appear in the early sixteenth-century rewritings and reprints of the late fifteenth-century lives, some writers, in particular those in humanist circles, were beginning to cast doubt on the truthfulness of the story that Saint Anne had been married three times.

The criticism had two thrusts: philological and historical arguments were employed to question the historical veracity of the *Trinubium*, while the idea that Anne had married three times was attacked as highly inappropriate behavior for the mother of the Virgin Mary. One of the first assaults took place in 1517, when the reform-minded Zwickau humanist cleric Sylvius Egranus, provoked by the Leipzig printer Melchior Lotter's reprinting of the late fifteenth-century *Legenda Sanctae Annae*, called the story "an impudent lie" (tam impudens mendacium).[1] In France the humanist Jacques Lefevre d'Etaples also called attention to the inappropriateness of the triple marriage, referring to the *Trinubium* as an example of sexual incontinence. Saint Paul said widows ought not to remarry, he observes, and surely a thrice-married mother is no example to the Virgin Mary. Anne had one husband, not the three mentioned in the popular verse: "Anna solet dici tres concepisse Marias / Quas genuere viri Joachim, Cleophas, Salomeque, / Has duxere viri, Joseph, Alpheus, Zebedeus."[2] Somewhat later, in 1533 in Germany and inspired by Lefevre d'Etaples, Henricus Cornelius Agrippa von Nettesheim also called the idea of a thrice-married Anne a slander on the dignity of the Virgin: "It is scandalous because it slanders the good morals and the lawful practices and observances of that time, and it defames the honorable parent of the bearer of God and the dignity of the Virgin Mary" (Scandalosum est, quia detrahit bonis moribus, detrahit consuetudini legali & observantiae illius temporis, detrahit honesti parentum deipare genitricis, & dignitati virginis Mariae).[3]

Criticism of the *Trinubium* did not spring out of nowhere. Trithemius had anticipated it, for he had pointedly excluded the subject of Anne's three husbands from the *De laudibus*, which, unlike the other new books about Anne, was intended to bring the learned around to her cause. And Petrus Dorlandus evidently felt called to justify the *Trinubium*, for he criticizes those who criticize it.[4]

Whether the emphasis some of the humanists laid on Anne's first husband, Joachim, the father of the Virgin, is evidence of leanings in this direction is a moot point, but certainly their interest in Joachim was considerable. In the late 1490s many of those who had written about Anne began turning their attention to him. Arnold Bostius wrote two lives of Joachim and in 1497 founded a brotherhood dedicated to him; Sebastian Brant wrote poems in his honor and lamented his neglect.[5] But they were not able to arouse the same enthusiasm for Joachim as for Anne, and when Anne eventually lost her place as the third person in the Holy Family, it was Joseph, not Joachim, who replaced her. But it was not for lack of trying.

The two other men who had shared Saint Anne's bed had always been somewhat shadowy figures, distinguishable one from another, like their sons-in-law, only by the number of little boys shown in their proximity. The presence in a good many paintings of banderoles that identify them (sometimes incorrectly) suggests that they did not make their mark on their medieval viewers. The new lives give Cleophas and Salome relatively little space, bringing them on stage to marry Anne so that she could produce the two additional daughters prophesied to her. Moreover, when Anne laments their deaths it sometimes seems less for sorrow than because the divine plan for her progeny appears to have been thwarted. Cleophas and Salome are often described as descended from the House of David and as good men. The Augsburg life says of Cleophas: "He is truly peaceful, upright, a keeper of God's commandments, and he has kept his body under strict control, chaste, with prayer, fasting, and watching. He also gives alms to the needy poor and to strangers, and setting a good example with his generosity and other good works he has encouraged many others to perform the same good works."[6] The earlier liturgical texts devoted to the Holy Kinship, which preceded the lives by over a decade, gave Cleophas and Salome equally short shrift; while these books contain numerous prayers to Anne's three daughters, to Joachim, and to Joseph, and sometimes to Mary's nephews, they contain only a very few to Cleophas, Salome, Alphaeus, and Zebedee.[7]

The men described in the texts are essentially the same men who appear in the images: sobriety and seriousness are made visible in the unsmiling expressions, while the thin faces and slender, weakly positioned bodies are consistent with a no-fleshly-lust approach to marital relations. At the same time, their passive demeanors might also have been seen as bespeaking calmness and self-control, a serious issue at this time when court records show that clerics and civic officials were concerned to restrain husbands from beating their wives.

Indeed, the way the men were portrayed may have had different meanings for different people, for on the one hand Cleophas and Salome are the necessarily weak consorts of the powerful females of the Kinship, but from a clerical point of view they may depict the ideal lay male: humble, passive, lacking in vigour and sexual vitality. Did the passive onlookers gazing at the holy scene portrayed in the Holy Kinship from the Thuringian church at Rabis embody a wish that the layman might learn his place vis-à-vis the church (fig. 16)?

By 1530, production of images of the *Trinubium* and the Holy Kinship had declined sharply. And some at least of the Anne texts produced later in the century make no mention of Cleophas and Salome, though their daughters are still present. *Dit is Sint Anna Cransken*, a devotional work published in Brussels in 1575, contains three prayers to Joachim, one to Mary Cleophas, and one to Mary Salome, but none to Salome or Cleophas.[8]

FIGURE 16. Holy Kinship from Rabis, Thuringia, ca. 1500. Thüringer Museum, Eisenach, on loan from the Evangelisch-Lutherischen Kirchgemeinde Schöngleina mit Rabis

Anne Loses Her Central Role in the Family

While the presence of Cleophas and Salome was being challenged in the texts, a different set of changes appeared in the visual arts. Though the majority continued to use the compositional formats and iconography developed several decades earlier, new elements were showing up in a small but significant group of images, particularly in prints. Although many prints, especially inexpensive woodcuts, used established formats, some woodcuts and engravings depicted Saint Anne in new and different ways. The producers of the new compositions included some of the best-known names of the early sixteenth century, among them Albrecht Dürer, Lucas Cranach, Albrecht Altdorfer, and Lucas van Leyden. These images were in the minority, numerically, but it was a significant minority because it foreshadowed major changes in Anne's cult.

Those who looked at the new prints carefully would have noticed that Anne's location in the composition was changing. Quite literally, she was being shifted away from her central position. Dürer's *Holy Kinship with the Lute-Playing Angels* at first glance might seem like a traditional bench-type work, with the male figures arranged around and behind the central trio (fig. 17). But Dürer has changed the position and angle of the bench so that, instead of sharing the central space with her mother, Mary now occupies it alone and Anne is off to one side and farther back.[9] In an Altdorfer work of the 1520s, it is height and contact that are altered: Mary holds the child while Anne sits on the floor, reaching up but not touching him.[10]

The depiction of the male figures of the Holy Kinship changes too, over a series of three stages. In the paradigmatic late medieval Kinships, artists arranged the husbands and sons-in-law in a row, sometimes behind a wall, along the back of the work of art, pointedly excluding them from the sacred space of the revised *Hortus Conclusus*, which the Virgin now shared with her chaste but sexually active half-sisters and their six sons. Occasionally one of the fathers or grandfathers will lean down and hand a piece of fruit to a child, but most often the husbands and sons-in-law have little involvement with the women and children.

FIGURE 17. Albrecht Dürer, *The Holy Kinship with the Lute-Playing Angels*, 1511. Woodcut. Staatliche Museen zu Berlin, Preussischer Kulturbesitz, Kupferstichkabinett/bpk

FIGURE 18. Daniel Mauch, *Saint Anne Altarpiece*, 1510. Bieselbach parish church, Chapel of St. Francis Xavier, Bieselbach

This changes in the early sixteenth century, as the men begin to take tentative steps out of the background and into the foreground. In the side panels of the altarpiece Daniel Mauch carved for the church in Bieselbach, the two Marys are shown with husbands who, their mannered uncommunicative facial expressions notwithstanding, are actually helping their wives with the children (fig. 18). The hitherto excluded husbands have stepped over the wall that separated them from the sacred space. Abandoning their former roles as holy drones who exist only to serve their beautiful, sexually problematic, but wondrously fertile wives, they take on the male roles that mark the newly dominant middle class and family: sexually active males who father and raise sons. Nonetheless, despite their participation in family activities, Mauch's Cleophas and Salome retain the weak bodies and passive postures that characterized their older counterparts.

Mauch's altarpiece marks one of the stages in a transition from one paradigm of marriage, family, and gender roles to another, for what we are witnessing in the

Anne imagery is a shift from compositions that embody a mythical/aristocratic model of family and female behavior through several transitions, to a middle-class model. The process takes place step by step, the first step in the images of the late fifteenth century, the second in the texts, still another in the new prints of the early sixteenth century. Texts and images do not move in synchronization. The Anne who dominates so many of the late fifteenth-century Holy Kinships shares traits with the aristocratic noblewoman who retains her own lineage identity and her own power, which is independent of her role in the marital household. Yet the books produced in the same years make a different point, for while they stress Anne's link with her lineage and her salvific power, they emphasize in addition her role as the wife whose sphere of action is the home. At times one seems to be witnessing an argument between competing paradigms, for the modest Anne of the texts does not correspond to the regal Anne of the works of art. Lyndal Roper, in her book *The Holy Household: Women and Morals in Reformation Augsburg*, describes the change, sometimes interpreted as the change from the Catholic to the Protestant family, as rather the adoption of the guild family as the new paradigm of family life.[11]

This is the family that appears in Lucas Cranach's 1509 woodcut of the Holy Kinship (fig. 19). In this work Anne's sons-in-law, Alphaeus and Zebedee, now

FIGURE 19. Lucas Cranach, *Holy Kinship*, 1509. Woodcut. Staatliche Museen zu Berlin, Preussischer Kulturbesitz, Kupferstichkabinett/bpk

interact with their sons. Instead of handing them bottles—an action that links Mauch's Zebedee and Alphaeus with the bumbling Joseph's ineffectual attempts to feed the Christ Child—they teach them to read. Their actions define the new family. The men are involved in family life, sharing the same physical space as their wives at the same time that they dominate that space. Anne and her daughters, no longer the sole caretakers of the male children, busy themselves caring for infants while the male members of the Kinship take over the raising of sons who are old enough to learn to read. The books that had formerly sometimes been held by Mary's sisters (as well as by Anne, who still keeps her book) are now in the hands of their husbands, along with slates and switches. The women, now seated on the floor, provide bodily care, while their husbands, one seated on a stool, the other standing, provide intellectual care. The work seems to express the new early modern view of the family in which husband and wife worked together, not in equality but in partnership, raising children in the fear of God and equipping them with the skills, manners, and gender-appropriate attitudes that will make them good members of the community. Thus the fifteenth-century paintings' location of holiness (and power) in the maternal generative lineage is succeeded by a paradigm in which Anne's holiness is located within the order of the family. The fact that Cranach's woodcut was later adopted as a Protestant representation of the importance of education says something of its resonance with contemporary perceptions.[12]

But the new and, regardless of its origins, "Protestant" image that presents the family as the site of holiness did not survive. Cranach's model was superseded by a different composition that was consistent with the new Catholic model of the Holy Family in which Anne is no longer a central, supernatural figure, but instead becomes a secondary human participant in a holy family in which Mary and the Christ Child are the central figures.

Anne Loses Her Salvational Power

Just as Anne loses her place as the center of the Holy Family, she also loses the power that had been embodied in her serene mature physical presence. In the new prints she becomes an old woman: lines and crevices appear on her face, and she stoops. And where formerly her fertility and generative activity had been emphasized in the compositions of the *Selbdritt*, now the physical space between Anne and the dyad of Jesus and Mary distances her from this role as well.

The change in her appearance also raises the possibility that the stereotype she was intended to contradict may have been stronger than we realized. The idea of the inappropriateness of the *Trinubium* had been made explicit in learned circles. But there is some evidence that these thoughts may have passed through less-elevated minds as well, for the possibility of shame may be behind the frequency with which the authors of the lives felt called upon to justify the triple marriage. The anonymous Franciscan author counsels Anne herself to put away feelings of shame: "Therefore put away all shame, for it was by the command and will of God that you married your third husband."[13] The story in the same life in which Saint Colette declines to honor Saint Anne because of her three marriages centers around the same theme. When the author admits that she has a valid, even if ultimately untenable, argument in rejecting Anne because of her three marriages, he may have been making a statement with which the vernacular reader would have sympathized.[14] And here, as in so many other places, the insistence that Anne did not marry out of "fleshly lust" serves not only to reconcile sanctity and marital sexuality but also as a recognition that her repeated marriages in fact required justification:

> O maiden, maiden, you who boast to yourself of your unspotted flesh, your faith is good but your devotion is small. You must know that I desired no man for fleshly reasons; I have always refused to live carnally with a man, for I resolved to remain a virgin. But because of the law and the predestination of God, I married and bore healing fruit.
>
> [O Jungkfraw Jungfraw die du dich rühmest wegen deines unbefleckten Fleisches: dein Glaub ist guet aber dein Andacht ist klein. Du solt wissen das ich keinen Mann dem Fleisch nach begert habe; fleischlich bey ihm zu wohnen hab ich allzeit abgeschlagen dann ich mir fuergenommen ein Jungkfraw zuuerbleiben: Aber auss zwang dess Gesatses vnd fuersehung Gottes hab ich mich verheyrat vnd hailsame früchten erlangt.][15]

Was Anne losing the argument? At least one early sixteenth-century print seems to allude to the idea of Anne as a less than desirable role model. In Lucas van Leyden's *Saint Anne with the Virgin and Child* of 1516, Anne is not merely placed on the sidelines; she comes perilously close to becoming the stereotype she was intended to counter (fig. 20). Her back is hunched now in true old age, her chin juts out so as to suggest toothlessness, and she holds a walking stick. Standing beside Mary, who is taller than she, she holds out to the Child an apple in what may strike the viewer as an obscene parody of Eve offering the apple of (sexual) sin to mankind.[16]

Anne as Recipient of Salvation
But the Lucas van Leyden print is not typical. Most often we see the new Anne not

FIGURE 20. Lucas van Leyden, *Saint Anne with the Virgin and Child*, 1516. Engraving. Staatliche Museen zu Berlin, Preussischer Kulturbesitz, Kupferstichkabinett/bpk

as menacing but as a comfortable grandmother admiring her holy grandson and perhaps helping her daughter by preparing or rocking a cradle. In Wolf Huber's *Holy Family* of 1515, Joachim's stance, with one leg up on a stool, and Anne's crossed legs create a convincing picture of warm family intimacy.[17] But what look like realistic depictions of family life are no less resonant with theological concepts. Anne's change of position within the family also changes her position in the economy of salvation. When Anne looks up to a Madonna and Child who are seated higher than she, or when she kneels before the Christ Child instead of sitting above him and his mother, she is no longer the giver (or mediator) of salvation—she is now its recipient.[18] Her role is reversed.

Thus over the course of slightly less than one hundred years, from 1480 to 1550, the image of Saint Anne went through a series of transformations. Beginning as the source of an important female generative line largely independent of men, with her own power to help save her devotees from hell, in effect a fertility deity with power

over the underworld, Anne passes through a series of stages in which conflicting
paradigms are held in suspension. Fertile but without "fleshly lust," powerful but
submissive, sexually voracious in the number of her husbands but sexually restrained
in her relations with them, Anne achieves sanctity through her role as a married
woman yet does not behave like a normal married woman. The progression culmi-
nates in a new image, which reverses the earlier one: marginalized now within the
family and disassociated from the fertility of Mary, old in appearance, no longer the
source of salvation for others, embodying the Counter-Reformation ideal of the saint
as model for rather than a helper of Christians, she is now dependent on her grandson for her own salvation. By the seventeenth century a new compositional format
had come into use in which Anne is typically shown kneeling before the Christ
Child, as she is in Dirck van Hoogstraten's 1630 painting in which the aged saint
folds her hands in prayer before her grandson in the arms of his mother (fig. 21).

FIGURE 21. Dirck van Hoogstraten, *Anna-te-Drieen*, 1630. Museum
Amstelkring, Amsterdam

9
The Images

Paintings, sculptures, and prints of the *Anna Selbdritt* and the Holy Kinship form the tangible remains of Saint Anne's late medieval cult in Germany, Flanders, and Holland. A number of these works of art have already
been introduced in the course of the foregoing chapters. This final chapter examines
them in more detail, addressing such things as the origins and development of the
different compositional types, the regional variations of the images, and the wealth
of iconographic details they contain.

Although a few early examples date to the late thirteenth and early fourteenth
centuries, the vast majority of *Anna Selbdritts* and Holy Kinships were produced
between the late 1470s and 1530, the years during which promotion of the cult was
at its height. Most of the sculpted images are of wood, though some are of stone,
and a small number in silver, ivory, and ceramic survive. Paintings on panel and also
on canvas are numerous, and woodcuts and engravings were widely produced. As
well, a substantial body of manuscript illustrations are extant, in particular in Flemish and Rhenish books of hours, along with a few drawings, most of which, if not
all, are studies for prints or paintings. The *Anna Selbdritt* also appears in stained glass
and on enamel plaques. Small objects bearing the image include coins and convent
seals.[1] Accompanied by inscriptions such as "Hilf Sint-Anne sulf-drit," Anne's image
was also used on church bells. And sometimes casts of pilgrimage tokens, themselves no longer extant, from Anne shrines, were affixed to church bells; inscriptions
on some bells indicate that Anne was seen as having power to disperse thunder-
storms. The *Anna Selbdritt* might also be found as a decoration on textiles or on
household furnishings, such as the chimneypiece in the Utrecht Museum or the
stag-horn lamp in the Detroit Institute of Arts.

Images of Saint Anne and her family generally display the same stylistic features
as other works produced in the periods and regions in question. The flattened folds
of Romanesque drapery are present in late thirteenth-century *Anna Selbdritts*; in the
fourteenth century the smiling eyes and mouth of the High Gothic style appear; the

fifteenth century presents the realism typical of this period, while some works from the early sixteenth century display the extravagant peculiarities of drapery and posture that mark some subschools of the very Late Gothic period. By the same token, regional characteristics that appear in other works are found in representations of Anne. The richly detailed paintings from Lower Saxony create perspective through height. The lively and handsome Holy Kinships from Lübeck are fond of the additive groupings, with lineups of figures, that characterize much sculpture of this region, though they also use circular compositions, which may be based on South Netherlandish imports. South Netherlandish works often show figures in action, whereas the South German masters imply and predict, rather than depict, interaction. And just as other works of art in early sixteenth-century Germany show the influence of the Italian Renaissance, so too is this the case with artworks depicting Saint Anne. Tilman Riemenschneider portrays Mary with a slender, narrow-shouldered Gothic body in the *Anna Selbdritt* he made for the Benedictine nuns at Kitzingen, but the nude Christ Child on her knee flexes his leg like a classical putto (fig. 1). Equally to be expected is that works from less-skilled ateliers sometimes show stylistic lags, as well as crudeness of design.

Given the extraordinarily large numbers of *Anna Selbdritt*s and Holy Kinships in churches, museums, and private collections, a full analysis of the development of their various forms and iconographic details will be possible only once separate regional studies are completed. Important steps have been taken in this direction though. Willemien Deeleman–van Tyen has cataloged the sculpted *Anna Selbdritt*s in Holland; Bernadette Mangold has done the same for Lower Bavaria; Peter Paul Maniurka, for Silesia. Werner Esser's dissertation on the Holy Kinship, while it eschews the task of cataloging the images, does include representative samplings from the various Germanic and Netherlandish regions.[2] But though much further research remains to be done, there is nonetheless a good deal that can be said about the origins and development of the *Anna Selbdritt* and the Holy Kinship in Northern Europe. The earliest extant examples of the *Anna Selbdritt* comprise a handful of sculptures that have been dated to the late thirteenth and early fourteenth centuries. Modeled in some cases on the Romanesque Throne of Wisdom, and in other cases on standing or seated Gothic Madonnas, these works give the impression that their creators, faced with the challenge of creating a new type of image—that is, Mary and her son, *plus* her mother—met it by combining (conceptually, not literally) a Madonna with a second, larger Mary.[3] The two figures in the late thirteenth-century *Anna Selbdritt* from Regensburg in the Bayerisches Nationalmuseum, one of the oldest surviving examples of the theme, are an example (fig. 22). Virtually identical

FIGURE 22. Bavaria, *Anna Selbdritt*, late fourteenth century. Bayerisches
Nationalmuseum, Munich

apart from size, Anne and Mary wear the same clothing and headdresses, and Anne
even has the same long braids as Mary. Similar resemblances in headdress, clothing,
age, facial features, and expression mark the large seated *Anna Selbdritt* (ca. 1300) in
the Nikolaikirche in Stralsund (fig. 11). This masterpiece of German High Gothic,
made of plaster formed in a mold, allowed to partially dry, and then sculpted, draws
its style from French Gothic via the art of the cathedral centers in Saxony, where
this process was widely used.[4]

The beauty and size of the Stralsund work, nearly eight and a half feet in height, suggest that it may have played a special role in Stralsund's civic life. This supposition is supported by a series of remarks in Stralsund's fourteenth-century civic records that provide an insight into how, on occasion, medieval people might use works of art. The records in question refer to the church giving food, clothing, and sometimes money to certain men in return for sitting in front of, "watching," and looking after the Saint Anne statue, and sometimes other images as well.[5] These cases may well have involved a type of *Leibdinge*, the annuities sold by churches and convents that entitled the holder to food and lodging for life in return for a fixed payment in advance, for some of the references say that the "watchers" are in fact to have food and clothing for life. In some instances, also, it seems the men paid a fee to the church in order to obtain the watcher's position: "Herman Dalsce, who is to be present in the chapel of Saint Anne, gave Saint Nikolai '40 mrc.den.,' for which office he shall receive sustenance for his temporal life, but if after his death any of these goods remain, they shall go back to the church of Saint Nicholas."[6] A partial explanation of what the Stralsund "watchers" did appears in a record of 1348, which mentions that one Lubbert von Soest is "to sit in front of the image and ask for alms, and to keep an eye on the building that is going on, as his predecessors have done."[7] Lubbert's job seems to have combined aspects of standard medieval fund-raising practices—alms boxes placed in front of images inside churches, and individuals taking relics and images on fund-raising ventures outside the church—with the *Leibdinge*.

Compositional Formats and Iconography

Though the earliest *Anna Selbdritt*s came from different parts of Germany, the Stralsund work being a striking example, a disproportionate number seem to be have come from the Rhineland—further evidence, along with the relic shrines, for a relatively early cult here. It may have been here too that the incorporation of the *Anna Selbdritt* into the Holy Kinship became solidly established. According to Esser, the Kinship as a visual image originated in a handful of late thirteenth- and early fourteenth-century manuscript paintings that used the Tree of Jesse as a format, an early fourteenth-century window in Regensburg Cathedral being the first example to combine the *Anna Selbdritt* with the families of Mary's sisters.[8] However, it seems to have been in the Rhineland that the Kinship first appeared as a row of figures, and it may be that the bench-type *Anna Selbdritt* developed out of its central position in row arrangements like those in the early fifteenth-century Middle Rhenish *Ortenberg Altarpiece* now in the Darmstadt Museum (fig. 23). The bench-type *Anna Selb-*

FIGURE 23. Master of the Ortenberg Altar, *Ortenberg Altar,* ca. 1420–30. Hessisches Landesmuseum, Darmstadt

dritt was to become the most widely used way of incorporating the three main figures into the Holy Kinships, though other compositional formats were also used. Other origins, however, have also been proposed for the bench *Anna Selbdritt*.[9]

Just as the *Ortenberg Altar* suggests a possible origin for the bench-type compositional format, so it contains a number of the iconographic details that will continue to be important in the imagery of Saint Anne, notably the fruit, which is held here by Jesus, Anne's book, and the slate held by one of Mary Cleophas's older sons. Often Mary or Anne holds out a round object, either the orb or a fruit, to the Christ Child; sometimes it is the Child who holds it. The fact that one of the German words for the orb is *Weltapfel*—the "world apple" (along with *Weltkugel*)—raises the possibility that the medieval viewer may have seen the orb and the apple as to some extent interchangeable. The apple is the fruit shown most often, though pomegranates, pears, and grapes are also shown, as well as cherries, peaches, and figs. In Dutch examples the fruit is sometimes contained in a basket, while Silesian *Anna Selbdritts* are virtually unique in sometimes having the fruit in a bowl.[10] The fruits undoubtedly had multiple significations. The association of the apple with Eve and the idea of Mary as the second Eve was certainly current in the Middle Ages. An Anne office published in Augsburg in 1479 refers to Eve as "corrupted by the apple."[11] However, though the trope was widespread, references to it in the Anne texts are in fact rare. A more tenable generalization, especially considering that in these images the fruit is often held not by Mary but by Anne or Jesus, is that it refers to the Christ Child. Jesus is of course the fruit of Mary's womb of the *Ave Maria*. But in the late medieval Anne texts the fruit is used to symbolize Jesus in a more extended tree image. The prophetic dream of the monks of Mount Carmel that advises Anne's mother Emerentia to marry presents its message through the metaphor of a tree: the tree is Emerentia, the branch is Anne, the flower is Mary, and the fruit is the Christ Child. The life of Saint Anne by the anonymous Franciscan describes the vision as follows:

> This most beautiful tree that she saw represents the visible purity of the virgin Emerentia. . . . that branch which outdoes the others in beauty means that she will bear a daughter named Anne; from her will come a flower that is a virgin full of grace named Mary who in all eternity will remain immaculate. From this flower that is the Virgin Mary the allsweetest and honey-flowing fruit, the Son of God and the redeemer of the whole race of men will come to the light of day and allow himself to be seen. . . . The other branches of this tree together with their twigs and fruits mean nothing other than her holy descendents and children's children who will be beneficial to the whole world.[12]

As the particular fruit is not specified in the dream, the choice of fruit in the artworks provokes a cautious search for additional meanings. The apple's association with Eve is clear enough, and it seems likely that the salvational connotation of Mary as the new Eve attached to the apples in the *Anna Selbdritts*. But on a more everyday level, the apple seems to have had another medieval signification as a particularly appropriate treat to give a child. A fourteenth-century text from the Dominican convent of Katharinenthal describes a vision in which the Christ Child comforts a weeping nun by reversing roles and giving her an apple: "So Our Lord gave her an apple in her hand."[13] When the mystic Henry Suso thought of apples, he thought of Mary feeding them to Jesus: "Large pieces of fruit he divided into four parts. Three parts he ate in the name of the Holy Trinity, the fourth part in the love with which the heavenly Mother gave her tender child Jesus an apple to eat. This part he would eat unpeeled because children usually eat it unpeeled. From Christmas day until some time thereafter he would not eat this fourth part. He offered it in his contemplation to the gentle Mother to give to her dear young Son."[14] The fact that in the Anne works the apples, and other fruits, are sometimes shown being given suggest this meaning, as does the fact that the recipient is not invariably the Christ Child. Zebedee in the altarpiece of the Georgenbruderschaft in Lübeck hands an apple down to Mary Salome so that she can pass it to John the Evangelist, who is raising his hands to reach for it.[15] In Jörg Breu the Elder's depiction of the Circumcision painted for the Melk Benediktiner-Stift, an attendant hands an apple to Jesus, presumably to distract him from the painful operation he is about to undergo.[16]

Grapes, another among the fruits Mary and Anne give Jesus, are often used in late medieval art as a eucharistic symbol. It is doubtful, though, that this is the usual meaning in the Anne works, for the grapes rarely appear with wheat or other bread symbols, nor do they correlate with the occasional appearance of the *ostentatio* position in which the Christ Child's body is spread out to recall the elevated host. Eucharistic symbols, apart from the Christ Child himself, do not seem to be widespread in the *Anna Selbdritt*, though there are some examples: in the Lower Rhine / Westfalian Holy Kinship in the Wallraf-Richartz Museum, John the Baptist's lamb bleeds into a chalice placed directly beneath the nude Christ Child; in a Dutch painted Holy Kinship, apples plucked from a tree are held by Anne in a chalice-shaped container.[17] And there is undoubtedly a eucharistic reference in a Holy Kinship by Hans Döring (ca. 1515) in which one of Mary Cleophas's sons picks cherries from a tree while another holds a flat golden plate full of the fruit.[18] The cherries represent Christ, who is the fruit of the tree described in the Anne lives, while the plate takes the form of the eucharistic paten. However, the fig that Joachim hands the Christ Child to encourage him to take his first step is probably not intended as a eucharistic allusion.

Like the fruit, the book that Anne is shown reading in the *Ortenberg Altar* has been the subject of various interpretations, and like it, the meanings intended or perceived by medieval people were probably various and multiple. The possibility that, like the book in the Annunciation, it refers to the biblical prophecies concerning Christ's birth seems reasonable enough. However, in some cases it is clear that the book represented is not the Bible but a book of hours. Is there an intention to encourage the reading of the Psalter? In the late medieval English *N-Town Play* Mary makes an enthusiastic speech about the Psalter, which is clearly intended to do this:

> It makyht sowles fayr that doth it say
> Angelys be steryd to help us ther with
> it lytenyth therkeness and puttyth develys Away.
>
> . . . .
>
> synne is put A-wey ther by
> It lernyth A man vertuysful to be

It feryth mannys herte gostly
who that it vsyth custommably
it claryfieth the herte and charyte makyth cowthe
he may not faylen of goddys mercy
that hath the preysenge of god evyr in his mowthe.[19]

The reading motif has other aspects too. Connections between the theme of the Education of the Virgin and the teaching of girls to read have been made by Pamela Sheingorn and Ayers Bagley.[20] However, it does not seem that this meaning is necessarily intended in the books held by Anne or Mary in the *Anna Selbdritts* or Holy Kinships, for the act of teaching, so easily discernible in some depictions of the theme known as the Education of the Virgin (which also exists in Germany), is not part of the repertoire of motifs found in the former. But though an overall interpretation of the book in the *Anna Selbdritt* and Holy Kinships as an allusion to the teaching of reading cannot be sustained, there are Holy Kinship images that do refer to teaching and learning. However, these do not involve Christ or Mary, and it is the teaching of boys, not girls, that is depicted. The best-known example is the Lucas Cranach woodcut (ca. 1510) in which the family of Frederick the Wise are shown as participant patrons and in which the fathers are shown teaching their sons to read (fig. 19). But the Cranach is far from the first instance of this interesting motif. In the *Ortenberg Altar* the two older sons of Mary Cleophas, at left, are shown with an open book and a schoolboy's slate or hornbook. Apostle children are also shown with writing tablets in a Westfalian Holy Kinship of ca. 1430 in the Hessisches Landesmuseum in Darmstadt and in a 1521 altarpiece by Martin Schaffner in the choir of Ulm Münster, and in a number of other works as well. The Schaffner work, in which Mary's sisters' husbands are ducal participant donor portraits, shows a writing tablet or hornbook in the hand of James the Greater.

But though only a small number explicitly refer to education, a large number of Holy Kinship paintings place emphasis on the act of reading. It is not infrequent to find several members of the Holy Kinship reading books. In an altarpiece by the Master of Frankfurt in the Frankfurt Historisches Museum, both of Mary's sisters have open books. Mary Salome reads hers while Mary Cleophas shows hers to two of her sons, her finger pointing to a specific line of text. In Quentin Massys's *Saint Anne Altarpiece* in Brussels, in which neither Mary nor Anne holds a book, two of Mary Cleophas's sons look at and touch the book on their mother's lap while a tiny John the Evangelist sits on the floor looking at a printed sheet that Christine Gottler suggests may be an indulgence sheet (fig. 24). The small, hand-colored single-sheet

FIGURE 24. Quentin Massys, *Triptych of the Saint Anne Confraternity at the Church of Saint Peter in Louvain,* 1509. Museés royaux des Beaux-Arts de Belgique, Brussels

prints on the floor depict Christ as the Lamb and the IHS, the monogram of Christ popularized by the fourteenth-century Italian preacher Bernardino of Siena. The book of hours is open at the penitential psalms, the illustration depicting David in prayer. John's rather sad and thoughtful little face suggests he may be meditating on the coming death of his cousin, and perhaps on the sinner's means of grace as well.[21] In all, nine people are engaged in reading in this studious Kinship. Several paintings depict the magnifying reading glasses that were in fairly widespread use in the fifteenth century. Anne wears them in the Geertgen Tot Sint Jans Holy Kinship in the Rijksmuseum in Amsterdam. Zebedee uses them to read a sheet of paper in a ca. 1470 Westfalian painting of the Holy Kinship in the Treasury of the Saint Servatius Church in Maastricht while James the Lesser holds his father's glasses.

In a small number of works the proposal that the book refers to Christ as the *Logos* is tenable, for example, in the right-hand panel of the *Saint Anne Altarpiece* from the Gerard David workshop, which shows Saint Anthony of Padua holding a cross in one hand, and in his left an open book on which sits a small naked Christ Child. But the fact that the book is not the attribute of a single individual—any one or several of the women in a Holy Kinship, and sometimes their children, may hold it—suggests that an exclusive intended meaning as the *Logos* is unlikely in the majority of examples.

The combination of the Holy Kinship or *Anna Selbdritt* with female saints is not uncommon, and in the *Ortenberg Altarpiece* we have Agnes holding up a lily to Mary, Barbara with the tower and the eucharistic chalice, and Dorothy with her basket of roses. Baby Jesus snuggles, atypically, up to his aunt Elizabeth (holding her own son John the Baptist), rather than to his grandmother, seated at Mary's left. The Christ Child is nude here, as he is in most though far from all fifteenth- and sixteenth-century works. The inclusion of only one husband, Joseph, invisible except for his head, in such a large Kinship is somewhat unusual. (The bishop at the far right is Servatius, a distant member of the kinship.)

A feature present in many Anne paintings, though not in the *Ortenberg Altar,* is the enclosed garden, the *hortus conclusus* of Mary's virginity. An unusual treatment of this theme appears in one of the panels of the Saint Anne altarpiece made for the confraternity at the Church of Saint Peter in Frankfurt, now in the Liebighaus Museum in Frankfurt, which depicts Anne and Joachim, the epitome of the prosperous bourgeois couple, at dinner in a loggia looking out onto a garden—clearly a reference to the virginity of the newborn Mary, whose birth scene can be glimpsed in the far corner of the panel (fig. 25). A mature but beautiful and smiling Anne, richly gowned, raises her hand in animated conversation with her kindly, attentive husband as the two sit together over roast chicken and meat pie. A dog gnaws a bone on the floor. The servants are handsomely dressed. And the pretty garden awaits an after-dinner stroll.

The various compositional types of the *Anna Selbdritt* and the Holy Kinship that developed over the course of the fifteenth century are not distributed equally throughout the territory under consideration—that is, present-day Germany, Austria, Switzerland, Belgium, and Holland. Preferences for certain compositional forms and iconographic features marked particular regions. The miniaturization of Mary is most widespread in Germany and rare in Holland. Conversely, the tendency to show Mary as or approximating normal size is most pronounced in Holland. In South Germany Anne frequently holds a child on either arm, whereas in the Rhineland and Flanders she typically holds both on one arm. The bench-type format with both women sitting on a bench or throne with the child between them, on the other hand, is found throughout the territory of the cult, though again certain differences in the positions of Anne and Mary characterize different regions. In Rhineland Kinships for example, the figures of Mary and Anne are often placed quite close together, as they are in the stone relief memorial commemorating the converted rabbi Victor von Carben in Cologne Cathedral carved ca. 1470. Von Carben, shown kneeling at Anne's feet, looks up toward the Christ Child, who holds out a bunch of grapes toward him in what may be a reference either to the shedding of his own blood or/and to the eucharist. Anne appears in several painted and sculpted grave monuments, among them the monument in the cloister of Augsburg Cathedral,

FIGURE 25. Flanders, *Anne and Joachim at Home* (Saint Anne Altarpiece),
late fifteenth century. Historisches Museum, Frankfurt am Main

which adorns the grave of the clockmaker Reichart Klieber (d. 1491) and his wife
Anna Freyin (d. 1498), but whether Anne played a special role in funerary culture
cannot yet be stated for sure, though there are indications she may have.[22]

A variety of factors seem to have been at work in shaping these regional variations, and in a given case it can be difficult to decide whether the use of a particular
format arose out of an underlying way of seeing and representing that was part of a
given culture, or whether it was the result of incidental factors. The Dutch liking for

compositions in which Mary is not miniaturized is certainly consistent with the fact that the Dutch life of Saint Anne by Jan van Denemarken is more realistic in its presentation of human feeling than the German lives. On the other hand, the use of a South German compositional type in the Saxon Erzgebirge may simply have been the result of the easy availability of woodcuts using this form.

Jesus and Mary as Attributes of Anne

One sometimes reads that the figures of Jesus and Mary in the *Anna Selbdritt* are intended as attributes whose function is to identify Anne.[23] In a sense this is true, as their presence does identify her, and their inclusion can sometimes be the only way of identifying Anne where she is included in a group of married female saints. But the figures of Jesus and Mary are much more than Anne's attributes. In a memorable way they call to mind the reason for her importance. The fact that the *Anna Selbdritt* was perceived as an image of three people, not one, is made clear by the references in the late fifteenth-century Anne texts and in several images to the practice of placing three candles rather than the usual single candle in front of the *Selbdritt*. At the same time—and in seeming contradiction to the above observation—the numerous references to "Anne with the two children" point to the primacy of Anne in perceptions of the image.[24] Is it possible that the story of the young man who was urged to place three candles in front of the image was intended to counter excessive attention to Anne?

The diversification of compositional types intensified following the enormous increase in production that began in the 1480s. But along with the new formats, older ones remained in use. The charming little *Anna Selbdritts* like the ca. 1520 example in the Utrecht Rijksmuseum Het Catharijneconvent, produced in quantity in Mechelen in the South Netherlands, repeat a format, including the smile, based on the standing High Gothic Madonna (fig. 26). According to Hans Nieuwdorp, small Mechelen figures of both the Madonna and the *Anna-te-Drieen* were sometimes incorporated into the *Mechelse Tuintjes* (little Mechelen gardens) made for sale by the beguines of the city.[25] In these small, glass-front shrine boxes whose descendants can be found in nineteenth-century convent handicrafts, statuettes bought ready-made were arranged with flowers and other decorations of silk, metal, and paper. Flowers are pervasive too in the prayers to Anne in books of hours produced in Holland and the Rhineland, with epithets comparing her to flowers, offerings of flower garlands of prayers, and illuminations combining the *Anna Selbdritt* with flowers.

In the Mechelen statue, Mary wears a crown, as she does in approximately half the *Anna Selbdritts* produced in Germany and the Netherlands. Some regions have

FIGURE 26. Brabant, Mechelen, *Anna-te-Drieen*, 1515–24.
Museum Catharijneconvent, Utrecht

both, others show a preference for one or the other. A rough survey suggests that
crowns are frequent in Bavaria, Lübeck, Saxony, and Holland, and infrequent in
Swabia, Franconia, the Rhineland, and North-Rhine Westfalia, though why this
should be the case I cannot say. Sometimes instead of a crown Mary wears a circlet
or garland that, according to Edwin Hall and Horst Uhr, may have been intended
as the *corona* of virginity described by Scholastic writers.[26] It cannot be assumed,
however, that sculptors necessarily used it with this intent.

The South German composition with a miniaturized Mary on one arm and a more or less normal-sized Christ Child on the other was used by the artist who made the sculptures for the small Swabian domestic altar, now in the Cloisters in New York City (fig. 27). The open book is held by Mary, its usual holder in this part of Germany. The small altar presents a favorite ensemble of powerful late medieval images: on the interior and exterior of the wings are the virgin supersaints Barbara and probably Katherine, with Ursula and Dorothy on the outside, while the predella bears the Veronica image. Inside the shrine the somewhat crudely carved *Anna Selbdritt* is flanked by two figures who are probably the patrons of the work. The furry clothing on the male figure identifies him as John the Baptist, and by inference the patron as Johann. The woman does not seem to be shown as a participant patron, but one wonders whether her name might have been Anne, for Anna Hoffman of Ingolstadt was not the only Anna who commissioned a representation of Saint Anne. Indeed, though no systematic study has been done, one has the impression that an unusually large proportion of Anne images and foundations were commissioned or funded by women named Anne.

The surprising number of small *Anna Selbdritt* altarpieces that survive suggest that these were popular objects in people's homes. A slightly larger but similarly designed mid-sixteenth-century Swabian work now in the chapel of Saint Markus in the Fuggerei in Augsburg, but formerly in the chapel of the Fugger House in Augsburg, depicts the coronation of Mary by the Trinity in the center, members of the Fugger family in the predella, and the *Anna Selbdritt* and Saint Michael in the wings, a pairing that has led Renate Kroos to posit salvational implications (fig. 14).[27]

Another Augsburg work—the *Anna Selbdritt* painted by Hans Holbein the Elder as part of the *Katharinenaltar* (1512), in the Augsburg Staatsgalerie, probably for the Dominican nuns of Saint Katherine in Augsburg, the same ones who took so much care over the acoustics of their new church—makes striking use of the bench format (fig. 9). The prescient sadness and the absence of connecting glances exemplify the implication of Anne and Mary in the salvational process that this book argues informs fifteenth-century German and Flemish Anne imagery. The white elevated figure of the Christ Child works as an *ostentatio* reference to the eucharist, and by extension to his crucified body. Given the profound presence of the eucharist in fifteenth-century devotion, all images of Christ can be seen as alluding to that sacrament. Nonetheless, as Barbara Lane and others have pointed out, some works, among them this one, seem to make a particular point of emphasizing the identity of Christ's physical body with his eucharistic body.[28] Is it going too far to wonder

FIGURE 27. Swabia, *Anna Selbdritt Private Devotional Altarpiece (Hausaltarchen)*, ca. 1490. Metropolitan Museum of Art, Cloisters Collection, New York

whether the cross-shaped woodwork of the bench that is painted to suggest a table-like altar refers to the Crucifixion?

Here, as is usually the case in fifteenth-century Germany and Flanders, Anne is depicted as mature rather than old. The reluctance to portray her as old may have been in part due to the negative associations attached to the image of the old woman in late medieval Germany.[29] It may also be the case that her continuing fertility, an essential feature of the Holy Kinship story and a justification of the *Trinubium*, is being alluded to through the absence of the signs of aging. The fact that in some cases Anne retains well-formed breasts visible under her tight-fitting bodice certainly suggests an intent to depict her as a mother, just as the anachronistic presence of noticeable breasts on the small Mary, as we see in the Riemenschneider sculpture (fig. 1), may be an allusion to her role as mother of Jesus. It is surely significant that Anne begins to age in artworks in the first few decades of the 1500s at the same time that her role as generator of the Redeemer through Mary began to be replaced by her role as human grandmother.

Though in some works Anne wears a gown and cloak of bright colors, more often she wears the sober clothing of an older woman (not a widow) of the upper levels of the merchant classes, and Mary Cleophas and Mary Salome wear the clothes and jewelry that would have been worn by young married women of the same class, as they do in the Quentin Massys altarpiece (fig. 24). As younger married women, they show more of their hair than Anne but less than Mary, who is of course a virgin. In some paintings they also wear more jewelry than might have been worn by women who had born several children. A book of advice for women printed in Augsburg in 1522 states that with each successive child a woman ought to wear less jewelry: "Have you two children from your marriage / Then wear your jewels no more."[30] Anne's traditional colors are sometimes said to be green and red, but though these colors are found in some paintings and original polychromy, other colors are often used.

While the bench composition goes back at least to the early 1400s, the emphasis on the child as a link between the two women seems to have originated somewhat later, possibly in a beautiful and perplexing sandstone *Anna Selbdritt* in the Bode Museum in Berlin (fig. 28). Believed to have been carved in Strasburg in the 1470s or early 1480s, this work was severely damaged in the bombardment of Berlin at the end of the Second World War but has since been reconstituted and restored. Formerly it was widely though not unanimously attributed to Nikolaus Gerhaert von Leyden, a remarkable, apparently Dutch, sculptor who worked in Germany, primarily in Strasburg. L. Fischel, who viewed Gerhaert as the inheritor of the French-Burgundian tradition, proposed that he influenced the whole range of South German sculpture in introducing to it Dutch realism and genre-like intimacy.[31]

But later art historians have rejected the attribution to Gerhaert. In 1987 Roland Recht attributed the *Anna Selbdritt* to another Strasburg sculptor, Lukas Kotter.[32] Hartmut Krohn makes a convincing argument on stylistic grounds that the work, while by an "outstanding artist," is not by Gerhaert, though it is by someone well acquainted with his work; Krohn goes on to say that it is not impossible that it is a copy of a Gerhaert work.[33] This seems highly likely, for the work treats the *Selbdritt*

FIGURE 28. Strasburg master, *Anna Selbdritt*, 1470–early 1480s. Sandstone. Staatliche Museen zu Berlin, Skulpturensammlung

theme very differently from other German examples of its period. Though the "caught in motion" quality of the action is consistent with German origins, the playful realism of the sculpture, in which the two women, each with the most delicate of smiles, delicately support the wobbling child, is not found in any other German example that I know of. However, both smiles and playful interaction are often found in Dutch *Anna-te-Drieens*. Indeed, one is reminded of the way in which the Dutch Anne sometimes seems to tease her grandson by, instead of handing him fruit, holding it just out of his reach, as she does in a beautiful sculpture (ca. 1500) from the Limburg area. Anne has a distinct smile on her face as she holds the grapes so far away that the child, supported by a standing Mary, is going to be forced to step on the book on Anne's lap if he is going to get the grapes. There is something of this interactive playfulness in the Berlin work's version of the "first steps" motif. Curious also is the fact that this Anne, beak-nosed and visibly wrinkled, is decidedly an old woman, very different from the mature but still handsome Anne of late fifteenth-century German art.

Wherever it originated, the "first steps" motif achieved widespread popularity. We see it in a Brussels Holy Kinship of ca. 1500–1510 in the Musée du Parc du Cinquantenaire in Brussels. This is an elaborate but not untypical example of the kind of altarpiece that was mass-produced in workshops in Brussels and Antwerp in the fifteenth and early sixteenth centuries (fig. 29). Characteristic of South Netherlandish Anne iconography are the round *bourrelet* hats on the women, the closed tunic of the Christ Child, the grapes in Anne's hand, and her long-tailed hood. Though the Christ Child is usually shown nude, he is sometimes dressed in a tunic as he is here, occasionally in a tunic fastened only at the neck so that it reveals the genitals, and rarely, in a loincloth, the latter probably a reference to the Crucifixion. The fact that the shirt often occurs in works from the Rhineland and the South Netherlands raises the possibility of a connection with the famous relic of the Holy Shirt at Trier, though in fact the shirts are more frequent in works from Antwerp and Brussels than in those made closer to Trier.[34] But Philippe de Vigneulles's description of the crowd's response is an indication of the widespread fame of this relic, which, according to the book published in 1520 to promote it, had been forgotten by Mary in the crib along with Jesus' diapers, found by the Empress Helena and given by her to "her friend Charlemagne."

Unusual in the Brussels Holy Kinship is the mixing rather than separation of men and women among the members of the Kinship, who in this case comprise the extended kinship. The most likely identifications for the numerous figures are as follows, clockwise from left to right: Mary Cleophas with her four sons; Eminym (or Emiu), grandson of Anne's sister Esmeria (son of her son Eliud) with his wife Memelia holding her son, the future Rhineland bishop Servatius; Efraim with his wife, Anne's sister Esmeria; the husbands of Anne's daughters, the three Marys. On the right-hand side of the throne, at the very back, are Anne's parents, Emerentia and Stollanus; in front of them are Anne's three husbands; Anne's cousin Elisabeth, Esmeria's daughter, holding John the Baptist, is shown with her husband, Zacharias; and seated at the bottom is Mary Salome with her two sons. The artist has skillfully arranged the figures, who are notable for their lively facial features and gesturing hands, to create a grouping that is both aesthetically harmonious and logically consistent.

Anna Selbdritts are sometimes mislabeled Holy Kinships. To be considered a Holy Kinship, the grouping must at least allude to Anne's other daughters and their

FIGURE 29. Brussels, *Holy Kinship*, 1500–1510. Musée du Parc du Cinquantenaire, Brussels

progeny. Thus at the very least Anne should be shown with her daughters if not with her daughters and their children. The usual complete kinship group includes Anne and her three husbands, Joachim, Cleophas, and Salome; the Virgin Mary with Joseph and Jesus; Mary Cleophas with her husband, Alphaeus, and their children, James the Greater, Simon, Jude, and Joseph the Just; and Mary Salome with her husband, Zebedee, and their sons, James the Lesser and John the Evangelist. It may also include Anne's sister Esmeria (Hismeria) and her daughter Elisabeth with the latter's son, John the Baptist, with or without his father, Zacharius.

Sometimes the Holy Kinship includes the great-grandson of Esmeria—Saint Servatius, Bishop of Maastricht—with his mother, Memelia, and sometimes his father, Emiu, and/or, more rarely, Esmeria's grandson Saint Maternus with or without his family. Occasionally Anne's parents, Emerentia and Stollanus, are also present. An *Anna Selbdritt* that includes Emerentia is called an *Anna Selbviert* or an *Emerentia Selbviert*.[35] Compositions in which the *Anna Selbdritt* is shown with her three husbands but without the three daughters are usually parts of larger works that include other panels showing Anne's daughters and grandchildren, according to Esser.[36] An *Anna Selbdritt* with the addition of Joseph is not a Holy Kinship.

In Rhineland bench-type *Anna Selbdritts*, Anne and Mary are often shown sitting very close together, Mary sometimes depicted as slightly shorter than Anne. This composition seems to be at the root of the rare and unusual version of the *Selbdritt*, the *Selbdritt Pietà* (Guelders/Limburg, ca. 1500) in the parish church of Saint Michael in the town of Waldniel in the German Rhineland (fig. 30). It is plain here why Mary and Anne no longer smile. The event adumbrated in the unmeeting gazes and unsmiling mouths has come to pass. The similarity between the two women, nearly identical in their drapery, facial features, pursed brows, and slightly open mouths, highlights the parallels between their roles in the salvational drama. Though it is Mary who holds Jesus, the left-curving position of his body links him in visual terms with Anne, who holds her book. In the only other German version of this remarkable composition, in the parish church of Gelsdorf, also in the Rhineland and probably by the same artist, Christ is held jointly by both women.[37]

Sculptors, perhaps especially in smaller centers, used, adapted, and sometimes misunderstood the image types and iconographic details they borrowed from their sources. Was the sculptor of the Holy Kinship (ca. 1520) from the parish church in Rabis near Jena, now in the Thüringer Museum in Eisenach, introducing a novelty or was he misunderstanding his models when he gave Mary two children to look after (fig. 16)? The swaddled infant would seem to be Jesus, while the naked boy hanging over her shoulder could be reasonably identified as one of the sons of Mary Cleophas since she is shown with only three (the foot of a missing badly damaged child is visible at Mary's left). Looking further at this curious work, one notices that the relationship between Anne and Mary suggests a conflating of two different compositions. Is it possible that the grouping of Anne, Mary, and the nephew between them is based on the bench *Selbdritt* with Jesus shown between the two women while the figure of Mary draws on a Madonna figure? And are the fingers over the face of one of Anne's husbands an attempt to show him resting his head on his hand? The husbands are typical of much fifteenth-century work, however, in

FIGURE 30. Lower Rhine, *Lamentation with the Anna Selbdritt*, ca. 1500. Church of St. Michael, Schwalmtal-Waldniel

being separated from the women by a physical barrier, here the back of the bench on which the women are seated.

Less widespread than bench compositions are those in which Mary and Jesus are seated below Anne in a vertical format resembling Throne of Grace depictions of the Trinity. In the panel from the Schlutuper Altar (ca. 1500) from the circle of Henning van der Heide in the Saint Annen-Museum in Lübeck, the C-shape of the Brussels Holy Kinship, in reverse form, encloses a Throne of Grace *Selbdritt* (fig. 31). Other signs of borrowing from imported South Netherlandish Holy Kinships include the numerous toys that the pudgy-cheeked apostle children play with,

FIGURE 31. Circle of Henning van der Heide, Schlutuper Altar, late fifteenth century. St. Annen-Museum, Lübeck

among them the cooking pot, drinking canister, puppy, and hobbyhorse. In the detail from the altar of the Gertrudenbruderschaft (Lübeck, late fifteenth century) we see a similar group of toys: two of Mary Cleophas's sons hold, respectively, a samovar-shaped drinking apparatus, and a spoon and small cauldron, while a third rides a hobbyhorse (fig. 32). The toys shown with the apostle children are often versions of their attributes: James the Greater is shown in the garb of a pilgrim with wallet, staff, and broad hat decorated with pilgrims' badges; Simon holds a saw, the instrument of his martyrdom; the golf club, a common toy in Holland in this period, held by Jude, represents the instrument of his martyrdom, the fuller's club. But sometimes the significance of the attributes is less clear. Both the Schlutuper and the 1509 Gertrudenbrudershaft altarpieces include a miniature cauldron, seemingly the cauldron in which John the Evangelist was boiled in oil. Yet in each case the cauldron is shown with the wrong child—one of Mary Cleophas's sons (John the Evangelist is a son of Mary Salome). By the same token, if the hobbyhorse ridden by one of Mary Cleophas's sons in the Gertrudenbrudershaft altar originated in the image of the mounted James the Greater, the *Matamoros* of Spanish iconography, then it too is shown with the wrong child. The puppy that James the Greater teaches to beg in the Gertrudenbruderschaft altarpiece may also be connected with the cult of Saint James, according to Francesca Sautman.[38] But it is also possible that the artist is simply depicting children at play. There are other objects that do not even provoke a hypothesis: who can explain the "meaning" of the pull toy in which a ball revolves in a kind of cage in Lucas Cranach's Torgauer Altar, in the Städelsches Kunstinstitut in Frankfurt am Main, or the game of marbles played by Mary Cleophas's three older boys in a painting in the Halberstadt Domschatz?[39]

FIGURE 32. Lübeck, *The Children of Mary Cleophas* (detail, Gertrudenbruderschaft Altar), late fifteenth century. St. Annen-Museum, Lübeck

What are we to make of the fact that Jude has a dreidel or die as well as a hobby-horse? Are there symbols in the combs occasionally wielded by Mary Cleophas and Mary Salome, or is this merely routine grooming—or are lice a problem even for the blessed cousins of the Christ Child? And is there something more to the unspillable samovar, or is it just a medieval version of a modern toddler's covered plastic juice cup?

The subsidiary children in the Holy Kinships have attributes too. In a Flemish triptych (ca. 1510) commissioned by Margarethe von Merode Petershem and Johann VII, Herr von Merode Petershem, in the Wallraf-Richartz Museum in Cologne, John the Baptist has his lamb on a leash. Servatius is usually dressed as a miniature bishop and is sometimes shown with the dragon that his legend tells us he killed. Servatius plays with his mother's gold key and chain in what is undoubtedly a reference to another incident in his *vita*, the translation of the relics of Peter.[40]

The Lübeck compositional forms, with their borrowings from South Netherlandish art, themselves moved along and across the Baltic, appearing in Scandinavia and along the coast.[41] The Late Gothic *Anna Selbdritt* in the Katholische Propsteikirche zur Hl. Mutter Anna in Schwerin employs a composition popular in Lübeck, the standing Anne holding Jesus with the standing young Mary reaching up to Jesus' hand, and the seven Holy Kinships from Mecklenburg and Pomerania illustrated by Esser all use forms popular in Lübeck, the ubiquitous horizontal bench and the vertical Throne of Grace arrangements.

The pomegranate is another fruit depicted in the Anne imagery. In the *Anna Selbdritt* by the Master of Rabenden (ca. 1515–20) in the Unterlinden Museum in Colmar, the infant Christ reaches for the pomegranate as though to embrace the suffering of the Cross, which is suggested by the ruby-colored seeds, which resemble not only drops of blood but also medieval depictions of Christ's side wound (fig. 33). At the same time, it is difficult to imagine that the medieval viewer might not also have perceived a sexual allusion in the placing of the partially opened pomegranate over Anne's womb, the same place the jewel was located in the Cluny reliquary. Indeed, the shape of the opening in the pomegranate is similar to the humorous lead vulva-shaped mock pilgrimage images that have been found in Holland, such as the one illustrated here in which a vulva holds a penis-shaped pilgrim staff (fig. 34).[42] The coral necklace Jesus wears in the Unterlinden work, like so many others seen in paintings of this period, is a protective charm. At left kneels the clerical patron who may have commissioned the work for a family or personal altar.

The compositional format of this work in which Anne holds the Christ Child while Mary stands to one side, though not as widespread as bench compositions or

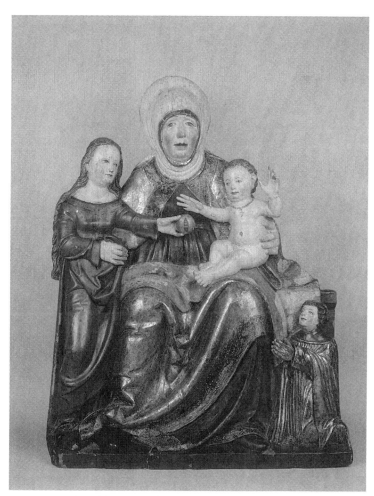

FIGURE 33. Atelier of the Master of Rabenden, *Sainte Anne, la Vierge et l'Enfant*, 1515–20. Musée d'Unterlinden, Colmar

works in which Anne holds the two children, is fairly widespread. It was especially popular in Swabia, Franconia, and Bavaria, and in Lübeck (where Anne usually stands), and it is among the most widespread *Anna-te-Drieen* compositions in Holland, where it manifests a number of subforms. In Jan van Steffeswert's sculpture (ca. 1500) in the Bonnefantenmuseum in Maastricht, Jesus has grabbed the bowl Mary is handing him, spilling its contents—an instance of characteristically Dutch humor (fig. 12). It is interesting in this connection to notice that most of the small number of *Anna Lactans* are Dutch. The smiles also identify this grouping as Dutch. Though the sober facial expressions and unmeeting gazes so frequent in German and Flemish fifteenth-century art are not absent in Dutch *Anna-te-Drieens*, the latter are noteworthy for an

FIGURE 34. Vulva as pilgrim with phallus staff and rosary, ca. 1375–1425. Stichting Middeleeuwse Religieuze en Profane Insignes. Found at Reimerswaal, Holland

unusually high proportion in which both gazes and body positions establish a sense of intimate contact: Anne and Mary sometimes look out jointly toward the viewer; bodies incline toward one another; smiles are frequent. Rather than portraying Anne as a figure of power, Dutch images are more apt to show her as an affectionate, down-to-earth grandmother. A sure sign of Dutch origins is a large, firm hand resting solidly on Anne's or Mary's back. Also consistent with this tendency to realism is the fact that outright miniaturization is less frequent in Dutch *Anna Selbdritt*s than in Flemish and German ones. And even when the sizes are unequal, Dutch sculptors will sometimes create an impression of natural size by careful adjustment of body position and placement. Here Van Steffeswert accomplished this by having Anne seated, the much smaller Mary standing.

Compositional formats were not the only thing artists copied. The shape of Mary Salome's dark underskirt in the panel from an altarpiece by Bernhard Strigel (ca. 1515–20, Washington, D.C., National Gallery of Art) recalls the dramatic dark green mass of Mary Cleophas's skirt in Massys's Louvain altarpiece (fig. 24), as does the pose of the leaning boy (fig. 35). But the white tunic of Strigel's James the Lesser creates an emphasis on the child that Massys did not choose to make, preferring instead a more even distribution of accents. The Strigel panel, by contrast, calls attention to the two apostles and to the two books, the one on Mary Salome's lap being read by the eager James, the other, the *Apocalypse* in the process of being written, or at any rate transcribed, by John the Evangelist as the haloed eagle dictates it to him. Strigel is here making witty use of the convention that shows the children of the Kinship playing with pets. Salome wears one of the many examples of contemporary Jewish headgear that are modeled in splendid variety by the men of the Kinships. It is not known who commissioned this multipanel altarpiece by the Memmingen painter Strigel, but there is no doubt that it is one of the most distinctive of all the Holy Kinships in the beauty of its conception and the individuality of its iconography. Strigel did a good deal of work for patrons in ruling circles, and this altarpiece may be among them, for some of the figures seem to be participant patrons; Cleophas in the panel matching the one shown is a portrait of Frederick the Wise.

The Strigel altarpiece is a reminder that Anne's popularity was by no means restricted to the urban middle classes. Countless sculptures and paintings in small rural churches, and the large body of works commissioned by, and sometimes depicting, aristocratic and royal patrons, testify to her popularity among other groups as well. All levels of society likely shared an interest in her salvational powers, a response to her motherly qualities, and an appreciation of her reputation for increasing wealth. But the upper levels had an additional reason for choosing to depict themselves with her: the identification of their family status with hers, the most exalted family of all.

Though the vast majority of the Saint Anne images consist of *Anna Selbdritts* and Holy Kinships, a small number drew directly on the new Anne texts. The increase in the production of images of Saint Anne had been spurred by the appearance of the new texts, but the content of the artworks in fact made little direct reference to them. The handful that do were commissioned by Rhineland clerics involved with the initial promotion of the cult. One of them, a panel depicting *Saint Colette's Devotion to the Holy Kinship* (from the Flemish *Saint Anne Altarpiece* now in the Historisches Museum in Frankfurt am Main, painted probably in the 1480s for one of the first confraternities founded by the Rhineland promoters, the one instituted by

FIGURE 35. Bernhard Strigel, *Saint Mary Salome and Her Family*, ca. 1520–28.
National Gallery of Art, Washington, D.C., Samuel H. Kress Collection

FIGURE 36. Flemish, *Saint Colette's Devotion to the Holy Kinship* (Saint Anne Altarpiece), late 1400s. Historisches Museum, Frankfurt am Main

Rumold Laupach, prior of the Carmelite convent in Frankfurt), is revealing in its depiction of an artwork in an original fifteenth-century setting (fig. 36) in a side chapel. The small, carved Holy Kinship altar shown in the painting takes the form of the widespread Rhineland *Anna Selbdritt* type, with Anne holding a miniaturized Madonna and Child on one arm.

The vision in the sky shows Anne collecting golden pennies from the saints, "alms" that she will use to bring to heaven the soul of the praying nun, who is identified in some lives as Saint Colette.

The Anna Selbdritt *Outside Germany and the Netherlands*

Though the majority of *Anna Selbdritts* and Holy Kinships were produced in Northern Europe, depictions of Anne with Mary and Jesus were also painted, carved, and printed in moderate to substantial numbers in Scandinavia, Spain, Poland, and other parts of eastern Europe, and France, in smaller numbers in Italy, and in much smaller numbers in England. The Scandinavian, Polish, and eastern European, and to a lesser degree the Spanish and French *Anna Selbdritts*, use compositions similar to the German, Flemish, and Dutch works. As many of the numerous images of Saint Anne in Sweden were imported from Germany and the South Netherlands, it is not surprising to find the influence of these styles strong in native Swedish works, though the latter have distinctive characteristics of their own. In France, Anne's late medieval cult, though it was by no means restricted to northeastern France, was especially strong there, with many distinctive examples of the *Saint Anne Trinitaire* produced there. The fairly numerous Spanish images, like other late medieval Spanish works of art, draw on Flemish, Italian, and indigenous sources. Italian depictions of Anne with Mary and Jesus by and large use formats different from those in use farther north, sharing neither the peculiarities of proportion nor the emphasis on the triple link that characterize the Northern *Anna Selbdritts*. It is not surprising that in Italy Anne does not seem to have any connections with salvation.[43] In England, Anna enjoyed a thriving late medieval cult, but surviving images of the *Anna Selbdritt* are extremely rare.[44]

Epilogue

Most of the images discussed in this chapter were produced during the fifty-year span from 1480 to 1530, the period in which Saint Anne's Northern cult blossomed, flourished, and declined. The late Northern phase of her cult thus parallels the development of pre-Reformation culture, the change from medieval to early modern thinking, and the intensification and coming to consciousness of those issues that were creating an openness to religious change. The Saint Anne of the 1480s was a distinctly medieval saint, more powerful than most with her unique ability to help the soul into heaven, but nonetheless a saint who answered prayers in response to gifts and devotion. The fact that her clerical and humanist promoters saw fit to exploit that salvific potential is in itself an aspect of medieval culture, a culture that saw power in objects and vicarious ritual, in contiguity and quantity. At a more down-to-earth level, the growing resentment at the pressure to give, in the hope of ensuring salvation, was a significant factor in creating receptivity to alternative ways of accessing salvation. The business of giving money to help one into heaven, whether via indulgences, bequests, or donations, was beginning to look like a shaky investment.

Another set of changes that affected Saint Anne was the move from the medieval to the early modern family structure described in Chapter 8. The powerful medieval Anne had no place in the new family structure, and the same decades of the early sixteenth century that saw the waning of confidence in her salvational efficacy saw the weakening of her visible physical power as artists began to transform the once powerful matron into an old woman and to separate her from the still powerful figures of her daughter and grandson. Our period ended with the first images in which Anne, no longer a provider of salvation, looks to her grandson to receive her own salvation.

This is not the end of Saint Anne's story. There are aspects of her imagery that this book has not looked at. Any one of the works of art that have been all too briefly discussed could be the subject of a study in its own right. Spain, eastern Europe, Scandinavia, and France have not been examined at all, England only briefly, and Italy barely. And Saint Anne's early history, in particular her role in Holy Land pilgrimage, stands in need of examination.

The tentative suggestions made by a few scholars that Anne and her daughters may have taken over characteristics from Roman and indigenous Northern goddesses might also be worth investigation.[45] Agricultural goddesses and trios of holy women were worshiped in the region west of the Rhine, where the cult of Anne and her daughters had old roots. While there is no narrative congruence between the story of Anne and her family and the legends of pre-Christian figures that I know of—apart from a story told by but not originating with Caesarius of Heisterbach, in which Saint Anne and two female companions wipe the sweat from the brows of harvest workers—there are small but provocative correspondences in compositional and iconographic details between some Anne images and Romano-Celtic goddess figures from the Rhineland.[46] The *Matronenstein*, as these stele and altars are called, sometimes depict trios of women seated on benches. Sometimes round headdresses resembling halos are worn. Sometimes one of the women holds a bowl of fruit.[47] The most curious coincidence is the presence in several *Matronenstein* of three men, possibly donors, who stand on the other side of a railing behind and above the women in a configuration reminiscent of the placement of the male figures in some

Holy Kinships. The correspondences, though irregular, are numerous enough to lead one to ask whether some elements in *Anna Selbdritts* or Holy Kinships might have derived from *Matronenstein* with or without an understanding of their original meanings.[48]

By the later sixteenth century, the Holy Kinship had largely passed out of the repertoire of Catholic themes. *Anna Selbdritts* were occasionally made, but a new iconography of Saint Anne was in the process of establishing itself. For a brief period, Northern Baroque sculptors produced majestic, aged, prophetic Annes with craggy faces and swirling draperies, but ultimately it was a more calmly dignified grandmother who prevailed. In sixteenth-century France a vigorous new phase of Saint Anne's cult flourished in Brittany, and it was from France that Anne was brought to Quebec, where she was associated, as she always had been, with marine rescue. Today, despite the decline in church attendance on the part of French Quebecers, the shrine of Sainte-Anne de Beaupré, founded in the seventeenth century with a statue and a relic brought from France, flourishes. The United States, where church-going among both Protestants and Catholics is much higher than in Canada, supplies some of the pilgrims to Sainte-Anne de Beaupré, as do the immigrant communities. And their numbers are swelled a little by the Native Canadian, Native American, and Gypsy pilgrims, all of whom have a special fondness for the grandmother saint.[49]

Notes

Introduction

1. E. Schaumkell, *Der Kultus der heiligen Anna am Ausgang des Mittelalters* (Freiburg: Akademische Verlagsbuchhandlung von J. C. B. Mohr, 1893); P.-V. Charland, *Les trois légendes de Madame Saincte Anne*, vol. 1: *Légende hagiographique (la vie)* (Quebec, 1898); vol. 2: *Légende historique (le culte)*, *Histoire de la dévotion à Sainte-Anne* (Lévis: Mercier & Cie, 1904); vol. 3: *Légende iconographique (les arts)*, *Madame Saincte Anne et son culte au moyen âge*, 2 vols. (Paris: Alphonse Picard & Fils, 1911 and 1913); *Le Culte de sainte Anne en Occident, second période, 1400 (environ) à nos jours* (Quebec: Imprimerie Franciscaine Missionaire, 1921); *Patronage de Sainte Anne en arts*, 2 vols. (Quebec: A.-O. Pruneau, 1923); Beda Kleinschmidt, *Die heilige Anna: Ihre Verehrung in Geschichte, Kunst und Volkstum* (Düsseldorf: Schwann, 1930).

2. Kathleen Ashley and Pamela Sheingorn, eds., *Interpreting Cultural Symbols: Saint Anne in Late Medieval Society* (Athens: University of Georgia Press, 1990); Werner Esser, "Die Heilige Sippe: Studien zu einem spätmittelalterlichen Bildthema in Deutschland und den Niederlanden" (Ph.D. diss., Rheinischen Friedrich-Wilhelms-Universität, Bonn, 1986); Ton Brandenbarg, *Heilig familieleven: Verspreiding en waardering van de Historie van Sint-Anna in de stedelijke cultuur in de Nederlanden en het Rijnland aan het begin van de moderne tijd* (Nijmegen: Sun, 1990). Brandenbarg's article "St. Anne and Her Family: The Veneration of St. Anne in Connection with Concepts of Marriage and the Family in the Early Modern Period" (in *Saints and She-Devils: Images of Women in the Fifteenth and Sixteenth Centuries*, ed. Lène Dresen-Coenders et al. [London: Rubicon Press, 1987], 101–27) summarizes some of the material in *Heilig familieleven*. His "Saint Anne: A Holy Grandmother and Her Children," an overview of some aspects of the cult (in *Sanctity and Motherhood: Essays on Holy Mothers in the Middle Ages*, ed. Anneke B. Mulder-Bakker, 31–65 [New York: Garland Publishing, 1995]), introduces some new material.

3. Willemien Deeleman–Van Tyen, "Sint Anna-te-Drieen: Een onderzoek naar vorm, inhoud en functioneren van het thema St. Anna-te-drieen in de nederlandse beeldhouwkunst der late middeleeuwen," 2 vols. (Master's thesis, Free University, Amsterdam, 1990); Bernadette Mangold, "Die Darstellung der heiligen Anna selbdritt in der gotischen Plastik Niederbayerns, 1380–1540" (Master's thesis, University of Passau, 1990); Peter Paul Maniurka, *Mater Matris Domini: Die heilige Anna Selbdritt in der gotischen Skulptur Schlesiens* (Altenberge: Oros Verlag, 2001); Angelika Dörfler-Dierken, *Die Verehrung der heiligen Anna in Spätmittelalter und früher Neuzeit* (Göttingen: Vandenhoek & Ruprecht, 1992); idem, *Vorreformatorische Bruderschaften der hl. Anna* (Heidelberg: Carl Winter Universitätsverlag, 1992). See also Brandenbarg, Deeleman–van Tyen, Lène Dresen-Coenders, and Léon van Liebergen, *Heilige Anna, Grote Moeder* (Nijmegen: Sun, 1992); and Dresen-Coenders, "Machtige grootmoeder, duivelse heks: Speurtocht naar de samenhang tussen heksenvervolging en de verering van grote moeder Anna op de drempel van de nieuwe tijd," *Jeugd en samenleving* 5 (1975), 213–47.

4. Gabrielle Spiegel may be right when she remarks that the text's "inevitable clash of codes" may defer "the material presence towards which it appears to be destined but at which it never arrives" ("History, Historicism, and the Social Logic of the Text," *Speculum* 65 [1990], 61–63), but the differ/deferences along the way are endlessly revealing. The fact that the author may not be in conscious control means that he or she speaks not *less* clearly but *more* clearly. Nor is the relationship of the sign, whether linguistic or pictorial, to its referent "ruptured," as some have asserted; it is only changed.

5. Peter Brown, *The Cult of the Saints: Its Rise and Function in Latin Christianity* (Chicago: University of Chicago Press, 1981).

6. Lynn Hunt, "Psychoanalysis, the Self, and Historical Interpretation," *Common Knowledge* 6, 2 (1997), 1.

7. Clifford Geertz puts it well: "Works of art are elaborate mechanisms for defining social relationships, sustaining social rules, and strengthening social values.... They materialize a way of experiencing; bring a particular cast of mind out into the world of objects, where men can look at it." "Art as a Cultural System," *Modern Language Notes* 91 (October–December 1976), 1475.

Chapter 1

1. For the text of the *Protevangelium*, see C. von Tischendorf, *Evangelia apocrypha* (1853; reprint, Hildesheim, 1966); M. R. James, *The Apocryphal New Testament* (Oxford: Clarendon Press, 1955); Oscar Cullman, "The Protevangelium of James," in *Gospels and Related Writings*, vol. 1: *New Testament Apocrypha*, ed. Edgar Hennecke and Wilhelm Schneemelcher, trans. R. M. Wilson (Philadelphia: Westminster Press, 1963).

2. Cullman, "The Protevangelium of James," 375.

3. Most medieval texts say explicitly or implicitly that the conception took place through normal sexual intercourse. The fifteenth-century preacher Geiler von Kaisersberg made this clear

in no uncertain terms: "Our dear lady was conceived in human fashion, not from the kiss as absurd people say." Cited in J. Janssen, *Erläuterungen und Ergänzungen zu Janssens Geschichte des deutschen Volkes*, vol. 6, part 1, ed. Ludwig Pastor (Freiburg im Breisgau: Herdersche Verlagshandlung, 1907), 17.

4. As the *Protevangelium* was not known in the West until relatively late, possibly only in the sixteenth century, Anne's story was disseminated through a Latin reworking of the *Protevangelium*, the *Pseudo-Gospel of Matthew*, a work that has been dated to between 550 and 700, and through works derived from it, of which *De nativitate sanctae Mariae* (attributed incorrectly to Jerome) was of particular importance. See Jan Gijsel, *Die unmittelbare Textüberlieferung des sogenannten Pseudo-Matthäus*, Verhandelingen van de Koninklijke Academie voor Wetenschappen, Letteren en schone Kunsten van Belgie, Klasse der Letteren, 43, 96 (Brussels: Koninklijke Academie, 1981). *De nativitate sanctae Mariae* is in J. Migne, *Patrologiae cursus completus, series latina*, 221 vols. (Paris, 1844–64), (hereafter PL) 30:307–15. There are translations of the relevant parts of the *Pseudo-Matthew* and *De nativitate sanctae Mariae* in E. D. O'Connor, ed., *The Dogma of the Immaculate Conception: History and Significance* (Notre Dame: University of Notre Dame Press, 1958), 515–22.

5. Hroswitha of Gandersheim, *Historia nativitatis laudabilisque conversationis intactae Dei genitricis, quam scriptam reperi sub nomine sancti Jacobi fratris Domini*, J. P. Migne, PL 137; Hroswitha, *The Nondramatic Works of Hroswitha*, trans. S. M. Gonsalva Wiegand (Saint Meinrad, Ind.: Abbey Press, 1936). In the late twelfth century the first Northern vernacular version appeared, a translation by the "Priester Wernher" entitled *Marienlied: Driu liet von der maget* of the rhymed *Vita beatae virginis Mariae et Salvatoris rhythmica*, a work based on the *Pseudo-Matthew*. *Vita beatae virginis Mariae et Salvatoris rhythmica*, ed. A. Vögtlin (Tübingen: n.p., 1988); Priester Wernher, *Maria. Bruchstücke und Umarbeitungen*, 2d ed., ed. Hans Fromm (Tübingen: Max Niemeyer Verlag, 1969).

6. Vincent of Beauvais, "Speculum Historiale," *Speculum Quadruplex sive Speculum Maius* (1624; reprint, Graz: Akademische Druck-u. Verlagsanstalt, 1965), 194–95; Jacobus de Voragine, "De nativitate beatae Mariae virginis," *Legenda Aurea*, ed. Th. Graesse (1890; reprint, Osnabrück: Otto Zeller, 1965), 585ff.; Jacobus de Voragine, *The Golden Legend*, 2 vols., trans. William Granger Ryan (Princeton: Princeton University Press, 1993), 2:150–52.

7. Andrew of Crete compares the generation of Mary with the weaving of the royal purple that will clothe the emperor: "In thy womb, O Anne, begins the weaving of the royal purple in which God and the King of all will dress Himself, when He appears to the mortals and defeats the foes who are fighting against us." Andrew of Crete, second Troparion of the seventh Ode, cited in O'Connor, *The Dogma*, 118. In England in the twelfth century, Osbert of Clare employs the motif in a discussion of the Immaculate Conception. Osbert of Clare, "Le Sermon sur Sainte Anne," in André Wilmart, "Les Compositions d'Osbert de Clare en l'honneur de Sainte Anne," *Auteurs spirituels et textes dévots du moyen age Latin* (1932; reprint, Paris: Etudes Augustiniennes, 1971), 274.

8. The Byzantine chronicler Procopius remarks on the building of a church dedicated to Anne: "In that section of the city which is called Deuteron he erected a most holy and revered church to Saint Anna, whom some consider to have been the mother of the Virgin and the grandmother of Christ. For God, being born a man as was His wish, is subjected to even a third generation, and His ancestry is traced back from His mother even as is that of a man." Procopius, *Procopius, Works, 7: Buildings*, trans. H. B. Dewing, Loeb Classical Library (Cambridge, Mass.: Harvard University Press, 1940), 1.3.11.

9. See *Lexikon der christlichen Ikonographie*, ed. Engelbert Kirschbaum Rome and Freiburg: Herder, 1968–76), 5:182; G. A. Wellen, *Theotokos: Eine ikonographische Abhandlung über das Gottesmuttersbild in frühchristlichen Zeit* (Utrecht and Antwerp: Uitgeverij het Spectrum, 1961), 198, 221.

10. See Jaroslav Folda, "The Church of Saint Anne," *Biblical Archaeologist* 54 (June 1991), 88–96. Geoffroy de Beaulieu reported that Louis IX visited the village of Sephoris in March 1251; ibid., 88–89.

11. Ibid., 88, 92, 94. Living rock is found at Calvary, in the Grotto of the Nativity, and in a number of other holy places in Palestine.

12. According to Kleinschmidt, the Heiligengeistkirche in Saint Gallen acquired a relic and a portion of Anne's house in the eleventh century. Hagenau in Alsace acquired an Anne relic in twelfth-century Württemberg in 1182. In 1199 Archibishop Hartwich returned to Bremen from a pilgrimage with an Anne relic. The Diocese of Basel received a relic from Constantinople in 1205. The head of Anne at Chartres was brought from Constantinople by Louis of Blois in 1204. Kleinschmidt, *Die heilige Anna*, 78–79.

13. O'Connor, *The Dogma*, 118–29. Suppressed following the Norman Conquest, the feast was reestablished in England in the early twelfth century.

14. Thomas Aquinas, "Quaestio 27. de sanctificatione beatae virginis," *Summa theologiae* 3, q. 27, a. 2 (New York: Blackfriars, 1964–67), 11–12.

15. Bernard of Clairvaux, *The Letters of St. Bernard of Clairvaux*, trans. Bruno Scott James (London: Burns & Oates, 1953), 293. Bernard argued against the metonymic basis of the reasoning that would say that because the birth was holy, the conception must have been holy: "It would certainly be true to say that the sanctification of what had already been conceived could be transmitted to the birth that followed, but it is quite impossible that the holiness of the birth could be retrospective and sanctify the conception which preceded it." Ibid., 292.

16. Thomas Aquinas, "Omnem quae de concubitu nascitur, carnem esse peccati," *Summa theologiae*, 3, q. 27, a. 2, 14–15.

17. Anselmus, *De conceptu virginali et originali peccato*, PL 158.451. See also PL 158.452–54. The same point is made in Anselm's *Cur Deus Homo* 2, PL 158.419.

18. John Duns Scotus, *Opera Omnia*, 26 vols. (1894; reprint, Westmead: Gregg International, 1969), vol. 23, 3, 3, q. 1, 263. Robert Grosseteste had proposed that Mary could have been "cleansed and sanctified in the very infusion of her rational soul. In this way, there would have been a purification, not from a sin which had at one time been present in her, but from one which would have been in her if she had not been sanctified in the very infusion of her rational soul." British Museum, MS Royal VII f. 2, fol. 48va–49va, cited in O'Connor, *The Dogma*, 199–204, citing E. Longpre, "Robert Grossetete et l'immaculée Conception," in *Archivum franciscanum historicum* 26 (1933), 551.

19. See O'Connor, *The Dogma*, 161–212.

20. There are examples of inconsistency in discussions of the doctrine. Even those who supported the Immaculate Conception sometimes used terms such as "cleansing" that imply a transition from uncleanness to cleanness. See O'Connor, *The Dogma*, esp. 189ff. Osbert of Clare himself speaks of sanctifying and cleansing in a letter to Anselm of Bury, *The Letters of Osbert of Clare*, ed. E. W. Williamson (New York: Oxford University Press, 1929), 66–67.

21. See Esser, "Die Heilige Sippe"; Max Förster, "Die Legende vom Trinubium der hl. Anna," *Probleme der Englischen Sprache und Kultur: Festschrift Johannes Hoops zum 60. Geburtstag Uberreicht von Freunden und Kollegen*, ed. Wolfgang Keller (Heidelberg: Carl Winter's Universitätsbuchhandlung, 1925), 105–30.

22. Haymo [of Halberstadt], *Historiae sacrae epitome*, PL 118.823–24. For the reattribution from Haymo of Halberstadt to Haymo of Auxerre, see J. de Gaiffier, "Le Trinubium Annae," *Analecta Bollandiana* 90 (1972), 289–98. Jerome's statement is in *De perpetua virginitate, adversus helvidium*, PL 23.193–216.

23. Esser, "Die Heilige Sippe," 17–24, traces the spread of the *Trinubium*. An account of the Holy Kinship from a twelfth-century prayer book (Würzburger Universitätsbibliothek, M.p.th.qu.46)

appears in Kurt Reindel's article "Ein Legendar des 12. Jahrhunderts aus dem Kloster Pomuc (Diöz. Prag)," in *Festschrift für Max Spindler zum 75. Geburtstag*, ed. Dieter Albrecht, Andreas Kraus, and Kurt Reindel (Munich: C. H. Beck'sche Verlagsbuchhandlung, 1969), 143–63.

24. On medieval saints, see among others Ronald C. Finucane, *Miracles and Pilgrims: Popular Beliefs in Medieval England* (London: J. M. Dent & Sons, 1977); Benedicta Ward, *Miracles and the Medieval Mind* (Philadelphia: University of Pennsylvania Press, 1982), chap. 6, 110–26, and passim; Thomas Head, "I Vow Myself To Be Your Servant," *Historical Reflections* 11 (1984), 215–51; Patrick Geary, *Living with the Dead in the Middle Ages* (Ithaca: Cornell University Press, 1994).

25. Charland, *Madame Saincte Anne*, 313. Charland quotes from the French translation published in the nineteenth century by Théodore Hersart de la Villemarque in *Chants populaires de la Bretagne*. He implies that the poem was written before the twelfth century. Ibid., 312.

26. Dörfler-Dierken, *Vorreformatorische Bruderschaften der hl. Anna*. For Saint Anne's Dutch patronages, see Ellen Muller's inventory in Deeleman–van Tyen, "Sint Anna-te-Drieen," 1:35–48. Muller lists two double patronages: "Meppel [Drente]: Anna-en Nicolaas-altaar, -vicarie, gesticht ca 1422 (35); "Zutphen [Gelderland]: Anna- en Nicolaus-vicarie in de Walburgiskerk" (36). Francesca Sautman addresses the theme of Anne as maritime patron in France in "Saint Anne in Folk Tradition," in *Interpreting Cultural Symbols*, ed. Ashley and Sheingorn, 69–94.

27. Monika Zmyslony, *Die Bruderschaften in Lübeck bis zur Reformation* (Kiel: Walter G. Mühlau Verlag, 1977), 88–90. A third Anne brotherhood in Lübeck was associated with the retailers (*Krämer*).

28. Dörfler-Dierken lists fifteen French confraternities in her *Vorreformatorische Bruderschaften der hl. Anna*. Charland's works contain numerous details on Anne's cult in France. See Myra Orth's article "Madame Sainte-Anne: The Holy Kinship, the Royal Trinity, and Louise of

Savoy" (in *Interpreting Cultural Symbols*, ed. Ashley and Sheingorn, 199–228) on political uses of the cult in the uncertain religious climate of early sixteenth-century France.

29. See Nicole Cloutier, "L'Iconographie de Sainte Anne au Québec," 2 vols. (Ph.D. diss., Université de Montréal, 1982).

30. Joseph Braun drew this conclusion about the late thirteenth-century Regensburg work in the Bayerisches Nationalmuseum in Munich in which the two figures are virtually identical apart from size, Anne having the same long braids and youthful appearance as Mary. Joseph Braun, *Tracht und Attribute der Heiligen in der Deutschen Kunst* (Stuttgart: J. B. Metzlersche Verlagsbuchhandlung, 1943), 78.

Chapter 2

1. Siegfried Hofmann, *Goldschmiedearbeiten in und aus Ingolstadt* (Ingolstadt: Stadtmuseum Ingolstadt, 1988), 50.

2. Theodor Müller and Wilhelm Reismüller, *Ingolstadt: Die Herzogsstadt, die Universitätsstadt, die Festung*, vol. 2 (Ingolstadt: Verlag Donau Courier Ingolstadt, 1974), 26, 27.

3. Hofmann, *Goldschmiedearbeiten in und aus Ingolstadt*, 50.

4. Müller and Reismüller, *Ingolstadt*, 1:279.

5. Hofmann, *Goldschmiedearbeiten in und aus Ingolstadt*, 50.

6. Müller and Reismüller, *Ingolstadt*, 1:248, 265; for gifts and endowments, see 256–70. The building of their church in the 1480s did leave them with debts (ibid., 250). But after 1500, references to regular consumption of wine appear along with increasing mentions of ducal visitors (264, 269–72).

7. A 1501 document endowing masses to be said at the Augsburg Carmelite church for Anna Swertzin and her family gives an idea of what was expected of these poor women who lived in endowed homes: "Die Feier ist den Sonntag zuvor im Gotteshaus zu verkündigen und den Seelfrauen in des Hyren Seelhaus anzusagen, deren eine ob dem Grab zu sitzen, zu beten und der kerzen zu warten hat, wofür sie 2 Gross zu 8 Pfenn. erhält; die übrigen drei erhalten für ihre Anwesenheit bei der Feier je 1 Gross und ausserdem erhalten die Seelfrauen 2 Mas Speiswein und 4 Conventsbrot, der Küster der Gotteshauses 1 Gross, den er seinem Knecht zu geben hat," no. 181, 1501, December 10, Matthias Fabri, *Copialbuch* 11, 102b (Stadtarchiv Augsburg, Reichstadt Schätze 95), in Eberhard Schott, "Beiträge zur Geschichte des Carmeliterklosters und der Kirche von St. Anna in Augsburg," *Zeitschrift des Historischen Vereins für Schwaben und Neuburg* 7 (1880), 183. The term *Seelfrau* is sometimes used with other meanings; some sources refer to the sisters of Saint Johannes Gnadenthal as *Seelschwester* and *Seelfrauen* during the period when they were a Franciscan tertiary convent. See Müller and Reismüller, *Ingolstadt*, 1:240–41.

8. Müller and Reismüller, *Ingolstadt*, 1:249.

9. The reliquary had been in the collection of Prince Soltykoff. Hofmann, *Goldschmiedearbeiten in und aus Ingolstadt*, 35.

10. Müller and Reismüller, *Ingolstadt*, 1:243, 265; Franz Xaver Ostermair, *Genealogische Nachrichten über verschiedene theils noch blühende, theils erloschene Geschlechter* (Ingolstadt, 1885), 46.

11. J. Müller, "Ein st. gallischer Josephsverehrer des 15. Jahrhunderts," *Zeitschrift für schweizerische Kirchengeschichte* 3, 3 (1909), 161–74. Two copies of the *Basler Offizium* containing the same annotations by Knüssli exist: one in the Saint Gallen Stiftsbibliothek (Ink. No. 1081c), the other in the Bayerische Staatsbibliothek in Munich (2 Inc. s.a. 657, Hain 8748 1993). Müller dates the Munich copy 1476, as this date appears on it in Knüssli's hand. However, Dörfler-Dierken (referring to Munich 2 Inc. s.a. 657, GWK 1993) notes that "because of the reference to the Konstitution 'Cum praeexcelsa' of 27 February 1476 the Incunabulum must have been printed after this date." Dörfler-Dierken, *Die Verehrung der heiligen Anna*, 281. Müller views the second copy as an attempt to spread the program of devotion. Though Müller

refers to the office as the *Basler Josephsoffizium*, the title of the Munich copy is *Historia tres de S. Anna, de S. Joachim et de S. Joseph*, and it gives at least equal attention to the Holy Kinship. These earliest offices predated Pope Sixtus V's official establishment of Anne's feast in 1478–81.

12. Knüssli had previously been pastor at Herisau. Müller, "Ein st. gallischer Josephsverehrer," 163–64. A document dated June 28, 1475, describes the establishment of the early mass "in praise and honor of: God the almighty, Mary the queen of heaven, Saint Anne her dear mother and all God's saints and angels, and also for the consolation of all believing souls and for the removal of their suffering, and for the gaining and furtherance of eternal joy for living Christian people." Three collects were to be said: "the first that of Our Lady, the others according to his [the celebrating priest's] desire and inclination, the third of Saint Anne and Saint Joachim, our dear Lady's father and mother." St.-A, Urkunde E3–A9, cited in ibid., 162.

13. Ibid., 166.

14. Ibid., 170, citing St.-A. tom. 63a, 198–99. Brotherhoods or confraternities were religious associations for laypeople, dedicated to a patron saint, serving religious and social ends. Their structure varied. Along the north coast—for example, in Lübeck and Hamburg, where they were very numerous—they were usually organized and run by laypeople, often occupation-related, and located in parish churches. Elsewhere they were more likely to be founded by convents or churches, though Dörfler-Dierken's research suggests that lay founders played a significant role in the Rhineland and that here too they were sometimes occupation-related—and sometimes associated with occupations of high social status. Angelika Dörfler-Dierken, "Vorreformatorische Patrozinien der heiligen Anna im Erzbistum Trier," *Archiv für mittelrheinische Kirchengeschichte* 44 (1992), 103–36. In Augsburg, where there were only a few brotherhoods, the Anne confraternity was run by the Carmelite convent, and membership was open to anyone.

15. Müller, "Ein st. gallischer Josephsverehrer des 15. Jahrhunderts," 167, citing St.-A, Urkunde E3–A12; tom. 3, f. 145a.

16. *Johannes Kesslers Sabbata mit kleineren Schriften und Briefen*, ed. Emil Egli and Rudolf Schoch (Saint Gallen: Fehr'sche Buchhandlung, 1902), 312.

17. Ibid., citing St.-A. E4–O2.

18. Ibid., 174, citing Stiftsbibliothek Saint Gallen Inc. 1082, Bl. 8a. Steven Sargent, noting the near absence of the name "Maria" in fifteenth-century Bavaria, seems thus to be correct in suggesting that the growing popularity of the name "Anna" at this time may have "resulted in part from people's desire to venerate Mary by naming girls in honour of her mother." Steven D. Sargent, "Saints' Cults and Naming Patterns in Bavaria, 1400–1600," *Catholic Historical Review* 76 (October 1990), 687.

19. Most if not all of the liturgical texts place considerable emphasis on the Holy Kinship, a feature that is not retained in the new lives. The office entitled *Historia nova pulchra devota et autentica de sancta anna matris dei genitricis marie* (Augsburg: Anton Sorg, 1479) is prefaced by an excerpt that argues against those who maintained that Joseph, Joachim, Maria Jacobi, and Maria Salome, and other Old Testament saints, ought not to be honored in the church. The defence of Anne, her kinship, and their feasts in the face of opposition is a recurring motif in the new texts. A kinship office (incipit "Sciendum sicuti laudare," Hain 8747 BSB 40 Inc s.a. 1029) printed in Switzerland after 1482 defends Joseph and Joachim against those who say they are not canonized by reference to a bull of Sixtus IV dated October 3, 1482, which makes reference to relics of Joachim in the Monastery of Saint Gall.

20. A mention of such an earlier office occurs in a Kitzingen endowment document of 1434 in a reference to the celebration of a feast of Saint Anne: "our dear lady's mother's day, which is annually celebrated on the day after Saint James the Greater, with the present office of Saint Anne,

singing and celebrating vespers and matins in the evening, and mass in the morning." Staatsarchiv Würzburg wu 42/131a, cited in Ludwig Remling, *Bruderschaften in Franken* (Würzburg: Kommissionsverlag Ferdinand Schöningh, 1986), 268.

21. Dörfler-Dierken, *Die Verehrung der heiligen Anna*, 147–53, 284. Brandenbarg raises the possibility in *Heilig familieleven* (119–22) and argues it with some force in "Saint Anne: A Holy Grandmother and Her Children" (in *Sanctity and Motherhood*, ed. Anneke B. Mulder-Bakker, 44–45). See also Brandenbarg, "Jan van Denemarken en Pieter Dorlant over de maagschap van de heilige moeder Anna / een veergelijkende studie," *Ons Geestelijk Erf*, parts 63 and 64 (June–December 1989, March–September 1990), 85–128.

22. *Historia nova pulchra devota et autentica de sancta anna: Das alte Regensburger Office in Liber missalis secundum chorum ecclesiae maioris* (Regensburg, 1479), excerpts in Joseph Seitz, *Die Verehrung des hl. Joseph in ihrer geschichtlichen Entwicklung bis zum Konzil von Trient dargestellt* (Freiburg im Breisgau: Herdersche Verlagshandlung, 1908), esp. 340–55.

23. Trithemius singles out the Carmelites as particular devotees of Anne in his treatise on Saint Anne. Johannes Trithemius, *De laudibus sanctissimae matris Annae* (Mainz: Peter Friedberg, 1494), chap. 12. Carmelite associations with Anne predate the fifteenth century. In 1374, John of Hildesheim stated that the order's first house was at the Golden Gate. Ioannes de Hildesheim, *Dialogus inter directorem et detractorem de ordine Carmelitarum*, 14, ed. Adrianus Staring, *Medieval Carmelite Heritage: Early Reflections on the Nature of the Order* (Rome: Institutum Carmelitanum, 1989), 374. I am indebted to Paul Chandler, O.Carm. for these references.

24. The older type of narrative continued to appear in accounts of the life of Christ, such as the German version of Ludolf of Saxony's *Vita Christi, Von der kinthait unnsers herren iesu cristi genant vita christi*, as well as in more specialized works like the late fifteenth-century *Der Sündenfall* of Arnold Immessen. Arnold Immessen, *Der*

Sündenfall, ed. Friedrich Krage (Heidelberg: Carl Winters Universitäts-Buchhandlung, 1913), 213–20.

25. Deposed as abbot of Sponheim in 1506, Trithemius had to leave his magnificent library behind when he moved to the monastery of Saint Jakob in Würzburg.

26. His *Compendium* on the origins of the Franks, the *Miracula beatae Mariae semper virginis in Ecclesia nova prope Dittelbach* (1511), and the *De laudibus et miraculis beatae Mariae in Urticeto factis* (1514–15), are in Joannis Trithemii, *Opera pia et spiritualia*, ed. Johannes Busaeus (Mainz, 1604, 1605). On Trithemius's life and publications, see Klaus Arnold's *Johannes Trithemius, 1462–1516, Quellen und Forschungen zur Geschichte des Bistums und Hochstifts Würzburg 23* (Würzburg: Kommissionsverlag Ferdinand Schöningh, 1991); see also Noel Brann, *The Abbott Trithemius, 1462–1516: The Renaissance of Monastic Humanism* (Leiden: E. J. Brill, 1981), and Ioan Couliano, *Eros and Magic in the Renaissance* (Chicago: University of Chicago Press, 1987).

27. Johannes Trithemius, *De laudibus*, chap. 13.

28. Poems in Anne's honor by Konrad Celtis, Theodore [Dietrich] Gresemund, Jodocus Badius Ascensius [Gandensis], Jodocus Beissellius, Rutger Sicamber von Venray, Rudolf von Langen, Adam Werner von Themar, Johannes Herbst, and Rudolf Agricola were published with the *De laudibus* and in other Anne texts. Agricola, elder statesman of the German humanists, had earlier, in the 1840s, written a long ex-voto poem to Saint Anne in gratitude for healing. Rudolf Agricola, "Anna Mater," *Opuscula, orationes, epistolae* (1539; reprint, Frankfurt, 1975), 297–306. Petrus Dorlandus wrote two lives of Anne, the *Historia perpulchra de anna sanctissima* (Antwerp: Govert Back, ca. 1498), which also exists in manuscript form as *Vita Beatissimae Matris Annae edita a venerabili et erudito Pater Petro Dorlando* (Cologne, Historisches Archiv, ms G.B40 197), and *Die historie van Sint-Anna* (Antwerp: Govert Back, 1501). The latter was translated into Latin as the *Vita gloriosissime matris Annae christipare virginis Marie genetricis ab ascensio in compendium redacta*

ex historia suavissima eiusdem matris Anne ab religiosissimo viro F. dorlando ordinis Carthusiensis in zelem
theuthonice prius edita and printed with the *Vita
Jhesu Christi* of Ludolf of Saxony, first in Paris in
1502. In collaboration with Dominicus van
Gelre, Dorlandus published the *Legenda sanctae
Annae,* a life of Anne by an anonymous Franciscan, which enjoyed great popularity in Germany.
It was published in Louvain in 1496, in Leipzig
in 1497, 1502, 1507, and 1517, and under the title
Quedam rara Legenda de sancta Anna in Strasburg
in 1511. See Brandenbarg, *Heilig familieleven,*
279–81. It also appears under the title *Hec est
quedam rara et ideo cara legenda de sanctam Anna et
de universa eius.* The Dutch secular priest Jan van
Denemarken, who was not a member of the
humanist circles, wrote a life of the same type,
*Die historie, die ghetiden ende die exempelen vander
heyligher vrouwen sint Annen,* first published by
Geraert Leeu in Antwerp in 1490–91. The various editions of lives and offices are not always
identical. Others involved in Trithemius's circle
were the Frankfurt Carmelite prior Rumold
Laupach, the Dominican Dominicus van Gelre,
the humanists Judocus Beisselius, Wouter Bor,
Konrad Celtis, Johannes Oudewater, the canon
of Saint Goedele in Brussels, Robert Gaguin,
Jodocus Badius, Johannes von Lambsheym, and
Jakob Wimpfeling. Trithemius wrote other
works on Anne, among them, in 1494 an elegiac
poem, in 1495 the no longer extant *Miracula s.
Annae,* in 1499 a rosary and other prayers to Saint
Anne for Cardinal Raymund Peraudi, and in
1500 a sequence for the Koblenz Anne confraternity and another for the Augsburg Carmelite
prior Johannes von Stark. See Arnold, *Johannes
Trithemius,* and Brandenbarg, *Heilig Familie.*

29. Brandenbarg, *Heilig familieleven,* 107.

30. Philippe de Vigneulles, *Gedenkbuch des
Metzer Bürgers Philippe von Vigneulles aus den Jahren
1471 bis 1522,* Bibliothek des Litterarischen Vereins
in Stuttgart 24, 1851), ed. Heinrich Michelant
(Amsterdam: Editions Rodopi, 1968), 179.

31. Ibid.

32. Ibid., 180.

33. Erwin Gatz, "Die Annaverhrung bis zum
Ende 18. Jahrhunderts," in *St.-Anna in Düren,* ed.
Erwin Gatz (Mönchengladbach: B. Kühlen
Verlag, 1972), 161.

34. Heinrich Appel, "Annareliquiar und
Annaschatz," in *St.-Anna in Düren,* ed. Gatz,
114–18.

35. For the official contemporary and near-
contemporary accounts of the acquisition of the
Düren relic, see Jos Habets, "Chronijck der landen
van Overmaas en der aangrenzende gewesten,
door eenen inwoner van Beek bij Maastricht," in
*Publications de la Société Historique et Archéologique
dans le duché de Limbourg à Maestricht* 7 (Ruhrmond, 1870), 101–8; *St.-Anna in Düren,* ed. Gatz;
Jacobus Polius, *Exegeticon historicum sanctae Annae
aviae Christi, magnae matris Deiparae, necnon sacri
capitis ejusdem marcoduram translati* (Cologne,
1640).

36. Erwin Gatz, "Die Dürener Annaverehrung bis zum Ende des 18. Jahrhunderts," in *St.-
Anna in Düren,* ed. Gatz, 163ff.

37. Ibid., 167ff. A German translation of the
bull appears in *500 Jahre St. Anna in Düren, 1501–
2001* (Düren: Hahne-Schloemer Verlag, n.d.),
29–34.

38. De Vigneulles, *Gedenkbuch,* 179.

39. Ibid., 176.

40. Ibid., 184.

41. Ibid., 180–81.

42. The first documented reference is from
1511; the convent showed no previous evidence of
special devotion to Anne. Angelika Dörfler-
Dierken, "Wunderheilungen durch das Limburger Annenheiltum / Mit Edition einer
Abschrift des Mirakelbuches von 1511 in der
Stadtbibliothek Trier," *Kurtrierisches Jahrbuch* 31
(1991), 83–107. At Limburg, as at most other
healing shrines, pilgrims normally came in
consequence of a vow to make a pilgrimage if
the requested cure was granted. Once at the
shrine, they were touched by the relic or they
drank special water.

43. Martin Luther, *Werke: Kritische Gesamtausgabe* (Weimar, 1883–1948), 47, 383. Hereafter, WA.

44. Martin Luther, *Tischreden* (Weimar, 1883–1948), 4, 440. Luther may have chosen Anne to appeal to because of her reputation as a disperser of storms.

45. "Ipsa [Anna] pene supra quam B. Virgo extollitur." Luther, "Decem praecepta Wittenbergensi praedicta populo, 1518," WA 1, 415.

46. Luther, WA 47, 581, and again in WA 45, 528–29.

Chapter 3

1. Of 231 confirmed late medieval Saint Anne brotherhoods, all but about a dozen make their first appearances in sources dating from 1479 or later. Dörfler-Dierken, *Vorreformatorische Bruderschaften der hl. Anna*, 182–87.

2. On Icelandic translations of German lives, see Marianne E. Kalinke, "Mariu saga og Onnu," *Arkiv för Nordisk Filologi* 109 (1994); *The Book of Reykjaholar: The Last of the Great Medieval Legendaries* (Toronto: University of Toronto Press, 1996).

3. Valerius Anshelmus, *Berner Chronik von Anfang der Stadt Bern bis 1526*, vol. 3 (Bern: L. A. Haller, 1825, 1827), 252. Anne's name also came readily to the lips of the notorious fraudulent pseudo-mystic Anna Laminit when she visited Augsburg in 1513 with her claims to live without eating. According to Wilhelm Rem, "Annalin Lamenittlin" maintained she had not eaten or drunk for fourteen or sixteen years, and "gave out that Saint Anne had talked with her and Augsburg would perish if pious people did not come forth with their prayers." Wilhelm Rem, "Ain cronica alter und neuer geschichten," *Die Chroniken der deutschen Städte vom 14. bis ins 16. Jahrhundert. Chroniken der schwäbischen Städte. Augsburg*, vol. 5, ed. Karl von Hegel and Friedrich Roth (Leipzig: Verlag von S. Hirzel, 1866), 11. On Laminit, see F. Roth, "Die geistliche Betrügerin Anna Laminit von Augsburg," *Zeitschrift für Kirchengeschichte* 43 (1924), 355–417.

4. Though many studies have noted that salvation played a role in Anne's cult, only Schaumkell calls attention to the fact that her wide range of powers included the ability to help in the hour of death: "Like Mary, she stepped into the place of the vanquisher of death, Jesus Christ." E. Schaumkell, *Der Kultus der heiligen Anna*, 67–74. Further, "Her dominant position in the religious consciousness of that time she owed not merely to the circumstance . . . that she was the grandmother of saints . . . on the contrary above all things she was held in such high honor because she stood in such close connection with the work of salvation." Ibid., 71.

5. Anne has no salvational power in the older German collections of saints' lives: *Der Heiligen Leben* of ca. 1400 (vol. 1: Der Sommerteil, ed. Margit Brand, Kristina Freienhagen-Baumgardt, Ruth Meyer, and Werner Williams-Krapp [Tübingen: Max Niemeyer Verlag, 1996], and *Die elsässische Legenda Aurea*, ed. Werner Williams-Krapp [Tübingen, 1983]).

6. The twelfth-century English Augustinian Osbert of Clare of Suffolk gave Anne a place in the scheme of redemption and honored her for her link with the Savior: "since through the fruit of her womb God sent redemption to his people." But he does not conclude that Anne acquires power through her links with Mary and Jesus. Osbert of Clare, "Le Sermon sur Sainte Anne," in André Wilmart, "Les Compositions d'Osbert de Clare en l'honneur de sainte Anne," 272.

7. In a fifteenth-century rhymed office, we find: "Hail, Anne, holy mother / Through you comes the way of life, / From you comes the door of heaven, / Through which the true light is arisen / Through this door make us go / And at God arrive." Guido Maria Dreves and Clemens Blume, *Analecta hymnica medii aevi*, 55 vols. (1888; reprint, Frankfurt am Main: Minerva, 1961), 5:112. These short rhymed offices and Latin liturgical hymns to Saint Anne, which appear primarily in manuscript sources, often monastic, of the thirteenth, fourteenth, fifteenth, and even early sixteenth centuries, seem to represent a separate

line of descent from the body of late medieval
Anne texts discussed in this book. Typically they
praise Anne, her illustrious ancestry, and her role
as the source of Mary and Jesus (but they do not
mention the *Trinubium*) and they associate her with
the successful achievement of heaven—but without
ascribing power to her. For examples, see Dreves,
e.g., 4:78, 79; 5:106–21; Franz Joseph Mone, *Lateinische Hymnen des Mittelalters*, 3 vols. (1853–55; reprint,
Aalen: Scientia Verlag, 1964), vol. 3, nos. 801, 197;
and Philipp Wackernagel, *Das Deutsche Kirchenlied von der ältesten Zeit bis zu Anfang des XVII
Jahrhunderts*, 5 vols. (1864–77; reprint, Hildesheim:
Georg Olms Verlagsbuchhandlung, 1964).

8. "Chronik des Burkard Zink," *Die Chroniken
der deutschen Städte vom 14. Bis ins 16. Jahrhundert.
Die Chroniken der schwäbischen Städte. Augsburg*, 2,
ed. Karl von Hegel and Friedrich Roth (Leipzig:
S. Hirzel Verlag, 1866), 45.

9. Martin Luther, "Ein Sermon vom Sakrament des Leichnams Christi u. von den Brüder-
schaften, 1519," WA 2, 754–55.

10. Ibid., 756.

11. Aufnahmeformular der Saint Annen-
bruderschaft in Augsburg vom Jahre 1494
(Augsburg: Erhard Ratdolt, 1499) at Augsburg
Staats und Stadtbibliothek. The document is
published in A. Haemmerle, "Das Aufnahmefor-
mular der St. Annenbrüder in Augsburg vom
Jahre 1494," *Vierteljahreshefte zur Kunst und
Geschichte Augsburgs* 4 (1947–48), 9.

12. Ibid.

13. *Ain gar nutzlichs büchlin von dem gantzen
geschlecht sant Anna vnd von sant Anna lobliche
brüderschafft. Vnnd von etlichen grossen wunderzaichen
sant Anna* (Augsburg, after 1494).

14. "Dit is sint Anna Cransken," in *De gulden
Letanien* (Antwerp: Heinrich Wouters, 1575), 1r.

15. *Das Leben und Wunderzaichen der allerseeligisten Frawen Annae* (Munich: Cornelius
Leyffert, 1627) (a translation of an anonymous
Franciscan's *Legenda sanctae Annae* [Louvain: Joh.
de Westfalia, 1496], 71; the *Legenda sanctae Annae*
was reprinted eight times in Leipzig alone.)

16. Quatrains on a woodcut of the *Anna
Selbdritt* by the Nuremberg artist Wolf Traut
link the same ideas: "O sacred propagation, from
you has been begotten / Anna, she from whom
the redemption of all has sprung" ("O sacra
propagacio. ex vobis procreata / Anna. de quae
redempcio est omnis emanata"). Published by
Valentinus Bannholtzer, 1507. Max Geisberg,
The German Single-Leaf Woodcut: 1500–1550, ed.
Walter L. Strauss (New York: Hacker Art
Books, 1974), 4, fig. 1362.

17. *Ain gar nutzlichs büchlin*. The image of
releasing the soul from the power of evil is also
found in some late medieval Marian prayers: "O
thou all-holy bride of the most high, console and
release me from the death of sin and obtain for
me the life of nature, of grace and of eternal
glory" (O du allerhailigste praut des allerober-
sten trosts erloess mich von dem todt der sünde
vnd erwirb mir das leben der nature der gnaden
vnnd der ewigen glori). *Der Gilgengart* (Augsburg: Hans Schönsperger, ca. 1520), in *Spatmitte-
lalter Humanismus Reformation: Texte und Zeugnisse*,
ed. Hedwig Heger (Munich: C. H. Beck'sche
Verlagsbuchhandlung, 1975).

18. *Libellus continens laudes et fraternitatum,
Officiam misse et oraciones de sancta Anna* (Heidelberg: Heinrich Knoblochtzer, probably after
1500).

19. *Historia nova pulchra devota et autentica de
sancta anna.*

20. In *Vita gloriosissime matris Annae christipare virginis Marie genitricis ab ascensio in compendium redacta ex historia suavissima eiusdem matris
Anne ab religiosissimo viro F. dorlando ordinis
Carthusiensis in zelem theuthonice prius edita*
(published with the *Vita Jesu Christi* of Ludolph
of Saxony) (Antwerp: Johannus Kerberg), 767.
According to Brandenbarg, this text is a translation and reworking of Petrus Dorlandus's *Die
historie van Sint-Anna* by the humanist Judocus
Badius. Brandenbarg, *Heilig Familieleven*, 284–85.
The "Rosarium" was also published in the *De
laudibus* and in other texts.

21. Johannes von Lambsheym, *Oraciones et alia pulcra ad sanctam Annam* (Heidelberg: Heinrich Knoblochtzer, n.d.).

22. Trithemius, *De laudibus.*

23. "Copia Babstlicher Bullenn das Jubeljahr vnnd sant Annen Brüderschafft belangende," in Adam Daniel Richter, *Chronica der im Meissnis-chen Ober-Erz-Gebürge gelegenen Königl. Churfl. Sächssischen freyen Berg-Stadt St. Annaberg* (Annaberg: August Valentin Friesen, 1746), 70.

24. *Ain gar nutzlichs büchlin.*

25. *Die wunderbare Meerfahrt des heiligen Brandan* (Augsburg: Anton Sorg, c. 1476). Nor are special powers ascribed to the Three Kings in *Die Hystori oder Legend von den Heiligen Dryen Koenigen. Faksimileausgabe eines Pilgerbuches von 1520 mit einem Verzeichnis der Drucke der Servatius Kruffter in Köln,* ed. Elisbeth Christern (Cologne: Bibliophilen-Gesellschaft, 1964). And the same is true of *Das leben verdienen und wunderwerck der hailigen Auspurger Bistumbs bischoffen sant Ulrichs vnd Symprechts auch der säligen martrerin sant Aphre irer müter Hilaria geschlecht vnd gesellschafft in unserm daselbst loblichen gotshaus rastend* (Augsburg, 1516).

26. Petrus Dorlandus, *De Nativitate Conver-sione & vita invictissimae martiris beatissimae virginis Katharinae* (Louvain: Theodericus Martinus Alostensis, 1513).

27. Kieckhefer continues: "Inward disposi-tion of the heart was not decisive; what counted most was the correct observance of outward forms." Richard Kieckhefer, *Magic in the Middle Ages* (New York: Cambridge University Press, 1989), 165.

28. Bernd Moeller, "Piety in Germany Around 1500," in *The Reformation in Medieval Perspective,* ed. Steven Ozment (Chicago: Quadrangle Books, 1971), 55.

29. Rolf Kiessling, speaking about the quan-titative aspect of these endowments, remarks: "Not only one such endowment was made, but several, for the more that was expended, the greater was the salvational value." Rolf Kiessling, *Bürgerliche Gesellschaft und Kirche in Augsburg im*

Spätmittelalter (Augsburg: Verlag H. Mühlberger, 1971), 247. Monika Zmyslony's study of Lubeck's brotherhoods speaks of the salvational function of charitable bequests: "The charitable activity of the spiritual brotherhoods belonged part and parcel to the religious sphere. Along with the ensuring of salvation through various churchly functions and endowments, care of the poor was added as a further means of rescue from the purgatorial fires." Zmyslony, *Die Bruderschaften in Lübeck,* 127–38.

30. *Niklaus Manuels Spiel evangelischer Freiheit: Die Totenfresser, "Vom Papst und seiner Priesterschaft"* (Leipzig: Ferdinand Vetter, 1523), 7–9, trans. from Steven E. Ozment, *The Reformation in the Cities* (1975; reprint, New Haven: Yale University Press, 1980), 113.

31. Charles A. Garside Jr., *Zwingli and the Arts* (New Haven: Yale University Press, 1966), 83–84. Thomas Tentler argues that consolation and provocation of guilt are related: "Sacramental confession was designed to cause guilt as well as cure guilt." Thomas Tentler, *Sin and Confession on the Eve of the Reformation* (Princeton: Princeton University Press, 1977), xiii; see also the section "Sorrow and the Keys," 223–301. Steven Ozment observes that one popular catechetical book, Dietrich Coelde's *The Mirror of Christian Faith* (1520), included "prescriptions for religious secu-rity" in the form of "a seemingly endless routine of self-examination and criticism" yet still assumed a final uncertainty. Ozment, *The Reformation in the Cities,* 31–32.

32. Heiko Oberman, *The Harvest of Medieval Theology: Gabriel Biel and Late Medieval Nominalism* (Cambridge, Mass.: Harvard University Press, 1963), 184. With respect to predestination, Biel believed: "Even if one could be certain of pos-sessing grace in the present, it would not neces-sarily follow that this would be true tomorrow or on the decisive last day of life. . . . For two reasons therefore certitude of salvation is beyond the reach of the viator: there is no way in which he can ascertain that he possesses the habit of grace; and furthermore, even if everything points

to his being in a state of grace, this may very well be only according to present justice which by no means implies his perseverance to the end." Ibid., 220.

33. Whereas German documents often specify that the masses are to continue forever, English wills tend to stipulate relatively short periods of time, or to state that masses are to be said for as long as the money holds out. It should be noted though that the absence of *perpetual* bequests in England is probably at least partly the result of English laws prohibiting or limiting bequests in *mortmain*. Though bequests for requiem services seem to have increased in Italy in the late Middle Ages, becoming after 1350 a major source of confraternity income according to Charles de la Roncière ("Les Confrèrieres à Florence et dans son Contado," *Le Mouvement Confraternel au Moyen Age, France, Italie, Suisse: Actes de la table ronde organisée par l'université de Lausanne, 1985* [Geneva: Librairie Droz, 1987], 320, 337), Italian confraternity documents leave the impression that salvation did not occupy the same place in the thoughts of fifteenth-century Italians as it did in those of fifteenth-century Germans. Ronald Weissman's study of Florentine confraternities suggests a relatively low level of anxiety about salvation. In contrast to the situation in Germany, where Christians were encouraged to worry about their salvation, the Italian confraternities, according to Weissman, offered a manageable program to achieve it in the form of a list of prescribed devotional tasks that "provided the confraternity members with a sense of religion and religious obligation that was within his ability to grasp and to fulfill." Ronald Weissman, *Ritual Brotherhood in Renaissance Florence* (New York: Academic Press, 1982), 79. See also Nicholas Terpstra, "Death and Dying in Renaissance Confraternities," *Crossing the Boundaries: Christian Piety and the Arts in Italian Medieval and Renaissance Confraternities*, ed. Konrad Eisenbichler, Medieval Institute Publications, Early Drama, Art, and Music Monograph Series 15 (Kalamazoo: Western Michigan University, 1991), 183–92. Lionel Rothkrug

comments that Marsilius of Padua (1277–1342) located civic virtue in a vision of communal immortality, creating "a vision of corporate or civic immortality free of all expiatory obligation, . . . an urban ideal that was destined to have a long life." Lionel Rothkrug, "Religious Practices and Collective Perceptions: Hidden Homologies in the Renaissance and Reformation," *Historical Reflections* 7 (Spring 1980), 161.

34. An examination of some statistics on endowments of masses and chantries, and of the findings of some historians who have examined English sources, suggests that the peak of attention to the ensuring of salvation through ritual actions had already passed by the late 1400s in England. Joel Rosenthal's study of the salvation-related chantries and bequests of the nobility in fourteenth-century England finds a "steady and significant increase in such acts as alienations in mortmain [for the purpose of funding such enterprises]" in the first half of the fourteenth century, with a decline setting in almost immediately after the plague, with in general a decline in the overall number of families within the peerage and a decline in the amount of activity per family after 1350. Joel Rosenthal, *The Purchase of Paradise: Gift-Giving and the Aristocracy, 1307–1485* (London: Routledge & Kegan Paul, 1972), 127. A breakdown of Rosenthal's figures, which cover the years 1307–1485, reveals that the highest activity, 3.62 grants per year, was in the period 1327–48, with a sharp decline immediately after to 1.86 per year, following which the number declined steadily downward—apart from a few fluctuations—to a figure of 1.16 for the period 1460–85. As well English devotional texts consistently present salvation as a matter of personal repentance and redemption, whereas the German ones place heavy emphasis on the help that could be obtained through powerful persons and rituals. For details on the complexities involved in the foundation charters for posthumous masses to be said by the Augsburg Franciscans, see "Augsburg Franziskaner-Konventualen," in *Bavaria Franziskana Antiqua* 5 (1961), 390, 392.

35. *The Golden Legend; or, Lives of the Saints as Englished by William Caxton* (London: J. M. Dent & Co., 1900), 2:126–28. The story of Bishop Elsinus was originally connected with the feast of the conception of Mary. See *Cursor Mundi: A Northumbrian Poem of the xivth Century*, part 2, ed. Richard Morris, Early English Text Society (hereafter, EETS) (1875; reprint, New York: Oxford University Press, 1966), 21. On the motif of the death of bishops who hinder their flocks from honoring saints, see Stephen Wilson, ed., *Saints and Their Cults: Studies in Religious Sociology, Folklore, and History* (New York: Cambridge University Press, 1983).

36. *Das Leben und Wunderzaichen*, 78. The virgin is Saint Colette.

37. Translated from Brandenbarg's citation of the text, published in Heinrich Hubert Koch, *Das Karmeliterkloster zu Frankfurt am Main: 13. bis 16. Jahrhundert* (Frankfurt, 1912), 80–90.

38. Allusions to cult practice further underline the importance of honoring all three figures together in devotional rituals. The office *Libellus continens laudes* speaks of the three personages being honored with three candles: "Some people also, devotees of Anne, in honor of Jesus, Mary, and Anne, are accustomed each Tuesday at her altar or in front of her image, to light three candles and to give alms three times" (Non nulli etiam anne cultores ad honorem iesu marie & anne omni feria tercia in eius altari seu ante ipsius ymaginem. tres solent incendere candelas & tres facere elemosinas).

39. "Si laudandus est dominus in sanctis suis, quanto magis in sanctissimis suis parentibus." *Legenda sanctae Annae* (Leipzig: Melchior Lotter, 1497). The phrase appears earlier in several of the offices, and Trithemius repeats the idea in the *De laudibus*, chap. 1.

40. *Das Leben und Wunderzaichen*, 100.

41. For the growing tendency to ascribe holiness to the relatives of saints in late medieval Germany, see Ortrud Reber, *Die Gestaltung des Kultes weiblicher Heiliger im Spätmittelalter / Die*

Verehrung der Heiligen Elisabeth, Klara, Hedwig, und Birgitta (Hersbruck: Kommissionsverlag, Karl Pfeiffer's Buchdruckerei & Verlag, 1963), 154.

42. For a description of some of these large collections, see Erich Egg, "Stiftungen-Heiltum-Ablässe," in *Heiltum und Wallfahrt*, ed. Gert Ammann, esp. 61–77 (Innsbruck: Tiroler Landesmuseum Ferdinandeum, 1988).

43. "Ich hab auch gelesen das etlich menschen habent all tag geeret sant anna und alles ires seligen geschlecht mit v pater noster und mit v ave maria. und do dise menschen solten sterben do ist sant anna mit allen iren seligen geschlecht kumen zu irem end. vnd haben in umb got erworben ain seligs end." *Ain gar nutzliches büchlin*.

44. Reber, *Die Gestaltung des Kultes weiblicher Heiliger*, 143. If a saint were not of royal birth, the hagiographer might elevate her, as did Johannes Frank when in the 1450s he referred to his city Augsburg's nonroyal patron Afra as "die hailig künigin und martrerin sant Affra mit aller irer geselschafft." Frank's description also emphasizes Afra's position as part of a group of holy people. "Johannes Franks Augsburger Annalen," in *Die Chroniken*.

45. In the Augsburg life, Anne is descended through Emerentia from the royal line of David and the priestly line of Aaron. All three of her husbands are of the House of David. *Ain gar nutzlichs büchlin*.

46. *Historia nova pulchra devota et autentica de sancta anna*.

47. *Hystoria pulcra de sancto Joachim patre dei matris Marie* (Augsburg: Anton Sorg).

48. Esser, "Die Heilige Sippe," 8.

Chapter 4

1. Miriam Usher Chrisman, *Lay Culture, Learned Culture: Books and Social Change in Strasbourg, 1480–1599* (New Haven: Yale University Press, 1981), 114. Hans-Jörg Kunast, *Getruckt zu Augspurg: Buchdruck und Buchhandel in Augsburg zwischen 1468 und 1555* (Tübingen: Max Niemeyer Verlag,

1997), 13. Augsburg was a center for late medieval vernacular printing, and saints' lives made up about 31.2 percent of this output, with fables and stories at 18 percent, history at 17.2 percent, moral tracts at 14.2 percent, school texts at 5.7 percent, poetry and satire at 4 percent, and journalistic works at 3.9 percent. Kunast, *Getruckt zu Augsburg,* 240–41.

2. Exceptions include the altarpiece of the Frankfurt Carmelites' Anne brotherhood in the Historisches Museum, Frankfurt (illustrated in Brandenbarg, *Heilig Familieleven,* 75–79, 92, 96); the *Legend of Saint Anne* in the museum of the Saint Salvator church in Bruges (ibid., 137); and the altarpiece painted for the canons of Saint Goedele in Brussels, where Johannes Oudewater was part of a humanist circle propagating devotion to Anne (ibid., 139).

3. Occasional iconographic references to salvation occur in *Anna Selbdritts.* Joanna Wolska-Wierusz discusses the cross-like formation in the woodwork of the bench found in some *Anna Selbdritts* (Joanna Wolska-Wierusz, "Adventus Salvatoris i altarskapet fran Hägerstad," *Fornvännen* 88 [1993], 9–25). Though not common, these cross motifs (sometimes combined with the Christ Child's outstretched arms), which are also found in Late Gothic Marian imagery (fig. 8), occur often enough that they can be considered intentional. For examples in Anne works, see Brandenbarg et al., *Heilige Anna, Grote Moeder,* 12, 54, 112.

4. For Mary's compassion in art, see Barbara Lane, *The Altar and the Altarpiece: Sacramental Themes in Early Netherlandish Painting* (New York: Harper & Row, 1984), 86, and Otto Georg Von Simson, "Compassio and Co-Redemptio in Rogier van der Weyden's *Descent from the Cross,*" *Art Bulletin* 35 (1953), 9–16.

5. Heiko Oberman, *The Harvest of Medieval Theology: Gabriel Biel and Late Medieval Nominalism* (Cambridge, Mass.: Harvard University Press, 1963), esp. 295ff. These ideas did not originate with Biel. The fourteenth-century Rhineland mystic Johannes Tauler, though he calls Mary mediatrix rather than co-redemptrix, assigned her a place in the salvational process: "As the heavenly Father offered his only Son, the living Host, on the altar of the cross, and still offers him daily in the sacrament for the salvation of men, so that he might be the perpetual intercessor between him and men; so he permitted his chosen Daughter, the most Blessed Virgin Mary, to suffer severely, and he received her oblation as an agreeable sacrifice for the advantage and salvation of the whole human race, so that she herself might be a mediatrix between God and men." *Exercita seu meditatio Optima Vitae et Passionis Jesu-Christi,* chap. 18, in Johannes Tauler, *Oeuvres complètes* 6, *Exercises ou méditations sur la vie et la Passion de Jésus-Christ,* ed. E.-P. Noel (Paris, 1912), 253ff., cited in Lane, *The Altar and the Altarpiece,* 86.

6. Among the Italian *metterze* that do show linking are G. Francesco Caroto's *Virgin and Child with Saints* (sixteenth century) in the Church of S. Fermo Maggiore in Verona; Luca Tomé's painting in the Accademia in Siena (reproduced in Ludwig Heinrich Heydenreich, "Le Saint Anne de Léonard de Vinci," *Gazette des Beaux-Arts* 10 [1933], 212); and the Benozzo Gozzoli *Sainte Anne, the Virgin, and Child* in the Museo Civico in Pisa (ibid., 211). An Italian work that follows the German model, the Saint Anne Altar dedicated in 1512 in the Church of Sant'Agostino in Rome, was commissioned by a German, the Trier humanist Johann Goritz, for his burial chapel. Here textual, contextual, and iconographic details combine to present a salvational message; however, Anne's salvational role is purely intercessory. The composition is an atypical version of the close Rhineland bench type in which Mary is smaller than Anne. See Virginia Anne Bonito, "The Saint Anne Altar in Sant'Agostino: A New Discovery," *Burlington Magazine* 122, 933 (December 1980), 805–11; and "The Saint Anne Altar in Sant'Agostino: Restoration and Interpretation," *Burlington Magazine* 124, 950 (May 1982), 268–76.

7. The letter is in A. Luzio, *I precettori di Isabella d'Este* (Ancona, 1887), 32 n. 1, in Peter Burke, *The Italian Renaissance: Culture and Society*

in Italy (1972; reprint, Princeton: Princeton University Press, 1986), 170.

8. "VERGINE: O Pilato, non fare lo figlio mio tormentare: / ch'io te posso mostrare como a torto è accusato. TURBA: Crucifige, crucifige! Omo che se fa rege, / secondo nostra lege, contradice al senato. VERGINE: Priego che m'entendàti, nel mio dolor pensàti: / forsa mò ve mutati da quel ch'avete pensato." Iacopone da Todi, "Pianto de la madonna de la passione del figliolo Iesu Cristo," *The Penguin Book of Italian Verse*, ed. George R. Kay (1958; reprint, Harmondsworth: Penguin Books, 1972), 8–13.

9. This is the picture of Florentine piety that emerges in Ronald Weissman, *Ritual Brotherhood in Renaissance Florence* (New York: Academic Press, 1982), and Richard Trexler, *Public Life in Renaissance Florence* (New York: Academic Press, 1980). On Anne's role as a civic patron associated with political liberty, see Roger J. Crum and David G. Wilkins, "In the Defense of Florentine Republicanism: Saint Anne and Florentine Art, 1343–1575," in *Interpreting Cultural Symbols*, ed. Ashley and Sheingorn (Athens: University of Georgia Press, 1990), 131–68.

10. See *The Middle English Stanzaic Versions of the Life of Saint Anne*, ed. Roscoe E. Parker, EETS, o.s. (New York: Oxford University Press, 1928); Osbern Bokenham, *Legendys of Hooly Wummen*, ed. Mary S. Serjeantson, EETS, o.s. (1938; reprint, Millwood, N.Y.: Kraus Reprint, 1971); *Cursor Mundi: A Northumbrian Poem of the XIVth Century*, part 2, ed. Richard Morris, EETS, o.s. (1875; reprint, London: Richard Clay, 1966), 75, 76; *The Early South-English Legendary*, ed. Carl Horstmann, EETS, o.s. (London: Trübner, 1887); *Ludus coventriae*, ed. K. S. Block, EETS, e.s. (1922; reprint, London: Oxford University Press, 1974).

11. *Mirk's Festial: A Collection of Homilies*, ed. Theodor Erbe, EETS, e.s. (1905; reprint, Millwood, N.Y.: Kraus Reprint, 1987), 216.

12. Van Denemarken's salvational allusions consist largely of half a dozen appearances of a prayer that requests Anne's help in our need "now and in the hour of our death."

13. E. Muller and W. Deeleman–van-Tyen list fewer than twenty late medieval Dutch brotherhoods dedicated to Anne (some of them of uncertain identification) in *Handleiding bij de kaarten over de verspreiding van de Annadevotie in Nederland tot 1800*, in Brandenbarg et al., *Heilige Anna, Groete Moeder*, 91. Only one Anne relic is recorded for Holland, in Maastricht. Ibid. Nine Dutch brotherhoods (eight without source documentation) are included in Dörfler-Diercken, *Vorreformatorische Bruderschaften der hl. Anna*.

Chapter 5

1. Anne Winston-Allen, *Stories of the Rose: The Making of the Rosary in the Middle Ages* (University Park: The Pennsylvania State University Press, 1997); Carol Schuler, "The Seven Sorrows of the Virgin," *Simiolus* 21, 1/2 (1992), 5–28.

2. Winston-Allen, *Stories of the Rose*, 120.

3. "The miracles attributed to the Virgin of Seven Sorrows provide evidence that many worshippers were primarily motivated by the belief in the salutary benefits of venerating the Virgin's sorrows, if not also in the apotropaic powers of the corresponding images." Schuler, "The Seven Sorrows," 28. For indulgences and other salvational aspects of the cult, see ibid., 14–13.

4. Arnold Bostius tried to incorporate Anne and Joachim in the Rosary movement. Klaus Arnold, *Johannes Trithemius*, 103. The life of Anne by an anonymous Franciscan, *Hec est quedam rara et ideo cara legenda de sancta Anna et de universa eius* (Strasburg, 1501), is followed in the same volume by a Rosary tract, "Incipit tractaculus novus et preciosus de fraternitate Rosarij gloriose Virginis Marie."

5. See Jean-Claude Schmitt, "La Confrérie du Rosaire de Colmar (1485)," *Archivum Fratrum Praedicatorum* 40 (1970), 97–124. On the invitation to women, see Winston-Allen, *Stories of the Rose*, 117; and "Tracing the Origins of the Rosary," *Speculum* 68 (July 1993), 634.

6. Johannes von Lambsheym, *Libellus perutilis de fraternitate sanctissima Rosarii et psalterij beate Marie virginis* (Mainz: Peter Friedberg, 1495).

7. Winston-Allen, *Stories of the Rose*, 137.

8. Anne Winston-Allen, "Tales of the Rosary in German Confraternity Handbooks, 1482–1515," conference paper, University of Western Michigan International Congress on Medieval Studies, Kalamazoo, 1993, 3.

9. Petrus Dorlandus, *Vita gloriosissime*, 767.

10. *Das Leben und Wunderzaichen*, 152ff.

11. See Brandenbarg, *Heilig familieleven*, 71, 135, and passim; and Dörfler-Dierken, *Vorreformatorische Bruderschaften der hl. Anna*, 42. Ludwig Remling finds that the upper levels of urban society predominated in most Franconian Anne brotherhoods. Remling, *Bruderschaften in Franken*, 258–77, esp. 274, 377–95.

12. Gustav Kawerau, *Johann Agricola von Eisleben* (Berlin: Wilhelm Hertz, 1881), 9, cited in Robert Scribner, *For the Sake of Simple Folk* (New York: Cambridge University Press, 1981), 15. "Mutter" is the most usual form of address in the prayer *incipits* in the Rhineland prayerbooks described in Karl Menne, *Deutsche und niederländische Handschriften* (Cologne: Verlag von Paul Neubner, 1937).

13. *Das Leben und Wunderzaichen*, 21. The description of Anne coincides with the advice in an early sixteenth-century rhyming "mirror" of instructions for women's behavior: "So point at no one with your finger, nor beckon with your hand . . . your conversation be not be loud. . . . Don't peer like an ostrich all around / and at a dance speak less than a mouse" (So solt du nyemants mit finger deüten / Nach wincken mit der hand herzuo . . . dein reden erschall nit überlaut . . . Nitt guck hin vnd her als ain strauss / Am dantz red minder dann ain mauss). *Der Frawen Spiegel* (Augsburg: Hanns Schoensperger am Weinmarckt, 1522).

14. Trithemius, *De laudibus*, chap. 6.

15. Brandenbarg, *Heilig familieleven*, 68.

16. Fouquart de Cambrai, Antoine du Val, and Jean d'Arras, *Les Evangiles des Quenouilles* (Bruges: Colard Mansion, ca. 1475), translated in England in the sixteenth century as *The Gospelles of Dystaves*, in *Distaves and Dames: Renaissance Treatises For and About Women*, ed. Diane Bornstein (Delmar, N.Y.: Scholars Facsimiles & Reprints, 1978). On the increasingly negative stereotype of the bad woman in the late fifteenth century, see Franz Brietzmann, *Die böse Frau in der deutschen Litteratur des Mittelalters* (1912; reprint, London: Johnson Reprint Company, 1967), 188. See also Dresen-Coenders, "Machtige grootmoeder, duivelse heks."

17. Lyndal Roper, *The Holy Household: Women and Morals in Reformation Augsburg* (Oxford: Clarendon Press, 1989), 84–85, 115–21, 130–31.

18. Dörfler-Dierken, *Die Verehrung der heiligen Anna*, 210ff. Anne and Joachim are presented as a loving couple in earlier presentations, such as those of Hroswitha and the Priester Wernher. However, these writers are not concerned primarily to present them as saints. See Hroswitha of Gandersheim, *Historia nativitatis laudabilisque*, PL 137.1065ff.; Wernher, *Maria: Bruchstücke und Umarbeitungen*. Kathleen Ashley discusses the transition between marital models in "Image and Ideology," in *Interpreting Cultural Symbols*, ed. Ashley and Sheingorn, 119.

19. Petrus Dorlandus, *Vita gloriosissime*, 766.

20. *Das Leben und Wunderzaichen der allerseeligsten Frwen Annae*, 33.

21. "Als Anna hatt ihren Mann Joachim in ehren gehalten als ihren Herren und geliebt als ihren Vatter Er aber hatt hergegen sein Haussfraw verehrt als sein Muetter und mit gebürender lieb umbfangen als sein Schwester." Ibid., 24.

22. Reber, *Die Gestaltung des Kultes weiblicher Heiliger im Spätmittelalter*, 194 and passim.

23. Van Denemarken, *Die historie, ende die exempelen*, 14r.

24. *Das Leben und Wunderzaichen*, 56.

25. Examples are numerous. Gertrud Schiller states: "The *Anna Selbdritt* can be understood as

an allusion to the Immaculate Conception or even a symbolic representation of it." Gertrud Schiller, *Ikonographie der christlichen Kunst* (Gütersloh: Verlagshaus Gerd Mohn, 1980), 4:2, 157. See also Mereth Lindgren, "De heliga änkorna," 69 (also 52); Remling, *Bruderschaften in Franken*, 258; Leo Steinberg, "The Metaphors of Love and Birth in Michelangelo's Pietàs," in *Studies in Erotic Art*, ed. Theodore Bowie and Cornelia V. Christenson (New York: Basic Books, 1970).

26. Kleinschmidt, *Die Heilige Anna*, 162. Franz Falk preceded Kleinschmidt in this belief. Franz Falk, *Geschichte der Marienverehrung und der Immakulata Tradition im Bistum Mainz und am Mittelrhein* (Mainz: Druckerei Lehrlinghaus, 1906), 103.

27. The decision by the University of Paris in the late fourteenth century to require adherence to the doctrine of the Immaculate Conception had led to a hardening of positions, and when the Council of Basel decided in 1439 to accept the feast, the level of dissension was raised, even though the council was later declared schismatic. The controversies did not abate when in 1477 the Franciscan pope Sixtus IV gave the doctrine official approval and introduced the feast in Rome. The actions of Sixtus followed on the publication in Milan in 1475 of the Dominican Vincenzo Bandelli's *Libellus recollectorius auctoritatum de veritate Conceptionis B. V. Mariae*, which had attacked the doctrine as heretical, wicked, and diabolical. In 1476 Sixtus had granted indulgences to those attending services on the feast, and in 1477 he sanctioned an office for the feast. The earliest extant holy kinship offices, some of which contain Immaculate Conception material, date from this decade; the earliest dated example is 1477. The *Historia nova pulchra devota et autentica de sancta anna*, an office published in Augsburg circa 1479, states that Anne "was made fruitful by her husband Saint Joachim without the stain of sin" (ex sancto joachim marito suo eciam sine peccati macula fecundari) and that her most blessed daughter "never committed actual sin and never contracted original sin" (hec filia vostra

beatissima a peccatum actuale nunquam commisit sic et ipsa peccatum originale nunquam contraxit). From the 1470s on, the doctrine's supporters and its Dominican opponents alternated in provoking, insulting, attacking, and counterattacking one another. The issue was debated in the German universities, first in Leipzig, subsequently in Heidelberg, and in print. See O'Connor, *The Dogma*, 232ff., and Franz Falk, *Zur Geschichte der Immaculata Tradition in der Mainzer Kirche*, 13, 15, and passim. The Dominicans celebrated the feast of December 8, but under the title not of *Conceptio* but of *Sanctificatio b. Mariae Virginis*. O'Connor, *The Dogma*, 139. It should be noted that the official title of the feast was, and remained for some centuries, simply *Conceptio b. Mariae Virginis*, but supporters of the doctrine celebrated it as the feast of the Immaculate Conception.

28. In a Braunschweig life the angel who prophesies the birth of Mary says she "shall be consecrated to God and sanctified in the body of her mother and filled with the holy ghost wherefore she shall not live with the common people but rather in the temple" (schal gode consecreret werden effte gehilliget werden vnde in dem liue oerer moder vor vullet myt dem hilgen geiste dar vmme se nicht myt dem gemeinem volcke wonen schal besunderen in dem tempel). *St. Annen Büchlein* (Braunschweig: Hans Dorn, 1509), cvii r, in. Kalinke, "Mariu saga og Onnu," 75. Dörfler-Dierken, notes that Anne confraternities were instituted at twelve Dominican convents. Dörfler-Dierken, *Vorreformatorische Bruderschaften*, 23. For rejection of the causal connection between Anne and the Immaculate Conception, see also Dörfler-Dierken, *Die Verehrung*, 45–66, and Brandenbarg, *Heilig familieleven*, 86–100.

29. "Thus the holy mother conceived through holy marriage; she conceived without original sin, she gave birth without fault. O holy and previously unheard-of conception" (Concepit ergo mulier sancta de coniuge sancto: concepit sine originali macula: peperit sine culpa. O sancta et prius inaudita conceptio). Trithemius, *De laudibus*, chap. 6.

30. "Supra natura est: qui naturam fecit." Ibid., chap. 7.

31. Bostius to Celtis, no. 147, 1497, February 8. *Die Briefwechsel des Konrad Celtis*, ed. Hans Rupprich (Munich: Kommission zur Erforschung der Geschichte der Reformation und der Gegenreformation, 1934), 246–47. Sebastian Brant is similarly unorthodox when he argues for Mary's virgin birth by citing the phenomenon of virgin birth in the animal kingdom. "Contra Iudeos et hereticos: Conceptionem virginalem fuisse possibilem argumentatios," cited in Sister Mary Rajewski, *Sebastian Brant: Studies in Religious Aspects of His Life and Works, with Special Reference to the Varia Carmina* (Washington, D.C.: Catholic University of America Press, 1944), 80.

32. Lambsheym, *Libellus perutilis.* Mirella Levi d'Ancona's *Iconography of the Immaculate Conception in the Middle Ages and Early Renaissance* (New York: College Art Association, 1957) is not a reliable guide to the iconography of the Immaculate Conception, nor is Bruno Borchert's "L'Immaculée dans l'iconographie du Carmel," *Carmelus* 2 (1955), 85–131.

33. Sancta Birgitta, *Revelaciones*, book 5, ed. Birger Bergh (Uppsala: Simlingar utgivna av Svenska Fornskriftsällskapet, 1971), 174. Nilsen states: "In another revelation (*Revelaciones* 1:9), the idea not unusual in this context emerges: that Mary was conceived without lust and that God subsequently inserted the soul in her body and at the same instant sanctified both." Anna Nilsen, "The Immaculate Conception of the Virgin Mary in Cult and Art During the Middle Ages with Special Reference to Swedish Material," 4, a translation by Alexander G. Davidson of "Marie obefläckade avlelse i kult och konst," *Konsthistorisk tidskrift* 56 (1987), 6–15.

34. A ca. 1500 woodcut depicting Birgitta with her family around her in a tree formation is borrowed from a Holy Kinship print by the Meister mit dem Dächlein (ca. 1450–75). Lindgren, "De heliga änkorna," 56–57, 70.

35. Birgitta of Sweden, *The Liber Celestis of St. Bridget of Sweden*, ed. Roger Ellis, EETS, o.s. (Oxford: Oxford Univerisity Press, 1987), 467.

36. Kleinschmidt had claimed Anne as a patroness of medieval women. Kleinschmidt, *Die heilige Anna*, 164. See Dörfler-Dierken's rebuttal of this claim in *Die Verehrung*, 100–101. In medieval England, Anne's help was sought for fertility, according to Gail McMurray Gibson, "Saint Anne and the Religion of Childbed: Some East Anglian Texts and Talismans," in *Interpreting Cultural Symbols*, ed. Ashley and Sheingorn, 95–110; see also Ashley and Sheingorn's introduction, on aspects of Anne's relationship with women, 1–68.

37. Anonymous Franciscan, *Hec est quedam rara et ideo cara legenda de sanctissima Anna et de universa eius* (Strasburg, 1501).

38. "Ain hisch lied von sant Anna, von den grossen wunder zaychen die sie zuo theürün thuot ganstlich zu singen" (Blatt 143, Heidelberger Bibl. no. 109). Wackernagel mistakenly identifies Theürün as Thuringia instead of Düren with its famous relic of Anne's head; as the song says, "Gen theürün für sant anna haüpte." Wackernagel, *Das Deutsche Kirchenlied*, vol. 2 nos. 1259, 1020.

39. Heinrich Appel, "Annareliquiar und Annaschatz," *St.-Anna in Düren*, ed. Gatz, 117.

40. Dörfler-Dierken, "Wunderheilungen durch das Limburger Annenheiltum," 87, 98.

41. The prayer is referred to in G.B. octavo 44, 223, cited in Menne, *Deutsche und niederländische Handschriften*, 454–55. Jodocus Beisselius's *Rosarium de sancta Anna* includes help in fertility in his list of Anne's patronages. Trithemius mentions help to women in childbirth but otherwise pays little special attention to women in his lengthy list. Johannes Trithemius, *De laudibus*, chap. 14. Kleinschmidt mentions a 1536 Halle text that recommends a Saint Anne shrine for easy childbearing. Kleinschmidt, *Die heilige Anna*, 165.

42. Martin Luther, WA 2, 69ff.

43. Kawerau, *Johann Agricola von Eisleben*, 9.

44. An exception is *Die historie van die heilige moeder santa anna ende van haer olders daer si van geboren is ende van horen leven ende hoer penitenci ende mirakelen mitten exempelen* (first published in Zwolle, 1499), which is a translation and reworking of the *Legenda sanctae Emerencianae* (MS, ca. 1496, KB Brussels, no. 4837). According to Brandenbarg, this work describes Anne in her later years following the mode of life of a desert ascetic. Brandenbarg, *Heilig familieleven*, 288. Jan van Denemarken occasionally mentions Anne's abstemiousness—she ate and drank only enough to stay alive—in her widowhood. Van Denemarken, *Die historie*, 66r,v.

45. Martin Luther, WA 17, 2, 400. See also ibid., 12, 458.

46. Brandenbarg, *Heilige Anna, Grote Moeder*, 42–44, states that Anne was honored in convents. A nativity play, probably dating to the early fifteenth century, in which Anne, Mary Cleophas, and Mary Salome visit Mary, Joseph, and the Christ Child, was written for a women's convent at Huy near Liège. "Fragment d'un mystère de la Nativité," in *Mystères et moralités du manuscrit 617 de Chantilly*, ed. Gustave Cohen (Paris: Librairie Edouard Champion, 1920), 27–38. On this work, see Kathleen Ashley, "Image and Ideology / Saint Anne in Late Medieval Drama and Narrative," in *Interpreting Cultural Symbols*, ed. Ashley and Sheingorn, 110–30. One of the lives by Petrus Dorlandus, the manuscript *Die historie der alder heilchster vrouwen Sijnte Anna (Dietse Historie)* (1500/1503, UB Ghent, hs. 895), which promotes the reforming of convents, was written for a women's convent, probably Sint-Anna-ter Woestijne near Bruges, according to Brandenbarg, *Heilige Anna: Grote Moeder*, 44–46; *Heilige Familieleven*, 282–83.

47. Menne, *Deutsche und niederländische Handschriften*, esp. 647–93.

48. Manfred Beck, *Untersuchungen zur geistlichen Literatur im Kölner Drück des frühen 16. Jahrhunderts* (Göppingen: Verlag Alfred Kümmerle, 1977), 120, 127, 129, 149.

49. Johannes Cochlaeus, *Brevis Germanie Descriptio*, 1512, ed. and trans. Karl Langosch (Darmstadt: Wissenschaftliche Buchgesellschaft, 1960), 156–57.

50. Brandenbarg, *Heilig familieleven*, 108.

Chapter 6

1. Rem, "Cronica newer Geschichten," 54.

2. Rolf Kiessling, in his study of three centuries of struggle as middle-class lay elements sought to wrest control of the city from noble clerical elements, remarks that at the turn of the century almost all the city's churches either began a new building or engaged in thoroughgoing renovation. Kiessling, *Bürgerliche Gesellschaft*, 246.

3. Rem, "Cronica newer Geschichten," 26–27.

4. Hieronymus Emser, "That One Should Not Remove Images of the Saints from the Churches Nor Dishonour Them, and That They Are Not Forbidden in Scripture" (Dresden, 1522), in *A Reformation Debate*, ed. Bryan D. Mangrum and Giuseppe Scavizzi (Toronto: University of Toronto Press, 1991), 87.

5. Kiessling. *Bürgerliche Gesellschaft*, 184–85; Albert Haemmerle, *Die Leibdingbuecher der Freien Reichsstadt Augsburg*, 1330–1500 (typescript, Munich, 1943).

6. "Fr. Johannes Franks Augsburger Annalen" and "Die Chronik von Clemens Sender," *Die Chroniken der deutschen Städte, Augsburg*, 302.

7. Other relics were uncovered as well; relics of Saint Adalbero had been discovered in 1480, while those of Saint Simprecht had been found in 1491 and ceremonially reburied in 1492. "Die Chronik von Clemens Sender," *Die Chroniken der deutschen Städte, Augsburg*, 60. The tomb of Simprecht, Bishop of Augsburg (d. 807), at Saints Ulrich and Afra, a pilgrimage site since the twelfth century, was the object of intensive promotion from 1450 on. In 1516 the monastery published a new miracle book for its three tomb saints: Ulrich, Afra, and Simprecht, *Das leben verdienen und wunderwerck der hailigen Auspurger Bistumbs bischoffen*.

8. Ibid., 302. See also Kiessling, *Bürgerliche Gesellschaft*, 290–91; Michael Hartig, *Das Benediktiner-Reichsstift Sankt Ulrich und Afra in Augsburg, 1012–1802* (Augsburg: Verlag Dr. Benno Filsner, 1923), 37. Burkard Zink also describes the digging up of bones: "Chronik des Burkard Zink," *Die Chroniken der deutschen Städte, Augsburg*, 294.

9. The Hohenwart finds were reported in the convent chronicle of 1489. Wilhelm Liebhart, "Historia Hohenwart: Eine Chronik von 1489 zur Gründung und Wallfahrtsgeschichte des Benediktinerinnenklosters aus dem Umkreis Kaiser Maximilians I," *Neuburger Kollektaneenblatt* 132 (1979), 297. Discoveries of hidden or lost relics, such as caches supposedly buried to avoid capture by enemies, were an established staple of the European relic discourse.

10. Kiessling, *Bürgerliche Gesellschaft*, 293. See also Wilhelm Liebhart on the economic basis behind Heilig Kreuz's defense of its miracle host. Wilhelm Liebhart, "Stifte, Klöster, und Konvente in Augsburg," in *Geschichte der Stadt Augsburg von der Römerzeit bis zur Gegenwart*, ed. G. Gottlieb, W. Barr, and Josef Beck (Stuttgart: Theiss, 1984), 198.

11. Trithemius, *De laudibus*, chap. 15.

12. Eberhard Schott, "Beitrag," 1882, "Beiträge zur Geschichte des Carmeliterklosters und der Kirche von Saint Anna in Augsburg," *Zeitschrift des Historischen Vereins für Schwaben und Neuburg* (ZHVS) (1882), 270–71. Schott published and summarized archival material on the Augsburg Carmelites in a series of five articles in the ZHVS published in 1878, 1879 (two articles), 1880, and 1882.

13. Schott gives the income of the convent in Rhenish florins (also called Rhenish guilders) as follows: 1401—190 florins; 1416—288; 1448—334; 1467—324; 1480—671; 1496—800; 1501—936; 1521—1386; and 1527–29—340 florins. (In 1404 the church paid 5 Rhenish florins for an altarpiece. In 1479 a horse cost 4 Rhenish florins.) Schott, "Beitrag 9," 272. He breaks

down the components as follows. *Oblaciones*, the offerings at divine service, dropped as a percentage of the total from almost one-third in 1401 to one-ninth, to one-tenth under Fabri's priorship (1479–97). Alms, which included offerings from boxes in front of images and at church doors, increased as a percentage of regular income from one-eleventh in 1401 to one-fifth in 1496. *Terminarii*, monks who collected for the convent in outlying districts in the dioceses of Augsburg, Freising, and Constance, in 1401 brought in more than one-seventh of its income, and in 1416 and 1448 brought in about one-third, with a further increase later in the century. The most profitable source of income consisted of the houses and properties given in the endowments for masses for departed souls, which increased from "sehr unbedeutend" in 1401 to one-eighth of the total income in 1498. The component from vigils, masses, and annual requiem masses increased significantly, accounting in 1496, at 116 florins, for approximately one-seventh of the total, and to 291 florins out of a total of 1,386 in 1521. In addition there was important income from gifts, bequests, money given for burial places or chapels, and membership in the Annenbruderschaft. Schott, ibid., 272–77. On the sales of *Leibdinge*, see ibid., 249.

14. Wilhelm Schiller, *Die St. Annakirche in Augsburg* (Augsburg: Evang. Luth. Pfarramt St. Anna and J. A. Schlosser'schen Buchhandlung, 1939), 21. In 1493 the bishop of Augsburg, Friedrich von Zollern, had granted the convent permission to offer an indulgence for the purpose of collecting funds for building. Schott, "Beitrag 10," 246.

15. *Aufnahmeformular der St. Annenbruderschaft* (Augsburg: Erhard Ratdolt, 1494).

16. *Ain gar nutzlichs büchlin*, a iii.

17. Schiller, *Die St. Annakirche in Augsburg*, 17–22, and Schott, "Beitrag," 1878, 238–39, 262. The convent buildings, which had suffered fire damage in 1460, had been rebuilt in the 1460s.

18. *Ain gar nutzlichs büchlin.* This work is based on one of the lives emanating from the Rhineland circles, *Hec est quedam rara et ideo cara legenda de sanctissima Anna et de universa eius,* by an anonymous Franciscan, first published by Joh. de Westfalia in Louvain in 1496 and republished many times subsequently in Germany. Embellished with local references and purportedly local stories, the Augsburg work is sufficiently different that it cannot be termed a translation or an adaptation. The brotherhood may have acquired additional indulgences, for the convent's account book of 1521 mentions a "tabula indulgentiarum pro fraternitate St. Annae." Leo Söhner, *Die Geschichte der Begleitung des gregorianischen Chorals in Deutschland* (Augsburg: Dr. Benno Filser Verlag, 1931), 8. Söhner notes references from 1513 onward to money deposited "pro trunco St. Annae." Ibid.

19. Fabri, *Copialbuch,* 2, 14, in Johannes Wilhelm, *Augsburger Wandmalerei 1368–1530* (Augsburg: Verlag H. Mühlberger, 1983), Beilage 4, 226–27.

20. See Conrad Rudolph, *The Things of Greater Importance: Bernard of Clairvaux's Apologia and the Medieval Attitude Toward Art* (Philadelphia: University of Pennsylvania Press, 1990). Encouragement to donate was widespread. A late medieval book on the pains of hell devotes an entire section to the blessings received by people who give alms to build or decorate churches: *Dis büchlin saget von den peinen so do bereit seint allen denen die do sterben in todsünden* (Strasburg, 1509).

21. Account Books (*Rechnungsbücher*), Hauptbuch 3, July 22, 1492, to 1511, Stadtarchiv, Augsburg, cited in Schott, "Beitrag," 1882, 247.

22. *Ain gar nutzlichs büchlin.* The Augsburg confraternity Holy Kinship included Elizabeth and John the Baptist, Eliud, Maternus, Emiu, Memelia, and Servatius.

23. Daily masses for Sabina Rölingerin were to be sung or read "in the choir at the St. Anne Altar." Fabri, *Copialbuch* 11, 116.b, May 2, 1505, cited in Schott, "Beitrag," 1880, 190.

24. Schott, "Beitrag," 1882, 260–62.

25. Cod. MS 20 153, Univ. Munich, cited by Leo Söhner, *Die Geschichte der Begleitung des gregorianischen Chorals in Deutschland,* 4.

26. Ibid., 7. The convent paid 100 guilders for the right to its yearly Anne procession. *Die Lutherstiege in Augsburg–St. Anna,* 20.

27. *Ain gar nutzlichs büchlin.*

28. Ibid.

29. Ibid. The sole Augsburg miracle, a story that looks as if it has been adapted from a type of frightening secular tale, tells about a person who honored Anne, fell into sin, and then with Anne's help was led to repentance after a dream or vision of hideous decapitated heads. Whatever credibility this grim exemplum might have had is weakened by a repeat appearance of the same story virtually identical except for the setting.

30. Ibid.

31. No Anne pilgrimages are mentioned in "Die übrigen Wallfahrten des Bistums Augsburg," in Ludwig Dorn, *Die Marien-Wallfahrten des Bistums Augsburg* (Augsburg: Verlag Winfried-Werk, 1957).

32. I know of no references to the church as the Annenkirche before the rededication of 1485. It is typically referred to as "the Church (or convent) of the Brothers of Our Lady" (vnser lieben Frauen Brüder Kirche, or Closter), and it was referred to by this name well into the 1500s. Dedication statements in endowment documents for the Augsburg Carmelites do not begin to mention Anne's name until the early 1500s, when the usual reference to God the Almighty, Mary the Queen of Heaven, and all the heavenly host is sometimes expanded to include Anne. The first references to the church as the Church of Saint Anne do not seem to appear until the second decade of the sixteenth century. Augsburg, Stadtarchiv, Reichstadt Schätze 95 111.

33. In addition, Jakob Fugger may have commissioned the small (13 cm) silver *Anna Selbdritt* dated 1513, now in the Hermitage, on the back of which are engraved representations of Saints Barbara and James the Greater, the

patron saints of his parents. At one time the Fugger arms were visible on the back. See Reiner Michaelis, *Dasein und Vision: Bürger und Bauern um 1500* (Berlin: Staatliche Museen zu Berlin, Berlin Henschelverlag, 1989), 48.

34. On the altar, see Alfred Schroeder, *Archiv für die Geschichte des Hochstifts Augsburg* (Dillingen, 1929), 6:288. The four fragments of Anne's bones along with pieces of Mary's veil, hair, clothing, and grave were contained in a Marian reliquary figure. M. Hartig, *Das Benediktiner-Reichsstift Sankt Ulrich und Afra*, 87. Johannes Wilhelm's study of Augsburg's medieval painted facades makes no mention of images of Anne. Johannes Wilhelm, *Augsburger Wandmalerei*.

35. *Das leben verdienen und wunderwerck der hailigen Auspurger Bistumbs bischoffen*, B iii. Philip Soergel observes that the German humanists fostered a hagiographical style that downplayed miracles and emphasized the saint's human fallibility and his value as a model. Philip M. Soergel, *Wondrous in His Saints* (Berkeley and Los Angeles: University of California Press, 1993), 96. Kiessling calls attention to the close relationship the Augsburg humanist circle enjoyed with the clergy of Saints Ulrich and Afra. Kiessling, *Bürgerliche Gesellschaft*, 34. However, cautious treatment of miracles and attention to inner development are not invariably present in humanist hagiography, according to James Michael Weiss, "Hagiography by German Humanists," *Journal of Medieval and Renaissance Studies* 15 (1985), 299–316.

36. *Das leben verdienen und wunderwerck der hailigen Auspurger Bistumbs bischoffen*, A vi.

37. Peter Segl, "Heinrich Institoris: Persönlichkeit und literarisches Werk," in *Der Hexenhammer / Entstehung und Umfeld des malleus maleficarum von 1487*, ed. Peter Segl (Cologne and Vienna: Böhlau Verlag, 1988), 114–16.

38. Reiner Michaelis identifies Saint Wolfgang as the Erzgebirg's mining patron. Reiner Michaelis, *Dasein und Vision*, 35. The altarpiece in the church of Saint Katherine in nearby Buchholz, which (unlike the Annaberg altarpiece) was commissioned by the largely miners' brotherhood of Saint Wolfgang, does not include Saint Anne, depicting instead Wolfgang, the Veronica image, the apocalyptic madonna, and Saints Peter, Katherine, and Paul, along with the legend of Daniel and the discovery of the ore. Ibid. See also Angelika Dörfler-Dierken, *Vorreformatorische Bruderschaften*, 49–55, 64, and *Die Verehrung der heiligen Anna*, 90–97.

39. Petrus Albinus, *Annabergische Annales de anno 1492 bis 1539 in Festschrift zum 25jährigen Bestehen des Vereins für Geschichte von Annaberg und Umgegend* (Annaberg, 1910), 18–19.

40. Many of the relevant documents are published in Adam Daniel Richter, *Umständliche aus zuverlässigen Nachrichten zusammengetragene Chronica Der im Meissnischen Ober-Erz-Gebürge gelegenen Königl. Churfl. Sächsischen freyen Berg=Stadt St. Annaberg* (Saint Annaberg: August Valentin Friesen, 1746).

41. Christian Gotthold Milisch, *Durch diese kurze Nachricht von der ehemahligen St. Annae-Bruderschafft* (Annaberg: Valentin Friesen, 1746). Milisch refers to the Jahr-Buechern of 1528 of Ienisius Milische, mentioning the "nie gedruckten Diplomate die Kirch-Einweihung zu St. Anna" in which Pope Leo X announces an indulgence for the brotherhood, dated May 2, 1528. The brotherhood had permission to enroll up to one thousand members, man and wife counting as a single individual. It was dedicated to Mary, Anne, Joachim, and Joseph, but it was Anne's fame that was paramount. Ibid., 66. Though the official documents give a date of May 24, 1517, other sources indicate that the brotherhood was in operation by 1508 if not by 1506, according to Bernhard Wolf, "Aus dem kirchlichen Leben Annabergs in vorreformatorische Zeit," in *Festschrift zum 25 jährigen Bestehen des Vereins für Geschichte von Annaberg und Umgegend* (Annaberg: n.p., 1910), 76. There was also a Rosary Brotherhood and a Jakobsbruderschaft. Richter, *Umständliche aus zuverlässigen Nachrichten*, 96ff.

42. Richter, *Umständliche aus zuverlässigen Nachrichten*, 165–84.

43. Hans Schneider, "Carmen von der Stadt Annaberg," in Milisch, *Durch diese kurze Nachricht*, 27–30.

44. Ibid.

45. The seventeenth-century historian Jacobus Polius relates that in Düren the pastor had one key to the shrine's offering box and the magistrates had the other keys. Erwin Gatz notes that in the shrines at Düren and Aachen the offerings were split between the city and the pastor. Erwin Gatz, "Die Dürener Annaverehrung bis zum Ende des 18. Jahrhunderts," *St.-Anna in Düren*, 176. On the division of the income from the Limburg Anne shrine, see Dörfler-Dierken, "Wunderheilungen durch das Limburger Annenheiltum," 83–107.

46. Wolf, "Aus dem kirchlichen Leben Annabergs," 68–72; Albinus, *Annabergische Annales*, 69–70; Aloys Schulte, *Die Fugger in Rom, 1495–1523* (Leipzig: Verlag von Duncker & Humblot, 1904), 1:143. Richter, *Umständliche aus zuverlässigen Nachrichten*, 78. Such arrangements were made elsewhere: the Nuremberg authorities wrote to Jakob Fugger on March 12, 1515, requesting that the indulgence for the Augsburg Dominicans not be preached in their city. Schulte, *Die Fugger in Rom*, 2:134–35.

47. Schulte, *Die Fugger in Rom*, 1:78; 2:201–2.

48. Richter, *Umständliche aus zuverlässigen Nachrichten*, 103.

49. Ibid., 64–66. The Latin bull is given on pp. 70–77; the confraternity form (*Brief*), which also describes the indulgence, is given on pp. 66–69. The indulgence (Arch. Vatic. reg. Vatic. 1204. fol. 239) is also in Schulte, *Die Fugger in Rom*, vol. 1, part 2, 170–77. Schulte states that the indulgence in Richter is "full of errors." Ibid., 170.

50. Richter, *Umständliche aus zuverlässigen Nachrichten*, 69–70. The Augsburg confraternity membership form does not contain a similar proviso. One has the impression that the post-mortem benefits automatically went into effect when the member died.

51. Richter (ibid., 119) says: "In the year 1718 the old sacristy [of the Saint Anne Church] was renovated. In the sacristy can be seen the great money chest of the famous Tetzel, its strong beams mounted with iron, of which he used to say 'As soon as the coin in the coffer klings, so soon the soul from the purgatorial fire into heaven springs' [So bald der Groschen im Kasten klingt, / So bald die Seel aus dem Feg Feuer im Himmel springt]."

52. Dörfler-Dierken reports a case of the dead being *forcibly* enrolled as members of an Anne brotherhood, though less for their benefit than for the financial benefit of the confraternity members. In 1503 the Koblenz brotherhood of notaries and other diocesan officials was given the right to enroll as members deceased persons whose wills they handled, presumably charging the appropriate fees. Dörfler-Dierken, *Vorreformatorische Bruderschaften*, 117.

53. Richter, *Umständliche aus zuverlässigen Nachrichten*, 69–70.

54. Albinus, *Annabergische Annales*, 19.

Chapter 7

1. *Das Leben und Wunderzaichen*, 115–16.

2. Ibid., 119.

3. Ibid., 123–24.

4. Ibid., 127–28.

5. *Ain gar nutzlichs büchlin*, bii. The same book describes another incident in which a widow with an only daughter sick of the plague tries medical help to no avail, finding healing only upon honoring an image of Anne with praises and a candle. These exempla are also found in other lives.

6. Emser, "That One Should Not Remove Images of the Saints," in *A Reformation Debate*, 86.

7. Anne occasionally appears in the main panels of high altars—for example, in the Holy Kinship that was formerly part of the altar of the Kreuzkirche in Hannover, now in the Hannover Landesgalerie.

8. *Ain gar nutzlichs büchlin;* and *Das Leben und Wunderzaichen,* 182.

9. Schott, "Beitrag," 1882, 250. Maximilian also joined Anne brotherhoods in Worms and Ghent. Dörfler-Dierken, *Vorreformatorische Bruderschaften,* 175.

10. *Das Leben der Schwestern zu Töss beschrieben von Elsbeth Stagel,* in *Deutsches Nonnenleben: Das Leben der Schwestern zu Töss und der Nonne von Engeltal Büchlein von der Gnaden Uberlast,* ed. Margarete Weinhandl (Munich: O. C. Recht, 1921), 156.

11. See Rosemary Hale, "Imitatio Mariae: Motherhood Motifs in Late Medieval German Spirituality" (Ph.D. diss., Harvard University, 1992).

12. Margery Kempe, *The Book of Margery Kempe,* trans. B. A. Windeatt (London: Penguin, 1985), 52–53. Anne makes a brief appearance of this type in Henry Suso's vision of the Passion when he leads the sorrowing Mary to be cared for at her mother's house. Henry Suso, *The Exemplar, with Two German Sermons,* trans. and ed. Frank Tobin (New York: Paulist Press, 1989), 86.

13. E. Sainte-Marie Perrin, *La belle Vie de Sainte Colette de Corbie, 1381–1447* (Paris: Librairie Plon, 1921), 64–65; Charles van Corstanje, Yves Cazaux, John Decavele, and Albert Derolez, *Vita Sancta Coletae, 1381–1447* (Leiden: Brill, 1982). And see Pamela Sheingorn, "Appropriating the Holy Kinship," in *Interpreting Cultural Symbols,* ed. Ashley and Sheingorn, 180. A similar story is told ca. 1450 of a backsliding devotee of Saint Katherine in *Mirk's Festial,* 277.

14. *Das Leben und Wunderzaichen,* 126.

15. Ibid., 133.

16. Jeffrey Hamburger, *Nuns as Artists: The Visual Culture of a Medieval Convent* (Berkeley and Los Angeles: University of California Press, 1977). Hamburger's study also calls attention to the importance of gesture and physical activity in medieval religious behavior and feeling.

17. Johann Geiler von Keisersberg, *Evangelibuch,* Strasburg 1515, fol. 180, cited in Johannes

Janssen, *Erläuterungen und Ergänzungen zu Janssens Geschichte des deutschen Volkes,* ed. Ludwig Pastor, vol. 6, part 1, "Beiträge zur vorreformatorischen Heiligen- und Reliquienverehrung" (Freiburg: Herdersche Verlagshandlung, 1907), 21–22.

18. Charles J. Garside describes the pilgrimages begun in 1507 to the miracle-working image of Anne at Ober-Stammheim near Zurich. Garside, *Zwingli and the Arts,* 167. The Zurich priest Ludwig Hätzer mentions Ober-Stammheim as an example of misplaced piety in an iconoclastic pamphlet written in 1523: "Item wir lauffent inen [idols] nach gen Stammen / Rom / Eynsidlen / Ach." Ludwig Hätzer, *Ain Urtayl Gottes vnsers eegemahels / wie man sich mit allen goetzen vnd Bildnussen halten soll / auss der hayligen geschrifft gezogen* (Zurich, 1523), C ii.c. A painting at Steinerberg was reputed to return to its place if moved. See Dörfler-Dierken, *Vorreformatorische Bruderschaften,* 160. Another wonder-working *Anna Selbdritt* supposed to have been located at the convent church of Saint Anna auf dem Schwandelberg in Luzern canton is described in L. Burgener, *Die Wallfahrtsorte der katholischen Schweiz* (Ingenbohl, 1864), 105.

19. Jan van Denemarken, *Die historie, die ghetiden;* and *Ain gar nutzlichs büchlin.*

20. By contrast, Trithemius describes gifts of wax, money, and clothing made to the wonder-working image of Mary at Dittelbach in the miracle book he wrote for this shrine. Johannes Trithemius, *Miracula beatae Mariae semper virginis in Ecclesia nova prope Dittelbach* (1511). Joannis Trithemii, *Opera pia et spiritualia, quotquot vel olim typis expressa vel m.ss. Reperiri potuerunt,* ed. Johannes Busaeus (Mainz, 1604, 1605), chap. 5, 1083. New construction was involved in this instance of pilgrimage promotion.

21. Catharina von Gebsweiler, *Lebensbeschreibungen der ersten Schwestern des Klosters der Dominikanerinnen zu Unterlinden,* trans. Ludwig Clarus (Regensburg: Verlag von Georg Joseph Manz, 1863), 38–39. The anecdote, which does not appear in Jeanne Ancelet-Hustache's edition of "Les vitae sororum d'Unterlinden: Edition critique

du manuscrit 508 de la Bibliothèque de Colmar," *Archives d'histoire doctrinale et littéraire du moyen age* 5 (1930), 317–517, is found in Elisabeth Kempf's fifteenth-century German version of Gebsweiler's lives.

22. *De historie von der hilligen moder sunte Anna und oren slechte* (Braunschweig: Hans Dorn, 1507), referred to by Marianne Kalinke as the *St. Annen-Büchlein*, oiii r, in Kalinke, "Mariu saga og Onnu," 69–70.

23. Fr. Johannes Franks Augsburger Annalen, "Die Chronik von Clemens Sender," in *Die Chroniken der deutschen Städte*, 303.

24. Kempe, *Book of Margery Kempe*, 113.

25. Lucas Rem, *Tagebuch des Lucas Rem*, 26–29.

26. "Chronik des Burkard Zink," *Die Chroniken der deutschen Städte, Augsburg*, 107; see also 122, 133, 135, 142, and passim.

27. *Huldrych Zwinglis Sämtliche Werke*, vol. 2 (Berlin and Zurich, 1905), 17–20, cited in Garside, *Zwingli and the Arts*, 134.

28. *Huldreich Zwinglis Sämtliche Werke*, vol. 4, cited in Carl Christensen, *Art and the Reformation in Germany* (Athens: University of Georgia Press, 1980), 22.

29. Ludwig Hätzer, *Ain Urtayl Gottes*, C iii.

30. Andreas Karlstadt, "On the Removal of Images," in *A Reformation Debate*, 21.

31. Ibid., 35–36.

32. Ibid., 21–22.

33. Ibid., 34.

34. *Akten der zweiten Disputation vom 26–28 Oktober 1523*, in *Huldrych Zwinglis Sämtliche Werke* (Berlin and Zurich: C. A. Schwetschke & Sohn, 1905), 872.

35. "Rutgerus venrai Canonicus regularis heynensis ad imaginem sancte anne," Johannes Trithemius, *De laudibus*.

36. An image of Saint Anne at the New Saint Peter's Church in Strasburg was "thrown into the charnel house." Christensen, *Art and the Reformation in Germany*, 88. Steven Ozment comments on the sense of deception unmasked, observing that "the outburst of iconoclasm at the inception of the Reformation may rather indicate the reaction of people who felt themselves fooled by something that they had not taken lightly at all but had in fact believed all too deeply." Steven Ozment, *The Reformation in the Cities: The Appeal of Protestantism to Sixteenth-Century Germany and Switzerland* (New Haven: Yale University Press, 1975), 44.

37. Robert W. Scribner, "Ritual and Reformation," in *The German People and the Reformation*, ed. R. Po-Chia Hsia (Ithaca: Cornell University Press, 1988), 133. Scribner cites a number of instances of images insulted as though they were people; beer, for example, was flung over a statue of Christ in the tavern of a tailors' guild. Ibid., 131ff. But his labeling of such actions as "satirical degradation" is open to question. An interpretation of such behavior as intended to shame and insult is more consistent with patterns of medieval social relations.

38. David Freedberg is in error when he states that Christian images acquired the power that people perceived in them through consecration. Freedberg's misunderstanding stems in part from an insistence on fitting his data to a set of vaguely formulated but rigorously predetermined theses, one of which seems to be that all images receive their power through consecration: "When we survey the history of images, we survey the history of consecration." Another is a belief that it is possible to discover a single ahistorical mode in which images function. Freedberg confuses treating an image as though it were alive with consecrating it. He concludes his argument by redefining consecration so that a consecrated image becomes synonymous with an image that is given special honors. David Freedberg, *The Power of Images* (Chicago: University of Chicago Press, 1989), 94.

39. Suso, *The Exemplar, with Two German Sermons*, 80.

40. "The Life of St. Anne," MS University of Minnesota Z.822, n. 81, in *The Middle English*

Stanzaic Versions of the Life of Saint Anne, ed. Parker, l.

41. "The Life of St. Anne," MS Trin. Coll. Camb. 601, in *Middle English Stanzaic Versions,* ed. Parker, 91.

42. Ibid., 93–94.

43. Ibid., 98.

44. "Many believe that image to be God, and many believe God's virtue subjectively to be therein, and thus they are more affected to one image than to another; that doubtless is idolatry, as true men say," wrote one Lollard. Margaret Aston, *Lollards and Reformers: Images and Literacy in Late Medieval Religion* (London: Hambledon Press, 1984), 151, citing *Apology for Lollard Doctrines,* 88.

45. H. F. B. Compston, "The Thirty-Seven Conclusions of the Lollards," *English Historical Review* 26 (1911), 743. See also Clifford Davidson, "The Anti-Visual Prejudice," in *Iconoclasm vs. Art and Drama,* ed. Clifford Davidson and Ann Eljenholm Nichols (Kalamazoo: Western Michigan University, Medieval Institute Publications, 1989), 33–46.

46. Robert Holcot, British Library, MS Harl. 2398, fol. 82r., in Aston, *Lollards and Reformers,* 155.

47. Kempe, *Book of Margery Kempe,* 113.

48. My proposal that English perceptions of images were moving into an early modern mode before this happened in most other parts of Europe is consistent with the arguments about the early disappearance of peasant society in England and its results made by Alan Macfarlane in *The Origins of English Individualism: The Family, Property, and Social Transition* (Oxford: Basil Blackwell, 1978).

49. G. H. Cook, *Letters to Cromwell on the Suppression of the Monasteries* (London: John Baker, 1965), 198, 65. Douglas Jones remarks: "There is surprisingly little direct evidence from Chester of that cult of relics which has been described as the true religion of the middle ages." Douglas Jones, *The Church in Chester* (Manchester: Chetham Society, 1957), 115.

50. On English enthusiasts Margaret Aston states: "The militant iconoclasts who, in the course of a century, managed to annihilate so much of England's artistic heritage, . . . may only have been a small minority of activists." Margaret Aston, "Iconoclasm in England: Official and Clandestine," in Davidson and Nichols, *Iconoclasm vs. Art and Drama,* 80.

51. Gert Grote, "A Treatise on Four Classes of Subjects Suitable for Meditation: A Sermon on the Lord's Nativity," in *Devotio Moderna: Basic Writings,* trans. John van Engen (New York: Paulist Press, 1988), 103.

52. Otto Pächt has brilliantly analyzed these and other qualities in the Late Gothic styles of the fifteenth-century North. Otto Pächt, "The Avignon Diptych and Its Eastern Ancestry," in *De Artibus Opuscula XL: Essays in Honor of Erwin Panofsky,* ed. M. Meiss (New York: New York University Press, 1961), 402–21.

53. See Jesse D. Hurlbut, "The Ghent Altarpiece Performed: Civic Appropriation of Art in 1458" (Conference paper, University of Western Michigan International Congress on Medieval Studies, Kalamazoo, 1993), 1.

Chapter 8

1. Egranus Sylvius [Johannes Wildenauer], *Apologia contra Calumniatores suos* (Leipzig, 1517).

2. Faber Stapulensis [Jacques Lefevre d'Etaples], *De Maria Magdalena, Tridvo Christi, Et ex tribus vna Maria, disceptatio* (Paris: Henricus Stephanus, 1518), 60, 67, 72. This work also argued against the identification of Mary Magdalene with Mary the sister of Martha. On Lefèvre and Saint Anne, see Myra D. Orth, "Madame Sainte Anne: The Holy Kinship, the Royal Trinity, and Louise of Savoy," in *Interpreting Cultural Symbols,* ed. Ashley and Sheingorn, 198–227.

3. Henricus Cornelius Agrippa, *De beatissimae Annae monogamia, ac unico puerperio propositiones abbreuiatae et articulate, iuxta disceptationem Iacobi Fabri Stapulensis in libro de tribus et una, intitulato* (Munich, 1533).

4. Dorlandus, *Vita gloriosissime matris Annae,* chap. 7.

5. On Bostius's promotion of Joachim, see Brandenbarg, *Heilig familieleven,* 122–24. And see Rajewski, *Sebastian Brant,* 103–9.

6. *Ain gar nutzlichs büchlin.*

7. Among the exceptions is the *Historia nova pulchra devota et autentica de sancta anna,* which recommends that a prayer be said to Joseph the Just, Cleophas, Salome, Alpheus, Zebedeus, Hysmeria, Elizabeth, and Zachary, "together with the others of the blessed kinship" for "the remission of sins, protection from all evil, and health of mind and body with participation in the celestial glory."

8. *Dit is Sint Anna Cransken.*

9. Brandenbarg notes changes in the representation of Anne. Brandenbarg, *Heilige familieleven,* 150.

10. Albrecht Altdorfer, *The Virgin and St. Anne at the Cradle,* ca. 1520–26, F. W. H. Hollstein, *German Engravings, Etchings, and Woodcuts* (Amsterdam: M. Hertzberger, 1954), 68.

11. The guild family, according to Roper, emphasizes the importance of the married man's mastery of workshop, household, and wife. Roper, *The Holy Household.* Brandenbarg discerns essentially the same model of marriage when he argues that the presentation of Anne as a model for sober, retiring, sexually restrained female behavior corresponded with the ethic of a rising middle and artisan class that had learned that unbridled sexual feelings could lead to alliances that disrupted the smooth running and handing down of business and property. Brandenbarg, *Heilig familieleven,* 141, 151, 165, 196. Dyan Elliott's study of celibate marriage also observes a late medieval rejection of an earlier Christian paradigm of the powerful wife who persuades her husband not to consummate the marriage, which came to be perceived as implying an undesirable independence in women, in favor of a submissive married woman. Dyan Elliott, *Spiritual Marriage: Sexual Abstinence in Medieval Wedlock*

(Princeton: Princeton University Press, 1993), 298–301.

12. Christiane D. Andersson, "Religiöse Bilder Cranachs im Dienste der Reformation," in *Humanismus und Reformation als kulturelle Kräfte in der deutschen Geschichte,* ed. L. W. Spitz (Berlin: Walter de Gruyter, 1981), 43–80.

13. *Das Leben und Wunderzaichen,* 64.

14. Ibid., 78.

15. Ibid., 83.

16. It also suggests the structurally similar motif of Snow White's stepmother offering the poisoned apple to Snow White.

17. Erwin Heinzle, *Wolf Huber* (*um,* 1485–1553) (Innsbruck: Universitätsverlag Wagner, 1953), 75.

18. This development parallels another development of the early modern period, the reduction of Mary's role as co-redemptrix. In sixteenth-century art, Mary begins to smile again.

Chapter 9

1. Kleinschmidt, *Die heilige Anna,* 147; Falk, *Geschichte der Marienverehrung und der Immakulata Tradition im Bistum Mainz,* 103.

2. Deeleman–van Tyen, "Sint Anna-te-Drieen"; Mangold, "Die Darstellung der heiligen Anna selbdritt"; Maniurka, *Mater Matris domini;* Esser, "Die Heilige Sippe." Deeleman–van Tyen is currently researching the theme of the *Anna själv tredje* in medieval wood sculpture in Sweden. Peter Rochhaus (University of Halle) is researching the *Anna Selbdritt* in Upper Saxony.

3. Unless otherwise stated, dates, regions, artists, and so on are those ascribed by the art historians or institutions who have published or who own the works. The same is true for non-generic titles of works of art. In some cases this chapter distinguishes between the North Netherlandish provinces of Flanders, where Bruges and Ghent are located, and Brabant, where Brussels and Antwerp are located. Elsewhere, unless

otherwise stated, the designation "Flanders" refers to the territory of present-day Belgium and Luxembourg.

4. Juliane von Fircks and Volkmar Herre, *Anna Selbdritt: Eine kolossale Stuckplastik der Hochgotik in St. Nikolai zu Stralsund* (Stralsund: Edition Herre, 1999), 18–20.

5. See *Das älteste Stralsundische Stadtbuch*, 1270–1310, ed. F. Fabricius (Berlin: Verlag von W. Weber, 1872). See also Otto Schmidt, "Die Stralsunder Anna Selbdritt," *Baltische Studien*, n.f., 33, 74; *Der Stralsunder Liber memorialis*, ed. Horst Diether Schroeder, I, fols. 1–60 (1320–42), Stralsund, 1903, no. 339, 68, this last cited in von Fircks and Herre, *Anna Selbdritt*, 17–19.

6. *Das älteste Stralsundische Stadtbuch*, 1270–1310, 150. An entry for June 24, 1307, reads: "Heinrich in front of Saint Anne has food during his life from Saint Nikolai." Ibid., 162. For information on the *Proven*, which were sold by confraternities in Lübeck and Bremen, and also in Hanseatic cities, see Zmyslony, *Die Bruderschaften in Lübeck bis zur Reformation*, 129–32; Dörflier-Dierken, *Vorreformatorische Bruderschaften*, 70–72.

7. "Et ipse debet sedere ante ymaginem s. Anne et petere in ecclesis cum imaginibus et videre ad structuram, sicut fecerunt sui alii antesessores." *Der Stralsunder Liber memorialis*, 68, cited in von Fircks and Herre, *Anna Selbdritt*, 18.

8. Esser, "Die Heilige Sippe," 55, 69. Tree format kinships continued in use, especially in Flanders, throughout the life span of the image. For a description of the theme of the *Stammbaum* or family tree of Mary, see Marita Lindgren-Fridell, "Der Stammbaum Maria aus Anna und Joachim," *Marburger Jahrbuch für Kunstwissenschaft* 2 (1938–39), 289–308.

9. Joanna Wolska-Wierusz suggests that coins bearing the image of the dual emperors on the double throne of the late Roman period may be the compositional source for the bench-type *Anna Selbdritt*, the immediate source being depictions of the Trinity seated on benches in books of hours. Joanna Wolska-Wierusz, "Adventus

Salvatoris i altarskapet fran Hägerstad," *Fornvännen* 88 (1993), 9–25. Jacqueline Lafontaine-Dosogne notes the similarity between Early Christian images in which a child is placed between two seated figures, and the *Anna Selbdritt*: "Anne et Marie, assises l'une près de l'autre et tenant l'Enfant entre elles, rappellent Joachim et Anne cajolant la petite Vierge [or David] dans la scène byzantine des Caresses." Jacqueline Lafontaine-Dosogne, *Iconographie de l'enfance de la Vierge* (Brussels: Académie royale de Belgique, 1964–65), III. Lafontaine-Dosogne believes the similarity is coincidental. Other possible sources include medieval depictions of presentations and circumcisions in which two adult figures flank the Christ Child.

10. See Deeleman-van Tyen, "Sint Anna-te-Drieen," for Dutch examples, and Maniurka's *Mater Matris Domini* for Silesian ones.

11. *Historia nova pulchra devota et autentica de sancta anna.*

12. Anonymous Franciscan, *Hec est quaedam rara.*

13. Anton Birlinger, ed., "Leben heiliger alemannischer Frauen des Mittelalters, 5: Die Nonnen von St. Katarinental bei Diessenhofen," *Alemannia* 15 (Bonn, 1887), 179.

14. Suso, *The Life of the Servant*, in Suso, *The Exemplar, with Two German Sermons*, 77. The presentation of tableaux vivants of the "Christ Child laughing with his mother" and the "Christ Child eating apples" were part of the "faerie or enchantments" put on by the bourgeoisie of Paris as part of *la grant feste* celebrating the knighting of Philip the Fair's sons at Pentecost of 1313. Elizabeth A. R. Brown and Nancy Freeman Regalado, "La grant Feste: Philip the Fair's Celebration of the Knighting of His Sons in Paris at Pentecost of 1313," in *City and Spectacle in Medieval Europe*, ed. Barbara A. Hanawalt and Kathryn L. Reyerson (Minneapolis: University of Minnesota Press, 1994), 68.

15. Reproduced in Jürgen Wittstock, *Kirchliche Kunst des Mittelalters und der Reformationszeit: St. Annen-Museum Lübeck* (Lübeck: Museum für Kunst & Kulturgeschichte, 1981), 177.

16. Cäsar Menz, *Das Frühwerk Jörg Breus des Alteren*, pl. 32.

17. Cologne, Wallraf-Richartz Museum, no. 398, reproduced in Marburger Index; *The Holy Kindred*, possibly by the Master of the Figdor Deposition (Zurich, Bührle Collection), reproduced in Albert Chatelet, *Early Dutch Painting: Painting in the Northern Netherlands in the Fifteenth Century* (Secaucus, N.J.: Wellfleet Press, 1980), 228.

18. Hans Döring, *Holy Kinship*, ca. 1515, 's-Heerenberg, Museum Huis Bergh, reproduced in *Heilige Anna, Grote Moeder*, cover and 109.

19. *Ludus coventriae*, 96.

20. Pamela Sheingorn, "'The Wise Mother': The Image of St. Anne Teaching the Virgin Mary," *Gesta* 32, no. 1 (1993); Ayers Bagley, "Mother as Teacher: St. Anne and Her Daughter," http://education.umn.

21. Christine Göttler, "Vom Sussen Namen Jesu," *Glaube Hoffnung Liebe Tod*, ed. Christoph Geissmar-Brand and Eleonora Louis (Vienna: Kunsthalle Wien, 1995), 292.

22. Knüssli's Anne chapel appears to have been located in the charnel house of the Saint Gallen Müster, and the Krell family's Saint Anne chapel at Saint Lorenz in Nuremberg functioned as a cemetery chapel according to Corinne Schleif (Donatio et Memoria, 425–26). Schleif states that at the beginning of the sixteenth century "cemetery chapels were frequently dedicated to Saint Anne." Ibid.

23. Stephan Beissel, *Die Verehrung der Heiligen und ihrer Reliquien in Deutschland im Mittelalter* (1890, 1892; reprint, Darmstadt: Wissenschaftliche Buchgesellschaft, 1991), 578.

24. The references are innumerable. An inscription on an *Anna Selbdritt* woodcut by Michel Schorpp of Ulm in which Anne holds a normal-size child Jesus and a semi-miniaturized child Mary reads: "O Saint Anne from whose womb was born Mary the Mother of Jesus Christ, with the two children on your arm, pray for us." Richard S. Field, "A New Woodcut of Saint Joseph by Ludwig of Ulm," *Cahiers de Joséphologie*

17 (July–December 1969). Typical is the reference to the *Anna Selbdritt* in a 1479 office as "Saint Anne painted with the two most holy children that ever were born." *Historia nova pulchra deuota et autentica de sancte Anna matre dei genitricis Marie.* Another office asks Anne to "pray for me with both those most glorious children." Johannes von Lambsheym, *Oraciones et alia pulcra ad sanctam Annam*, (Heidelberg: Heinrich Knoblochtzer, n.d.).

25. Hans M. J. Nieuwdorp, "Drie Mechelse huisaltaartjes," *Musees royaux des Beaux-Arts de Belgique Bulletin* 1–2 (1969), 7.

26. Aquinas, summarizing the tradition, writes that along with the *aurea* (halo) granted to all the blessed, additional *aureolae* were granted to martyrs, virgins, and doctors. In the fifteenth century the small crown was often replaced by the circlet or garland. Edwin Hall and Horst Uhr, "*Aureola super Auream*: Crowns and Related Symbols of Special Distinction for Saints in Late Gothic and Renaissance Iconography," *Art Bulletin* 67 (December 1985), 567–603.

27. Letter to the author, January 31, 1994, Markus Graf Fugger.

28. Barbara Lane, *The Altar and the Altarpiece: Sacramental Themes in Early Netherlandish Painting*, esp. chap. 3.

29. See Franz Brietzmann on the negative connotations of the old woman in late medieval Germany. *Die böse Frau in der deutschen Litteratur des Mittelalters*, 190–95.

30. "Gewinst du zway kindlein in der ee / darnach so trag dein geschmuck nit mee." *Der Frawen Spiegel*. I am indebted to Tamara Chaplin's research on clothing in Holy Kinships. Tamara Chaplin, "The Saint Anne Holy Kinship: Costume and Class Level" (unpublished paper, Concordia University, Montreal, 1992).

31. L. Fischel, *Nicolaus Gerhaert und die Bildhauer der deutschen Spätgotik* (Munich: Verlag F. Bruckmann, 1944). See also Wilhelm Pinder, *Die Deutsche Plastik von ausgehenden Mittelalter bis zum Ende der Renaissance*, 2 vols. (Potsdam: Akademische Verlagsgesellschaft Athenaion, 1929).

32. Roland Recht, *Nicolas de Leyde et la sculpture à Strasbourg, 1460–1525* (Strasbourg: Presses Universitaires de Strasburg, 1987), 373.

33. *Tilman Riemenschneider: Master Sculptor of the Late Middle Ages*, ed. Julien Chapuis (Washington, D.C.: National Gallery of Art, 1999), 188–91.

34. *Die Hystori oder Legend von den Heiligen Dryen Koenigen*, 7. In Cologne Heinrich von Neuss published the *Rock Jesu Christi* ca. 1512, 20.

35. In an example from Hildesheim in the Metropolitan Museum in New York, Emerentia stands behind a bench-type formation in which the Child sits on Mary's knee. The fourth figure was formerly identified as Afra, patron saint of Augsburg, no doubt because she grasps a slender tree trunk with cut-off branches similar to the tree depicted with Afra in the life of Saints Afra, Ulrich, and Simprecht published in Augsburg to promote the cult of these local saints in the early sixteenth century (*Das leben verdienen und wunderwerck der hailigen Auspurger Bistumbs bischoffen*). The figure, however, is identified on the sculpture as Emerentia.

36. Esser, "Die Heilige Sippe," 73.

37. Heinrich Appel, "Die Vesperbilder von Heimnach und Drove: Ein Nachtrag," *Jahrbuch der Rheinischen Denkmalpflege* 24 (1962), 181–88. The subject is also depicted in a work by Luca della Robbia (1400–1482) in the convent of the Observant Franciscans in Siena. Ibid.

38. Francesca Sautman, "Saint Anne in Folk Tradition," in *Interpreting Cultural Symbols*, ed. Ashley and Sheingorn, 73–74.

39. Hans Georg Gmelin, *Spätgotische Tafelmalerei in Niedersachsen und Bremen* (Munich: Deutscher Kunstverlag, 1974), 473.

40. A. M. Koldeweij, *De gude Sente Servas* (Assen: Van Gorcum, 1985).

41. On the export of Flemish altarpieces, see Lynn F. Jacobs, *Early Netherlandish Carved Altarpieces, 1380–1550: Medieval Tastes and Mass Marketing* (Cambridge: Cambridge University Press, 1998).

42. H. J. E. van Beuningen, A. M. Koldeweij, *Heilig en Profaan: 1000 Laatmiddeleeuwse Insignes uit de collectie H. J. E. van Beuningen*, Rotterdam Papers 8 (Cothen: Stichting Middeleeuwse Religieuze en Profane Insignes, 1993), 264. The opening in the pomegranate also resembles images of the side wound of Christ. See *Psalter and Hours of Bonne of Luxembourg*, in Jeffrey Hamburger, "The Visual and the Visionary: The Image in Late Medieval Monastic Devotions," *Viator* 20 (1989), fig. 23.

43. See Roger J. Crum and David G. Wilkins, "In the Defense of Florentine Republicanism: Saint Anne and Florentine Art, 1343–1575," *Interpreting Cultural Symbols*, ed. Ashlely and Sheingorn, 131–68. On the *Anna Selbdritt* carved by Andrea Sansovino (1486–1570) for the Northern humanist, the Apostolic Protonotary Johann Goritz, for the church of Sant'Agostino in Rome, see Bonito, "The Saint Anne Altar in Saint'Agostino: Restoration and Interpretation," *Burlington Magazine* 124, 950 (May 1982), 268–76.

44. Some works designated as (possibly) English may have been imported. For example, the style and iconographic details of the *Anna Selbdritt* from Bude Castle in the Victoria and Albert Museum in London and the *Anna Selbdritt* in the Lady Chapel of Exeter Cathedral suggest South Netherlandish origins. See Paul Williamson, *Northern Gothic Sculpture, 1200–1450* (London: Victoria and Albert Museum, 1988), 71; and P. Lasko and N. J. Morgan, eds., *Medieval Art in East Anglia, 1300–1520* (Norwich, 1973), nos. 108–10.

45. See Matthias Zender, "Matronen und verwandte Gottheiten," in *Ergebnisse eines Kolloquiums veranstaltet von der Göttinger Akademiekommission für die Altertumskunde Mittel- und Nordeuropas* (Cologne: Rheinland-Verlag GMBH, 1987), 213–28. Ton Brandenbarg raises additional points: *Heilig Familieleven*, 17–22; "Sint-Anna in Zeeland: Een verkenning," *Bulletin / Stichting Oude Zeeuwse Kerken* 29 (November 1992). Lène Dresen-Coenders notes correspondences in "Machtige grootmoeder, duivelse heks." See also

Lina Eckenstein, *Women Under Monasticism* (1896; reprint, New York: Russell & Russell, 1963), esp. 15–28, 38.

46. Caesarius of Heisterbach, *Dialogue of Miracles*, vol. 1, trans. H. von E. Scott and C. C. Swinton Bland (London: George Routledge & Sons, 1929), 25.

47. See H. Borger, S. Seiler, and W. Meier-Arendt, *Colonia Antiqua: Fouilles archéologues à Cologne* (Brussels: Crédit Communal de Belgique, 1977), 74. An image of Nehalennia in the Catherijnenkonvent Museum in Utrecht (RMCC b39, 40) bears an inscription from the donor, a merchant named Caius Crescentius Floras, asking the goddess' protection for his business. See also Emile Espérandieu, *Receuil Général des Bas-Reliefs, statues et Bustes de la Gaule Romaine*, vol. 5 (Paris: Presses Universitaires de France, 1966), 95.

48. Matthias Zender cites the seventeenth-century Luxemburg Jesuit scholar Alexander Wiltheim, an early investigator of possible connections between Christian and pre-Christian deities, who "remembered a Matronenstein in Metz and other images of gods, which in his homeland could be found in streets and attached to houses." Matthias Zender, "Matronen und verwandte Gottheiten," 214; see also 227.

49. Native Canadians honor Anne at several other Canadian shrines too, among them Lac Saint-Anne in Manitoba, where her feast on July 26 is celebrated by pilgrimage and immersion in the waters of the lake, and the Mi'Kmaq shrine at Lennox Island in Prince Edward Island.

Bibliography

Primary Sources

ABBREVIATIONS: ASSB   Augsburg Staats- und Stadtbibliothek
                 BSB   Bayerische Staatsbibliothek
                 EETS   Early English Text Society
                 PL   Migne, J. P. *Patrologiae cursus completus . . . series latina.* 221 vols. Paris: Migne, 1844–80.

Agricola, Rudolf. *Opuscula, orationes, epistolae.* Cologne, 1539. Reprint, Frankfurt, 1975.

Agrippa, Henricus Cornelius. *De beatissimae Annae monogamia, ac unico puerperio propositiones abbreuiatae et articulate, iuxta disceptationem Iacobi Fabri Stapulensis in libro de tribus et una, intitulato.* Munich, 1533.

Ain gar nutzlichs büchlin von dem ganzen geschlecht sant Anna vnd von sant Anna lobliche brüderschafft: Vnnd von etlichen grossen wunderzaichen sant Anna. Augsburg, after 1494. (BSB)

Albinus, Petrus. *Annabergische Annales de anno 1492 bis 1539: Festschrift zum 25 jährigen Bestehen des Vereins für Geschichte von Annaberg und Umgegend.* Annaberg, 1910.

Das älteste Stralsundische Stadtbuch, 1270–1310. Edited by F. Fabricius. Berlin: Verlag von W. Weber, 1872.

Anonymous Franciscan. *Hec est quedam rara et ideo cara legenda de sancta Anna. et de universa eius.* Strasburg, 1501. Published with the Rosary tract, "Incipit tractaculus novus et preciosus de fraternitate Rosarij gloriose Virginis Marie." (ASSB)

Anselmus of Canterbury. *De conceptu virginali et originali peccato.* Migne, PL 158.

Anshelmus, Valerius. *Berner Chronik von Anfang der Stadt Bern bis 1526.* Bern: L. A. Haller, 1825, 1827.

Aquinas, Thomas. *Summa theologiae.* New York: Blackfriars, 1964–67.

Aufnahmeformular der St. Annenbrüder in Augsburg vom Jahre 1494. Augsburg: Erhard Ratdolt, 1494. (ASSB) Published in A. Haemmerle, "Das Aufnahmeformular der St. Annenbrüder in Augsburg vom Jahre 1494," *Vierteljahreshefte zur Kunst und Geschichte Augsburgs* 4 (1947–48), 9.

Augsburg, Reichstadt Schätze 95 II, III. (Augsburg Stadarchiv)

Bernard of Clairvaux. *The Letters of St. Bernard of Clairvaux.* Translated by Bruno Scott James. London: Burns & Oates, 1953.

Birgitta of Sweden. *The Liber Celestis of St. Bridget of Sweden.* Edited by Roger Ellis. EETS, o.s. New York: Oxford University Press, 1987.

———. *Revelaciones.* Edited by Birger Bergh. Uppsala: Simlingar utgivna av Svenska Forn-skriftsällskapet, 1971.

Birlinger, Anton, ed. "Leben heiliger alemannischer Frauen des Mittelalters 5: Die Nonnen von St. Katarinental bei Diessenhofen." *Alemannia* 15. Bonn, 1887.

Bokenham, Osbern. *Legendys of Hooly Wummen.* Edited by Mary S. Serjeantson. EETS, O.S. 1938. Millwood, N.Y.: Kraus Reprint, 1971.

Die Briefwechsel des Konrad Celtis. Edited by Hans Rupprich. Munich: Kommission zur Erforschung der Geschichte der Reformation und der Gegenreformation, 1934.

Brussels MS II 3636. Centrum voor de Studie van het Verluchte Handschrift in de Nederlan-den, Katholieke Universiteit, Louvain. Files pertaining to the *Anna Selbdritt.*

Das Büchlin wirt genannt die himelisch Funtgrüb. (ASSB)

Dis büchlin saget von den peinen so do bereit seint allen denen die do sterben in todsünden. Strasburg, 1509. (BSB)

Caesarius of Heisterbach. *Dialogue of Miracles.* 2 vols. Translated by H. von E. Scott and C. C. Swinton Bland. London: George Routledge, 1929.

Die Chroniken der deutschen Städte vom 14. bis ins 16. Jahrhundert: Chroniken der schwäbischen Städte, Augsburg. Edited by Karl von Hegel and Friedrich Roth. Leipzig: Verlag von S. Hirzel, 1862–1931.

Cochlaeus, Johannes. *Brevis Germanie Descriptio, 1512.* Edited and translated by Karl Lan-gosch. Darmstadt: Wissenschaftliche Buchgesellschaft, 1960.

Cohen, Gustave, ed. *Mystères et moralités du manuscrit 617 de Chantilly.* Paris: Librairie Edouard Champion, 1920.

Corstanje, Charles van; Yves Cazaux; John Decavele; and Albert Derolez. *Vita Sancta Coletae, 1381–1447.* Leiden: Brill, 1982.

Cullman, Oscar. "The Protevangelium of James." In *Gospels and Related Writings,* vol. 1: *New Testament Apocrypha.* Edited by Edgar Hennecke and Wilhelm Schneemelcher. Translated by R. M. Wilson. Philadelphia: Westminster Press, 1963.

Cursor Mundi: A Northumbrian Poem of the XIVth Century. Part 2. Edited by Richard Morris. EETS, O.S. 1875. London: Richard Clay, 1966.

Denemarken, Jan van. *Die historie, die ghetiden ende die exempelen vander heyligher vrouwen sint Annen.* Antwerp: Geraert Leeu, 1490–91. (Brussels, Bibliothèque Royale)

Die elsässische Legenda Aurea. Edited by Werner Williams-Krapp. Tübingen, 1983.

Der Frawen Spiegel. Augsburg: Hanns Schoensperger am Weinmarckt, 1522. (ASSB)

Der Gilgengart. (Augsburg: Hans Schönsperger, ca. 1520) In *Spätmittelalter Humanismus Refor-mation: Texte und Zeugnisse.* Edited by Hedwig Heger. Munich: C. H. Beck'sche Verlagsbuchhandlung, 1975.

De gulden Letanien. Antwerp: Heinrich Wouters, 1575. (Brussels, Bibliothèque Royale)

Der Heiligen Leben. Edited by Margit Brand, Kristina Freienhagen-Baumgardt, Ruth Meyer, and Werner Williams-Krapp. Tübingen: Max Niemeyer Verlag, 1996.

Devotio Moderna: Basic Writings. Translated by John van Engen. New York: Paulist Press, 1988.

Distaves and Dames: Renaissance Treatises For and About Women. Edited by Diane Bornstein. Delmar, N.Y.: Scholars Facsimiles & Reprints, 1978.

Dorlandus, Petrus. *De nativitate conversione & vita invictissimae martiris beatissimae virginis Katharinae.* Louvain: Theodericus Martinus Alostensis, 1513. (ASSB)

————. *Vita beatissimae Matris Annae edita a venerabili et erudito Pater Petro Dorlando.* Manuscript GB 4° 197, ff. 65r–152r. (Cologne, Historisches Archiv)

————. *Vita gloriosissime matris Annae christipare virginis Marie genetricis ab ascensio in compendium redacta ex historia suavissima eiusdem matris Anne ab religiosissimo viro F. dorlando ordinis Carthusiensis in zelem theuthonice prius edita.* Printed with Ludolf of Saxony, *Vita Jhesu Christi.* Antwerp: Johannus Kerberg, n.d. (BSB)

Dreves, Guido Maria, and Clemens Blume. *Analecta hymnica medii aevi.* 55 vols. 1886–1922. Frankfurt am Main: Minerva, 1961.

Duns Scotus, John. *Opera omnia.* 26 vols. 1894. Reprint, Westmead: Gregg International, 1969.

The Early South-English Legendary. Edited by Carl Horstmann. EETS, o.s. London: Trübner, 1887.

Egranus Sylvius [Johannes Wildenauer]. *Apologia contra Calumniatores suos.* Leipzig, 1517. (ASSB)

Faber Stapulensis [Jacques Lefevre d'Etaples]. *De Maria Magdalena, Tridvo Christi, et ex tribus vna Maria, disceptatio.* Paris: Henricus Stephanus, 1518. (BSB)

Fugger, Markus Graf. Letter to the author. January 31, 1994.

Gebsweiler, Catharina von. *Lebensbeschreibungen der ersten Schwestern des Klosters der Dominikanerinnen zu Unterlinden.* Translated by Ludwig Clarus. Regensburg: Verlag von Georg Joseph Manz, 1863.

Habets, Jos. "Chronijck der landen van Overmaas en der aangrenzende gewesten, door eenen inwoner van Beek bij Maastricht." *Publications de la Société Historique et Archéologique dans le duché de Limbourg à Maestricht,* 7:101–8. Ruhrmond, 1870.

Haemmerle, Albert. *Die Leibdingbuecher der Freien Reichsstadt Augsburg, 1330–1500.* Typescript, Munich, 1943. (ASSB)

Hätzer, Ludwig. *Ain Urtayl Gottes vnsers eegemahels wie man sich mit allen goetzen vnd Bildnussen halten soll auss der hayligen geschrifft gezogen.* Zurich, 1523. (ASSB)

Haymo [of Halberstadt]. *Historiae sacrae epitome.* PL 118.

Hildesheim, Ioannes de. *Dialogus inter directorem et detractorem de ordine Carmelitarum 14.* Edited by Adrianus Staring. In *Medieval Carmelite Heritage: Early Reflections on the Nature of the Order.* Rome: Institutum Carmelitanum, 1989.

Historia nova pulchra devota et autentica. Augsburg: Anton Sorg, 1479 (Berlin Staatsbibliothek Preussischer Kulturbesitz). This work is entitled *Officia parentelae Christi* in the Berlin *Inkunabelkatalog.*

Hroswitha of Gandersheim. *Historia nativitatis laudabilisque conversationis intactae Dei genitricis, quam scriptam reperi sub nomine sancti Jacobi fratris Domini.* PL 137.

————. *The Nondramatic Works of Hroswitha.* Translated by S. M. Gonsalva Wiegand. Saint Meinrad, Ind.: Abbey Press, 1936.

Hystoria pulcra de sancto Joachim patre dei matris Marie. Augsburg: Anton Sorg. (ASSB)

Die Hystori oder Legend von den Heiligen Dryen Koenigen: Faksimileausgabe eines Pilgerbuches von 1520 mit einem Verzeichnis der Drucke der Servatius Kruffter in Köln. Edited by Elisabeth Christern. Cologne: Bibliophilen-Gesellschaft, 1964.

Iacopone da Todi. "Pianto de la madonna de la passione del figliolo Iesu Cristo." In *The Penguin Book of Italian Verse*, edited by George R. Kay, 8–13. 1958. Reprint, Harmondsworth: Penguin Books, 1972.

Immessen, Arnold. *Der Sündenfall*. Edited by Friedrich Krage. Heidelberg: Carl Winters Universitäts-Buchhandlung, 1913.

James, M. R. *The Apocryphal New Testament*. Oxford: Clarendon Press, 1955.

Jerome. *De perpetua virginitate, adversus Helvidium*, PL 23.

Kempe, Margery. *The Book of Margery Kempe*. Translated by B. A. Windeatt. London: Penguin, 1985.

Kessler, Johannes. *Johannes Kesslers Sabbata mit kleineren Schriften und Briefen*. Edited by Emil Egli and Rudolf Schoch. St. Gallen: Fehr'sche Buchhandlung, 1902.

Lambsheym, Johannes von. *Libellus perutilis de fraternitate sanctissima Rosarii et psalterij beate Marie virginis*. Mainz: Peter Friedberg, 1495. (ASSB)

———. *Oraciones et alia pulcra ad sanctam Annam*. Heidelberg: Heinrich Knoblochtzer, n.d. Hain 12029. (BSB)

Das Leben der Schwestern zu Töss beschrieben von Elsbeth Stagel, Deutsches Nonnenleben: Das Leben der Schwestern zu Töss und der Nonne von Engeltal Büchlein von der Gnaden Uberlast. Edited by Margarete Weinhandl. Munich: O. C. Recht, 1921.

Das Leben und Wunderzaichen der allerseeligisten Frawen Annae. Munich: Cornelius Leyffert, 1627. (A translation of Anonymous Franciscan, *Legenda sanctae Annae* [Louvain: Joh. de Westfalia, 1496].) (BSB)

Das leben verdienen und wunderwerck der hailigen Auspurger Bistumbs bischoffen sant Ulrichs vnd Symprechts auch der säligen martrerin sant Aphre irer müter Hilaria geschlecht vnd gesellschafft in unserm daselbst loblichen gotshaus rastend. Augsburg, 1516. (ASSB)

Legenda sanctae Annae. Leipzig: Melchior Lotter, 1497.

Libellus continens laudes et fraternitatum: Officiam misse et oraciones de sancta Anna. Heidelberg: Heinrich Knoblochtzer, probably after 1500. (BSB)

Ludus coventriae. Edited by K. S. Block. EETS, e.s. London: Oxford University Press, (1922) 1974.

Luther, Martin. *Tischreden*. Weimar: Bölhaus, 1883–1948.

———. *Werke: Kritische Gesamtausgabe*. 90 vols. Weimar: Bölhaus, 1883–1948.

Middle English Stanzaic Versions of the Life of Saint Anne. Edited by Roscoe E. Parker. EETS, o.s. London: Oxford University Press, 1928.

Migne, J. P. *Patrologiae cursus completus . . . series latina*, 221 vols. Paris: Migne, 1844–80.

Milisch, Christian Gotthold. *Durch diese kurze Nachricht von der ehemahligen St. Annae-Bruderschafft*. Annaberg: Valentin Friesen, 1746.

Mirk's Festial: A Collection of Homilies. Edited by Theodor Erbe. EETS, e.s. 1905. Reprint, Millwood, N.Y.: Kraus Reprint, 1987.

Mone, Franz Joseph. *Lateinische Hymnen des Mittelalters*. 3 vols. 1853–55. Reprint, Aalen: Scientia Verlag, 1964.

Northern Renaissance Art, 1400–1600: Sources and Documents. Edited by Wolfgang Stechow. 1966. Reprint, Evanston, Ill.: Northwestern University Press, 1989.

Polius, Jacobus. *Exegeticon historicum sanctae Annae aviae Christi, magnae matris Deiparae, necnon sacri capitis ejusdem marcoduram translati.* Cologne, 1640.

Procopius. *Procopius, Works: Buildings.* Translated by H. B. Dewing. Loeb Classical Library. Cambridge, Mass.: Harvard University Press, 1940.

A Reformation Debate. Edited by Bryan D. Mangrum and Giuseppe Scavizzi. Toronto: University of Toronto Press, 1991.

Rem, Lucas. *Tagebuch des Lucas Rem aus den Jahren, 1494–1541: Ein Beitrag zur Handelsgeschichte der Stadt Augsburg.* Edited by B. Greiff. Augsburg: J. N. Hartmann'schen Buchdruckerei, 1861.

Richter, Adam Daniel. *Umständliche aus zuverlässigen Nachrichten zusammengetragene Chronica der im Meissnischen Ober-Erz-Gebürge gelegenen Königl.churfl. Sächssischen freyen Berg-Stadt St. Annaberg.* Annaberg: August Valentine Friesen, 1746.

Sainte-Marie Perrin, E. *La belle vie de Sainte Colette de Corbie, 1381–1447.* Paris: Librairie Plon, 1921.

"Sciendum sicuti laudare." Switzerland, after 1482. (BSB)

Suso, Henry. *The Exemplar, with Two German Sermons.* Edited and translated by Frank Tobin. New York: Paulist Press, 1989.

Tischendorf, C. von. *Evangelia apocrypha.* 1853. Reprint, Hildesheim, 1966.

Trithemius, Johannes. *Joannis Trithemii: Opera pia et spiritualia.* Edited by Johannes Busaeus. Mainz, 1604, 1605. (University of Toronto, Robarts Library)

————. *De laudibus sanctissimae matris Annae.* Mainz: Peter Friedberg, 1494. (ASSB)

Vigneulles, Philippe de. *Gedenkbuch des Metzer Bürgers Philippe von Vigneulles aus den Jahren 1471 bis 1522.* Edited by Heinrich Michelant. 1851. Reprint, Amsterdam: Editions Rodopi, 1968.

Vincent of Beauvais. "Speculum Historiale." *Speculum Quadruplex sive Speculum Maius.* 1624. Reprint, Graz: Akademische Druck-u. Verlagsanstalt, 1965.

Vita beatae virginis Mariae et salvatoris rhythmica. Edited by A. Vögtlin. Tübingen, 1988.

Von der kinthait unnsers herren iesu cristi genant vita christi. (BSB)

Voragine, Jacobus de. *The Golden Legend.* 2 vols. Translated by William Granger Ryan. Princeton: Princeton University Press, 1993.

————. *The Golden Legend; or, Lives of the Saints as Englished by William Caxton.* London: J. M. Dent & Company: Aldine House, 1900.

————. *Legenda Aurea.* Edited by Th. Graesse. 1890. Reprint, Osnabrück: Otto Zeller, 1965.

Wackernagel, Philipp. *Das Deutsche Kirchenlied von der ältesten Zeit bis zu Anfang des XVII Jahrhunderts.* 5 vols. 1864–77. Reprint, Hildesheim: Georg Olms Verlagsbuchhandlung, 1964.

Wernher, Priester. *Maria. Bruchstücke und Umarbeitungen.* Edited by Hans Fromm. Tübingen: Max Niemeyer Verlag, 1969.

Wie hebt sich an sant Brandons Buch was er wunders erfaren hat. 1476. (ASSB)

Williamson, E. W., ed. *The Letters of Osbert of Clare.* New York: Oxford University Press, 1929.

Die wunderbare Meerfahrt des heiligen Brandan. Augsburg: Anton Sorg, c. 1476. (ASSB)

Zwingli, Huldrich. *Akten der zweiten Disputation vom 26–28 Oktober 1523, Huldrych Zwinglis Sämtliche Werke.* Berlin and Zurich: C. A. Schwetschke & Sohn, 1905.

Secondary Sources

Andersson, Christiane D. "Religiöse Bilder Cranachs im Dienste der Reformation." Edited by L. W. Spitz. *Humanismus und Reformation als kulturelle Kräfte in der deutschen Geschichte.* Berlin: Walter de Gruyter, 1981.

Appel, Heinrich Appel. "Die Vesperbilder von Heimnach und Drove: Ein Nachtrag." *Jahrbuch der Rheinischen Denkmalpflege* 24 (1962), 181–88.

Arnold, Klaus. *Johannes Trithemius, 1462–1516.* Quellen und Forschungen zur Geschichte des Bistums und Hochstifts Würzburg, 23. Würzburg: Kommissionsverlag Ferdinand Schöningh, 1991.

Ashley, Kathleen. "Image and Ideology: Saint Anne in Late Medieval Drama and Narrative." In *Iconoclasm vs. Art and Drama,* edited by Clifford Davidson and Ann Eljenholm Nichols. Kalamazoo: Western Michigan University, Medieval Institute Publications, 1989.

Ashley, Kathleen, and Pamela Sheingorn, eds. *Interpreting Cultural Symbols: Saint Anne in Late Medieval Society.* Athens: University of Georgia Press, 1990.

Aston, Margaret. "Iconoclasm in England: Official and Clandestine." In *Iconoclasm vs. Art and Drama,* edited by Clifford Davidson and Ann Eljenholm Nichols. Kalamazoo: Western Michigan University, Medieval Institute Publications, 1989.

———. *Lollards and Reformers: Images and Literacy in Late Medieval Religion.* London: Hambledon Press, 1984.

"Augsburg Franziskaner-Konventualen." *Bavaria Franziskana Antiqua* 5 (1961).

Bagley, Ayers. "Mother as Teacher: St. Anne and Her Daughter." http://education.umn.

Beck, Manfred. *Untersuchungen zur geistlichen Literatur im Kölner Drück des frühen 16. Jahrhunderts.* Göppingen: Verlag Alfred Kümmerle, 1977.

Beissel, Stephan. *Die Verehrung der Heiligen und ihrer Reliquien in Deutschland im Mittelalter.* 1890, 1892. Reprint, Darmstadt: Wissenschaftliche Buchgesellschaft, 1991.

Beuningen, H. J. E. van , and A. M. Koldeweij. *Heilig en Profaan: 1000 Laatmiddeleeuwse Insignes uit de collectie H. J. E. van Beuningen* (Rotterdam Papers). Cothen: Stichting Middeleeuwse Religieuze en Profane Insignes, 1993.

Bonito, Virginia Anne. "The Saint Anne Altar in Sant'Agostino: A New Discovery." *Burlington Magazine* 122, 933 (December 1980), 805–11.

———. "The Saint Anne Altar in Sant'Agostino: Restoration and Interpretation." *Burlington Magazine* 124, 950 (May 1982), 268–76.

Borchert, Bruno. "L'Immaculée dans l'iconographie du Carmel." *Carmelus* 2 (1955), 85–131.

Borger, H., S. Seiler, and W. Meier-Arendt. *Colonia antiqua: Fouilles archéologues à Cologne.* Brussels: Crédit Communal de Belgique, 1977.

Brandenbarg, Ton. *Heilig familieleven: Verspreiding en waardering van de Historie van Sint-Anna in de stedelijke cultuur in de Nederlanden en het Rijnland aan het begin van de moderne tijd.* Nijmegen: Sun, 1990.

———. "Jan van Denemarken en Pieter Dorlant over de maagschap van de heilige moeder Anna / een veergelijkende studie." *Ons Geestelijk Erf,* parts 63 and 64 (June–December 1989, March–September 1990), 85–128.

———. "Saint Anne: A Holy Grandmother and Her Children." In *Sanctity and Motherhood: Essays on Holy Mothers in the Middle Ages,* edited by Anneke B. Mulder-Bakker, 31–65. New York: Garland Publishing, 1995.

———. "Sint-Anna in Zeeland: Een verkenning." *Bulletin / Stichting Oude Zeeuwse Kerken* 29 (November 1992), n.p.

———. "St. Anne and Her Family: The Veneration of St. Anne in Connection with Concepts of Marriage and the Family in the Early Modern Period." In *Saints and She-Devils: Images of Women in the Fifteenth and Sixteenth Centuries,* edited by Lène Dresen-Coenders, 101–27. London: Rubicon Press, 1987.

Brandenbarg, Ton, Willemien Deeleman–van Tyen, Lène Dresen-Coenders, and Léon van Liebergen. *Heilige Anna, grote Moeder.* Nijmegen: Sun, 1992.

Brann, Noel. *The Abbott Trithemius, 1462–1516: The Renaissance of Monastic Humanism.* Leiden: E. J. Brill, 1981.

Braun, Joseph. *Tracht und Attribute der Heiligen in der deutschen Kunst.* Stuttgart: J. B. Metzlersche Verlagsbuchhandlung, 1943.

Brietzmann, Franz. *Die böse Frau in der deutschen Litteratur des Mittelalters.* 1912. Reprint, London: Johnson Reprint Company, 1967.

Brown, Elizabeth A. R., and Nancy Freeman Regalado. "La grant Feste: Philip the Fair's Celebration of the Knighting of His Sons in Paris at Pentecost of 1313." In *City and Spectacle in Medieval Europe,* edited by Barbara A. Hanawalt and Kathryn L. Reyerson. Minneapolis: University of Minnesota Press, 1994.

Brown, Peter. *The Cult of the Saints: Its Rise and Function in Latin Christianity.* Chicago: University of Chicago Press, 1981.

Burgener, L. *Die Wallfahrtsorte der katholischen Schweiz.* Ingenbohl, 1864.

Burke, Peter. *The Italian Renaissance: Culture and Society in Italy.* 1972. Reprint, Princeton: Princeton University Press, 1986.

Chaplin, Tamara. "The Saint Anne Holy Kinship: Costume and Class Level." Unpublished paper. Concordia University, Montreal, 1992.

Charland, P. V. *Le culte de sainte Anne en Occident, seconde période: De 1400 (environ) à nos jours.* Quebec: Imprimerie Franciscaine Missionaire, 1921.

———. *Patronage de Sainte Anne en arts,* 2 vols. Quebec: A.-O. Pruneau, 1923.

———. *Les trois légendes de Madame Saincte Anne.* Vol. 1: *Légende hagiographique (la vie),* Quebec: Pruneau & Kirouac, 1898. Vol. 2: *Légende historique (le culte), Histoire de la dévotion à Sainte-Anne,* Lévis: Mercier & Cie, 1904. Vol. 3: *Légende iconographique (les arts), Madame Saincte Anne et son culte au moyen âge,* 2 vols., Paris: Alphonse Picard & Fils, 1911, 1913.

Chatelet, Albert. *Early Dutch Painting: Painting in the Northern Netherlands in the Fifteenth Century.* Secaucus, N.J.: Wellfleet Press, 1980.

Chrisman, Miriam Usher. *Lay Culture, Learned Culture: Books and Social Change in Strasbourg, 1480–1599.* New Haven: Yale University Press, 1981.

Christensen, Carl. *Art and the Reformation in Germany.* Athens: University of Georgia Press, 1980.

Cloutier, Nicole. "L'Iconographie de Sainte Anne au Québec." 2 vols. Ph.D. diss. Université de Montréal, 1982.

Compston, H. F. B. "The Thirty-Seven Conclusions of the Lollards." *English Historical Review* 26 (1911).

Cook, G. H. *Letters to Cromwell on the Suppression of the Monasteries.* London: John Baker, 1965.

Couliano, Ioan P. *Eros and Magic in the Renaissance.* Chicago: University of Chicago Press, 1987.

Crum, Roger J., and David G. Wilkins. "In the Defense of Florentine Republicanism: Saint Anne and Florentine Art, 1343–1575." In *Interpreting Cultural Symbols: Saint Anne in Late Medieval Society,* edited by Kathleen Ashley and Pamela Sheingorn, 131–68. Athens: University of Georgia Press, 1990.

Davidson, Clifford. "The Anti-Visual Prejudice." In *Iconoclasm vs. Art and Drama,* edited by Clifford Davidson and Ann Eljenholm Nichols, 33–46. Kalamazoo: Western Michigan University, Medieval Institute Publications, 1989.

Deeleman–Van Tyen, Willemien. "Sint Anna-te-Drieen: Een onderzoek naar vorm, inhoud en functioneren van het thema St. Anna-te-Drieen in de nederlandse beeld-houwkunst der late middeleeuwen." 2 vols. Master's thesis, Free University, Amsterdam, 1990.

Dörfler-Dierken, Angelika. *Die Verehrung der heiligen Anna in Spätmittelalter und früher Neuzeit.* Göttingen: Vandenhoek & Ruprecht, 1992.

———. *Vorreformatorische Bruderschaften der hl. Anna.* Heidelberg: Carl Winter Universitäts-verlag, 1992.

———. "Vorreformatorische Patrozinien der heiligen Anna im Erzbistum Trier." *Archiv für mittelrheinische Kirchengeschichte* 44 (1992), 103–36.

———. "Wunderheilungen durch das Limburger Annenheiltum / Mit Edition einer Abschrift des Mirakelbuches von 1511 in der Stadtbibliothek Trier." *Kurtrierisches Jahrbuch* 31 (1991), 83–107.

Dorn, Ludwig. *Die Marien-Wallfahrten des Bistums Augsburg.* Augsburg: Verlag Winfried-Werk, 1957.

Dresen-Coenders, Lène. "Machtige grootmoeder, duivelse heks: Speurtocht naar de samen-hang tussen heksenvervolging en de verering van de grote moeder Anna op de drempel van de nieue tijd." *Jeugd en Samenleving* 5 (1975), 213–47.

Eckenstein, Lina. *Women Under Monasticism.* 1896. Reprint, New York: Russell & Russell, 1963.

Egg, Erich. "Stiftungen-Heiltum-Ablässe." In *Heiltum und Wallfahrt,* edited by Gert Ammann. Innsbruck: Tiroler Landesmuseum Ferdinandeum, 1988.

Elliott, Dyan. *Spiritual Marriage: Sexual Abstinence in Medieval Wedlock.* Princeton: Princeton University Press, 1993.

Espérandieu, Emile. *Receuil général des bas-reliefs, statues et bustes de la Gaule romaine.* 10 vols. Paris: Presses Universitaires de France, 1966.

Esser, Werner. "Die Heilige Sippe: Studien zu einem spätmittelalterlichen Bildthema in Deutschland und den Niederlanden." Ph.D. diss., Rheinischen Friedrich-Wilhelms-Universität, Bonn, 1986.

Falk, Franz. *Geschichte der Marienverehrung und der Immakulata Tradition im Bistum Mainz und am Mittelrhein.* Mainz: Druckerei Lehrlinghaus, 1906.

———. *Zur Geschichte der Immaculata Tradition in der Mainzer Kirche.* Mainz: Verlag von Kirghheim & Company, 1904.

Field, Richard S. "A New Woodcut of Saint Joseph by Ludwig of Ulm." *Cahiers de Joséphologie* 17 (July–December 1969), 237–72.

Finucane, Ronald C. *Miracles and Pilgrims: Popular Beliefs in Medieval England.* London: J. M. Dent & Sons, 1977.

Fircks, Juliane von, and Volkmar Heere. *Anna Selbdritt: Eine kolossale Stuckplastik der Hochgotik in St. Nikolai zu Stralsund.* Stralsund: Edition Herre, 1999.

Fischel, L. *Nicolaus Gerhaert und die Bildhauer der deutschen Spätgotik.* Munich: Verlag F. Bruckmann, 1944.

500 Jahre St. Anna in Düren, 1501–2001. Düren: Hahne-Schloemer Verlag, n.p.

Folda, Jaroslav. "The Church of Saint Anne." *Biblical Archaeologist* 54 (June 1991), 88–96.

Förster, Max. "Die Legende vom Trinubium der hl. Anna." In *Probleme der Englischen Sprache und Kultur: Festschrift Johannes Hoops zum 60. Geburtstag Überreicht von Freunden und Kollegen,* edited by Wolfgang Keller, 105–30. Heidelberg: Carl Winter's Universitätsbuchhandlung, 1925.

Freedberg, David. *The Power of Images.* Chicago: University of Chicago Press, 1989.

Gaiffier, J. de. "Le Trinubium Annae." *Analecta Bollandiana* 90 (1972), 289–98.

Garside, Charles A., Jr. *Zwingli and the Arts.* New Haven: Yale University Press, 1966.

Gatz, Erwin, ed. *St.-Anna in Düren.* Mönchengladbach: B. Kühlen Verlag, 1972.

Geary, Patrick. *Living with the Dead in the Middle Ages.* Ithaca: Cornell University Press, 1994.

Geertz, Clifford. "Art as a Cultural System." *Modern Language Notes* 91 (October–December 1976), 1473–99.

Geisberg, Max. *The German Single-Leaf Woodcut, 1500–1550.* 4 vols. Edited by Walter L. Strauss. New York: Hacker Art Books, 1974.

Gijsel, Jan. *Die unmittelbare Textüberlieferung des sogenannten Pseudo-Matthäus.* Verhandelingen van de Koninklijke Academie voor Wetenschappen, Letteren en Schone Kunsten van Belgie. Vols. 43 and 96. Brussels: Koninklijke Academie, 1981.

Gmelin, Hans Georg. *Spätgotische Tafelmalerei in Niedersachsen und Bremen.* Munich: Deutscher Kunstverlag, 1974.

Göttler, Christine. "Vom Süssen Namen Jesu." *Glaube Hoffnung Liebe Tod,* edited by Christoph Geissmar-Brand and Eleonora Louis, 292–95. Vienna: Kunsthalle Wien, 1995.

Grimme, Ernst G. *Europäische Bildwerke vom Mittelalter zum Barock.* Cologne: DuMont Buchverlag, 1977.

Hale, Rosemary. "Imitatio Mariae: Motherhood Motifs in Late Medieval German Spirituality." Ph.D. diss., Harvard University, 1992.

Hall, Edwin, and Horst Uhr. "*Aureola super Auream:* Crowns and Related Symbols of Special Distinction for Saints in Late Gothic and Renaissance Iconography." *Art Bulletin* 67 (December 1985), 567–603.

Hamburger, Jeffrey. *Nuns as Artists: The Visual Culture of a Medieval Convent.* Berkeley and Los Angeles: University of California Press, 1977.

———. "The Visual and the Visionary: The Image in Late Medieval Monastic Devotions." *Viator* 20 (1989), 161–82.

Hartig, Michael. *Das Benediktiner-Reichsstift Sankt Ulrich und Afra in Augsburg, 1012–1802.* Augsburg: Verlag Dr. Benno Filsner, 1923.

Head, Thomas. "I Vow Myself To Be Your Servant." *Historical Reflections* 11 (1984), 215–51.

Heinzle, Erwin. *Wolf Huber um 1485–1553.* Innsbruck: Universitätsverlag Wagner, 1953.

Heydenreich, Ludwig Heinrich. "Le Sainte Anne de Léonard de Vinci." *Gazette des Beaux-Arts* 10 (1933): 207–19.

Hofmann, Siegfried. *Goldschmiedearbeiten in und aus Ingolstadt.* Ingolstadt: Stadtmuseum Ingolstadt, 1988.

Hollstein, F. W. H. *German Engravings, Etchings, and Woodcuts.* 61 vols. Amsterdam: M. Hertzberger, 1954–68.

Hunt, Lynn. "Psychoanalysis, the Self, and Historical Interpretation." *Common Knowledge* 6, 2 (1997), 10–17.

Hurlbut, Jesse D. "The Ghent Altarpiece Performed: Civic Appropriation of Art in 1458." Conference Paper, University of Western Michigan International Congress on Medieval Studies, Kalamazoo, 1993.

Jacobs, Lynn F. *Early Netherlandish Carved Altarpieces, 1380–1550: Medieval Tastes and Mass Marketing.* Cambridge: Cambridge University Press, 1998.

Janssen, Johannes. *Erläuterungen und Ergänzungen zu Janssens Geschichte des deutschen Volkes.* Edited by Ludwig Pastor. Freiburg im Breisgau: Herdersche Verlagshandlung, 1907.

Jones, Douglas. *The Church in Chester.* Manchester: Chetham Society, 1957.

Kalinke, Marianne E. *The Book of Reykjaholar: The Last of the Great Medieval Legendaries.* Toronto: University of Toronto Press, 1996.

———. "Mariu saga og Onnu." *Arckiv för Nordisk Filologi* 109 (1994), 43–99.

Kawerau, Gustav. *Johann Agricola von Eisleben.* Berlin: Wilhelm Hertz, 1881.

Kieckhefer, Richard. *Magic in the Middle Ages.* Cambridge: Cambridge University Press, 1989.

Kiessling, Rolf. *Bürgerliche Gesellschaft und Kirche in Augsburg im Spätmittelalter.* Augsburg: Verlag H. Mühlberger, 1971.

Kirschbaum, Engelbert. *Lexikon der christlichen Ikonographie.* 8 vols. Rome and Freiburg: Herder, 1968–76.

Kleinschmidt, Beda. *Die heilige Anna: Ihre Verehrung in Geschichte, Kunst, und Volkstum.* Düsseldorf: Schwann, 1930.

Koch, H. H. *Das Karmeliterkloster zu Frankfurt am Main, 13. bis 16. Jahrhundert.* Frankfurt, 1912.

Koldeweij, A. M. *De gude Sente Servas.* Assen: Van Gorcum, 1985.

Kunast, Hans-Jörg. *Getruckt zu Augspurg: Buchdruck und Buchhandel in Augsburg zwischen 1468 und 1555.* Tübingen: Max Niemeyer Verlag, 1997.

Künstle, Karl. *Ikonographie der christlichen Kunst.* 2 vols. Freiburg: Herder, 1926–28.

Lafontaine-Dosogne, Jacqueline. *Iconographie de l'enfance de la Vierge.* Brussels: Académie royale de Belgique, 1964.

Lane, Barbara. *The Altar and the Altarpiece: Sacramental Themes in Early Netherlandish Painting.* New York: Harper & Row, 1984.

Lasko, P., and N. J. Morgan, eds. *Medieval Art in East Anglia, 1300–1520.* Norwich, 1973.

Levi d'Ancona, Mirella. *The Iconography of the Immaculate Conception in the Middle Ages and Early Renaissance.* New York: College Art Association, 1957.

Liebhart, Wilhelm. "Historia Hohenwart: Eine Chronik von 1489 zur Gründung und Wallfahrtsgeschichte des Benediktinerinnenklosters aus dem Umkreis Kaiser Maximilians I." *Neuburger Kollektaneenblatt* 132 (1979), 284–98.

————. "Stifte, Klöster, und Konvente in Augsburg." In *Geschichte der Stadt Augsburg von der Römerzeit bis zur Gegenwart*, edited by G. Gottlieb, W. Barr, and Josef Beck, 193–201. Stuttgart: Theiss, 1984.

Lindgren, Mereth. "De heliga änkorna: S. Annakultens framväxt, speglad i birgittinsk ikonografi." *Konsthistorisk tidskrift* 59 (1990), 52–75.

Lindgren-Fridell, Marita. "Der Stammbaum Maria aus Anna und Joachim." *Marburger Jahrbuch für Kunstwissenschaft* 2 (1938–39), 289–308.

Macfarlane, Alan. *The Origins of English Individualism: The Family, Property, and Social Transition.* Oxford: Basil Blackwell, 1978.

Mangold, Bernadette. *Die Darstellung der heiligen Anna Selbdritt in der gotischen Plastik Niederbayerns, 1380–1540.* Master's thesis, University of Passau, 1990.

Maniurka, Peter Paul. *Mater Matris Domini: Die heilige Anna Selbdritt in der gotischen Skulptur Schlesiens.* Altenberge: Oros Verlag, 2001.

McMurray Gibson, Gail. "Saint Anne and the Religion of Childbed: Some East Anglian Texts and Talismans." In *Interpreting Cultural Symbols: Saint Anne in Late Medieval Society*, edited by Kathleen Ashley and Pamela Sheingorn, 95–110. Athens: University of Georgia Press, 1990.

Menne, Karl. *Deutsche und niederländische Handschriften.* Cologne: Verlag von Paul Neubner, 1937.

Menz, Cäsar. *Das Frühwerk Jörg Breus des Älteren.* Augsburg: Kommissionsverlag Bücher Seitz, 1982.

Michaelis, Reiner. *Dasein und Vision: Bürger und Bauern um 1500.* Berlin: Staatliche Museen zu Berlin, Berlin Henschelverlag, 1989.

Moeller, Bernd. "Piety in Germany Around 1500." In *The Reformation in Medieval Perspective*, edited by Steven Ozment, 50–75. Chicago: Quadrangle Books, 1971.

Müller, J. "Ein st. gallischer Josephsverehrer des 15. Jahrhunderts." *Zeitschrift für schweizerische Kirchengeschichte* 3, 3 (1909), 161–74.

Müller, Theodor, and Wilhelm Reismüller. *Ingolstadt: Die Herzogsstadt, die Universitätsstadt, die Festung.* Ingolstadt: Verlag Donau Courier Ingolstadt, 1974.

Nieuwdorp, Hans M. J. "Drie Mechelse huisaltaartjes." *Musées Royaux des Beaux-Arts de Belgique Bulletin* 18, 1–2 (1969), 7–15.

Nilsen, Anna. "The Immaculate Conception of the Virgin Mary in Cult and Art During the Middle Ages with Special Reference to Swedish Material." Translated by Alex. G. Davidson of "Marie obefläckade avlelse i kult och konst." *Konsthistorisk Tidskrift* 56 (1987), 6–15.

Oberman, Heiko. *The Harvest of Medieval Theology: Gabriel Biel and Late Medieval Nominalism.* Cambridge, Mass.: Harvard University Press, 1963.

O'Connor, E. D., ed. *The Dogma of the Immaculate Conception: History and Significance.* Notre Dame: University of Notre Dame Press, 1958.

Orth, Myra. "Madame Sainte-Anne: The Holy Kinship, the Royal Trinity, and Louise of Savoy." In *Interpreting Cultural Symbols: Saint Anne in Late Medieval Society*, edited by Kathleen Ashley and Pamela Sheingorn, 119–228. Athens: University of Georgia Press, 1990.

Ostermair, Franz Xaver. *Genealogische Nachrichten über verschiedene theils noch blühende, theils erloschene Geschlechter.* Ingolstadt, 1885.

Ozment, Steven E. *The Reformation in the Cities.* 1975. Reprint, New York: Yale University Press, 1980.

Pächt, Otto. "The Avignon Diptych and Its Eastern Ancestry." In *De Artibus Opuscula* XL, *Essays in Honor of Erwin Panofsky,* edited by M. Meiss, 402–21. New York: New York University Press, 1961.

Pinder, Wilhelm. *Die Deutsche Plastik von ausgehenden Mittelalter bis zum Ende der Renaissance.* 2 vols. Potsdam: Akademische Verlagsgesellschaft Athenaion, 1929.

Rajewski, Sister Mary. *Sebastian Brant: Studies in Religious Aspects of His Life and Works with Special Reference to the Varia Carmina.* Washington, D.C.: Catholic University of America Press, 1944.

Reber, Ortrud. *Die Gestaltung des Kultes weiblicher Heiliger im Spätmittelalter: Die Verehrung der Heiligen Elisabeth, Klara, Hedwig und Birgitta.* Hersbruck: Kommissionsverlag, Karl Pfeiffer's Buchdruckerei und Verlag, 1963.

Recht, Roland. *Nicolas de Leyde et la sculpture à Strasbourg, 1460–1525.* Strasburg: Presses Universitaires de Strasbourg, 1987.

Reindel, Kurt Reindel. "Ein Legendar des 12. Jahrhunderts aus dem Kloster Pomuc (Diöz. Prag)." In *Festschrift für Max Spindler zum 75. Geburtstag,* edited by Dieter Albrecht, Andreas Kraus, and Kurt Reindel, 143–63. Munich: C. H. Beck'sche Verlagsbuchhandlung, 1969.

Remling, Ludwig. *Bruderschaften in Franken.* Würzburg: Kommissionsverlag Ferdinand Schöningh, 1986.

Roncière, Charles de la. "Les Confrèrieres à Florence et dans son Contado." *Le mouvement confraternel au moyen age, France, Italie, Suisse: Actes de la table ronde organisée par l'université de Lausanne, 1985.* Geneva: Librairie Droz S.A., 1987.

Roper, Lyndal. *The Holy Household: Women and Morals in Reformation Augsburg.* Oxford: Clarendon Press, 1989.

Rosenthal, Joel. *The Purchase of Paradise: Gift-Giving and the Aristocracy, 1307–1485.* London: Routledge & Kegan Paul, 1972.

Roth, F. "Die geistliche Betrügerin Anna Laminit von Augsburg." *Zeitschrift für Kirchengeschichte* 43 (1924), 355–417.

Rothkrug, Lionel. "Religious Practices and Collective Perceptions: Hidden Homologies in the Renaissance and Reformation." *Historical Reflections* 7 (Spring 1980).

Rudolph, Conrad. *The Things of Greater Importance: Bernard of Clairvaux's Apologia and the Medieval Attitude Toward Art.* Philadelphia: University of Pennsylvania Press, 1990.

Sargent, Steven D. "Saints' Cults and Naming Patterns in Bavaria, 1400–1600." *Catholic Historical Review* 76 (October 1990), 672–95.

Sautman, Francesca. "Saint Anne in Folk Tradition." In *Interpreting Cultural Symbols: Saint Anne in Late Medieval Society,* edited by Kathleen Ashley and Pamela Sheingorn, 69–94. Athens: University of Georgia Press, 1990.

Schaumkell, E. *Der Kultus der heiligen Anna am Ausgange des Mittelalters.* Freiburg: Akademische Verlagsbuchhandlung von J. C. B. Mohr, 1893.

Schiller, Gertrude. *Ikonographie der christlichen Kunst.* 5 vols. Gütersloh: Gerd Mohn, 1966–90.

Schiller, Wilhelm. *Die St. Annakirche in Augsburg.* Augsburg: Evang. Luth. Pfarramt St. Anna and J. A. Schlosser'schen Buchhandlung, 1939.

Schmidt, Otto. "Die Stralsunder Anna Selbdritt." *Baltische Studien,* n.f., 33.

Schmitt, Jean-Claude. "La Confrérie du Rosaire de Colmar, 1485." *Archivum Fratrum Praedicatorum* 40 (1970), 97–124.

Schott, Eberhard. "Beiträge zur Geschichte des Carmeliterklosters und der Kirche von St. Anna in Augsburg." *Zeitschrift des Historischen Vereins für Schwaben und Neuburg,* 1878, 1879 (two articles), 1880, and 1882.

Schroeder, Alfred. *Archiv für die Geschichte des Hochstifts Augsburg* 6. Dillingen, 1929.

Schuler, Carol. "The Seven Sorrows of the Virgin." *Simiolus* 21, 1/2 (1992), 5–28.

Schulte, Aloys. *Die Fugger in Rom, 1495–1523.* 2 vols. Leipzig: Verlag von Duncker & Humblot, 1904.

Scribner, Robert W. "Ritual and Reformation." In *The German People and the Reformation,* edited by R. Po-Chia Hsia, 122–26. Ithaca: Cornell University Press, 1988.

Segl, Peter. "Heinrich Institoris: Persönlichkeit und literarisches Werk." In *Der Hexenhammer / Entstehung und Umfeld des malleus maleficarum von 1487,* edited by Peter Segl. Cologne and Vienna: Böhlau Verlag, 1988.

Seitz, Joseph. *Die Verehrung des hl. Joseph in ihrer geschichtlichen Entwicklung bis zum Konzil von Trient dargestellt.* Freiburg im Breisgau: Herdersche Verlagshandlung, 1908.

Sheingorn, Pamela. "The Wise Mother: The Image of St. Anne Teaching the Virgin Mary." *Gesta* 32, 1 (1993), 69–80.

Silver, Larry. *The Paintings of Quentin Massys.* Montclair: Allanheld & Schram, 1984.

Simson, Otto Georg von. "Compassio and Co-Redemptio in Rogier van der Weyden's *Descent from the Cross.*" *Art Bulletin* 35 (1953), 9–16.

Soergel, Philip M. *Wondrous in His Saints: Counter-Reformation Propaganda in Bavaria.* Berkeley and Los Angeles: University of California Press, 1993.

Söhner, P. Leo. *Die Geschichte der Begleitung des gregorianischen Chorals in Deutschland.* Augsburg: Dr. Benno Filser Verlag, 1931.

Spiegel, Gabrielle. "History, Historicism, and the Social Logic of the Text in the Middle Ages." *Speculum* 65 (1990), 59–86.

Steinberg, Leo. "The Metaphors of Love and Birth in Michelangelo's Pietàs." In *Studies in Erotic Art,* edited by Theodore Bowie and Cornelia V. Christenson, 231–339. New York: Basic Books, 1970.

Terpstra, Nicholas Terpstra. "Death and Dying in Renaissance Confraternities." In *Crossing the Boundaries: Christian Piety and the Arts in Italian Medieval and Renaissance Confraternities,* edited by Konrad Eisenbichler, 179–200. Medieval Institute Publications Early Drama, Art, and Music Monograph Series, 15. Kalamazoo: Western Michigan University, 1991.

Tilman Riemenschneider: Master Sculptor of the Late Middle Ages. Edited by Julien Chapuis. Washington, D.C.: National Gallery of Art, 1999.

Trexler, Richard. *Public Life in Renaissance Florence.* New York: Academic Press, 1980.

Ward, Benedicta. *Miracles and the Medieval Mind.* Philadelphia: University of Pennsylvania Press, 1982.

Weiss, James Michael. "Hagiography by German Humanists." *Journal of Medieval and Renaissance Studies* 15 (1985), 299–316.

Weissman, Ronald. *Ritual Brotherhood in Renaissance Florence.* New York: Academic Press, 1982.

Wellen, G. A. *Theotokos: Eine ikonographische Abhandlung über das Gottesmuttersbild in frühchristlichen Zeit.* Utrecht and Antwerp: Uitgeverij het Spectrum, 1961.

Wilhelm, Johannes. *Augsburger Wandmalerei, 1368–1530.* Augsburg: Verlag H. Mühlberger, 1983.

Williamson, Paul. *Northern Gothic Sculpture, 1200–1450.* London: Victoria and Albert Museum, 1988.

Wilmart, Andre. *Auteurs spirituels et textes dévots du moyen age latin.* 1932. Reprint, Paris: Etudes Augustiniennes, 1971.

Wilson, Stephen, ed. *Saints and Their Cults: Studies in Religious Sociology, Folklore, and History.* Cambridge: Cambridge University Press, 1983.

Winston-Allen, Anne. *Stories of the Rose: The Making of the Rosary in the Middle Ages.* University Park: The Pennsylvania State University Press, 1997.

———. "Tales of the Rosary in German Confraternity Handbooks, 1482–1515." Conference paper, University of Western Michigan International Congress on Medieval Studies, Kalamazoo, 1993.

———. "Tracing the Origins of the Rosary." *Speculum* 68 (July 1993), 634.

Wittstock, Jürgen. *Kirchliche Kunst des Mittelalters und der Reformationszeit: St. Annen-Museum Lübeck.* Lübeck: Museum für Kunst & Kulturgeschichte, 1981.

Wolf, Bernhard. "Aus dem kirchlichen Leben Annabergs in vorreformatorische Zeit." In *Festschrift zum 25 jährigen Bestehen des Vereins für Geschichte von Annaberg und Umgegend,* 76. Annaberg: n.p., 1910.

Wolska-Wierusz, Joanna. "Adventus Salvatoris i altarskapet fran Hägerstad." *Fornvännen* 88 (1993), 9–25.

Zender, Matthias. "Matronen und verwandte Gottheiten." In *Ergebnisse eines Kolloquiums veranstaltet von der Göttinger Akademiekommission für die Altertumskunde Mittel- und Nordeuropas,* 213–28. Cologne: Rheinland-Verlag GMBH, 1987.

Zmyslony, Monika. *Die Bruderschaften in Lübeck bis zur Reformation.* Kiel: Walter G. Mühlau Verlag, 1977.

Index

CPSIA information can be obtained at www.ICGtesting.com
Printed in the USA
BVOW07s2212191213

339675BV00002B/98/P

9 780271 058122